Workshop on Figurative Language Processing 2018

New Orleans, Louisiana, USA
6 June 2018

ISBN: 978-1-5108-6358-3

NAACL HLT 2018

Figurative Language Processing

Proceedings of the Workshop

6 June 2018
New Orleans, Louisiana

Introduction

Figurative language processing is a rapidly growing area in Natural Language Processing (NLP), including processing of metaphors, idioms, puns, irony, sarcasm, as well as other figures. Characteristic to all areas of human activity (from poetic to ordinary to scientific) and, thus, to all types of discourse, figurative language becomes an important problem for NLP systems. Its ubiquity in language has been established in a number of corpus studies and the role it plays in human reasoning has been confirmed in psychological experiments. This makes figurative language an important research area for computational and cognitive linguistics, and its automatic identification and interpretation indispensable for any semantics-oriented NLP applications.

This workshop builds upon the successful start of the Metaphor in NLP workshop series (at NAACL–HLT 2013, ACL 2014, NAACL–HLT 2015, NAACL–HLT 2016), expanding its scope to incorporate the rapidly growing body of research on various types of figurative language such as sarcasm, irony and puns, with the aim of maintaining and nourishing a community of NLP researchers interested in this topic. The workshop features both regular research papers and a shared task on metaphor detection. We received 22 research paper submissions and accepted 10 (6 oral presentations and 4 posters). The papers cover a range of aspects of figurative language processing such as metaphor identification (Bizzoni and Ghanimifard; Mykowiecka, Marciniak and Wawer; Pramanick and Mitra; Stowe and Palmer; Zayed, McCrae and Buitelaar), metaphor interpretation (Bizzoni and Lappin; Rosen), identification of idiomatic expressions in essays written by non-native speakers (Flor and Beigman Klebanov), crowdsourcing for generating figurative language (Gero and Chilton) and linguistic features for estimating metaphor and sarcasm quality (Skalicky and Crossley).

A novel feature of this workshop is the shared task on token-level metaphor detection. The shared task attracted 11 teams, of whom 8 submitted a paper describing their system; these system papers appear in the proceedings of this workshop. The best performing systems showed improvement over strong baselines from recent published work. Almost all participants experimented with deep learning architectures; some of these incorporated linguistic information as well. Analysis of the results is presented in the summary paper by Leong, Beigman Klebanov, and Shutova; consistently across participating systems performance was best for verbs, and there were large differences in performance across texts from different genres.

Two distinguished researchers working on figurative language will give the invited talks at the workshop. Tony Veale, Department of Computer Science at the University College Dublin, will talk about metaphor generation "When You Come To A Fork In The Road, Take It: Complementary Approaches to Metaphor Generation", and Marilyn Walker, Department of Computer Science, University of California Santa Cruz, will talk about sarcasm detection "Hyperbole, Rhetorical Questions and Sarcasm: Figurative Language in Social Media".

We wish to thank everyone who showed interest and submitted a paper, all of the authors for their contributions, the members of the Program Committee for their thoughtful reviews, the invited speakers for sharing their perspectives on the topic, and all the attendees of the workshop. All of these factors contribute to a truly enriching event!

Workshop co–chairs:
Beata Beigman Klebanov, Educational Testing Service, USA
Ekaterina Shutova, University of Amsterdam, Netherlands
Patricia Lichtenstein, University of California, Merced, USA
Smaranda Muresan, Columbia University, USA
Chee Wee (Ben) Leong, Educational Testing Service, USA

Organizers:

Beata Beigman Klebanov, Educational Testing Service, USA
Ekaterina Shutova, University of Cambridge, UK
Patricia Lichtenstein, University of California, Merced, USA
Smaranda Muresan, Columbia University, USA
Chee Wee (Ben) Leong, Educational Testing Service, USA

Program Committee:

Yulia Badryzlova, National Research University Higher School of Economics, Russia
Susan Brown, University of Colorado at Boulder, USA
Paul Cook, University of New Brunswisk, Canada
Gerard de Melo, Rutgers University, USA
Ellen Dodge, ICSI, UC Berkeley, USA
Jonathan Dunn, Illinois Institute of Technology, USA
Anna Feldman, Montclair State University, USA
Elena Filatova, CUNY, USA
Michael Flor, Educational Testing Service, USA
Debanjan Ghosh, Rutgers University, USA
Mark Granroth-Wilding, University of Helsinki, Finland
Dario Gutierrez, IBM Research, USA
Eduard Hovy, Carnegie Mellon University, USA
Hyeju Jang, University of British Columbia, Canada
Aditya Joshi, IITB-Monash Research Academy, India
Valia Kordoni, Humboldt University Berlin, Germany
Mark Last, Ben-Gurion University of the Negev, Israel
Mark Lee, University of Birmingham, UK
Xiaofei Lu, The Pennsylvania State University, USA
Jean Maillard, University of Cambridge, UK
James H. Martin,University of Colorado at Boulder, USA
Rada Mihalcea, University of Michigan Ann Arbor, USA
Saif Mohammad, National Research Council Canada, Canada
Michael Mohler, Language Computer Corporation, USA
Preslav Nakov, Qatar Computing Research Institute, HBKU, Qatar
Srini Narayanan, Google, Switzerland
Ani Nenkova, University of Pennsylvania, USA
Diarmuid O'Seaghdha, Apple, UK
Gözde Özbal, FBK-irst Trento, Italy
Thierry Poibeau, Ecole Normale Superieure and CNRS, France
Paul Rayson, Lancaster University, UK
Marek Rei, University of Cambridge, UK
Ellen Riloff, University of Utah, USA
Paolo Rosso, Universitat Politècnica de València, Spain
Victoria Rubin, University of Western Ontario, CA
Eyal Sagi, University of St. Francis, USA
Agata Savary, Université François Rabelais Tours, France
Sabine Schulte im Walde, University of Stuttgart, Germany
Samira Shaikh, University of North Carolina at Charlotte, USA

Carlo Stapparava, Fondazione Bruno Kessler, Italy
Mark Steedman, University of Edinburgh, UK
Tomek Strzalkowski, SUNY Albany, USA
Marc Tomlinson, Language Computer Corporation, USA
Yulia Tsvetkov, Carnegie Mellon University, USA
Tony Veale, University College Dublin, Ireland
Aline Villavicencio, Federal University of Rio Grande do Sul, Brazil

Invited Speakers:

Tony Veale, University College Dublin, Ireland
Marilyn Walker, University of California, Santa Cruz, USA

Table of Contents

Workshop Program

Friday, June 6, 2018

9:00–9:10   *Opening remarks*

9:10–10:10   *Invited Talk: Tony Veale "When You Come To A Fork In The Road, Take It: Complementary Approaches to Metaphor Generation"*

10:10–10:30   *Challenges in Finding Metaphorical Connections*
Katy Gero and Lydia Chilton

10:30–11:00   *Coffee break*

11:00–11:20   *Linguistic Features of Sarcasm and Metaphor Production Quality*
Stephen Skalicky and Scott Crossley

11:20–11:40   *Leveraging Syntactic Constructions for Metaphor Identification*
Kevin Stowe and Martha Palmer

11:40–12:00   *Literal, Metphorical or Both? Detecting Metaphoricity in Isolated Adjective-Noun Phrases*
Agnieszka Mykowiecka, Malgorzata Marciniak and Aleksander Wawer

12:00–12:20   *Catching Idiomatic Expressions in EFL Essays*
Michael Flor and Beata Beigman Klebanov

12:20–14:00   *Lunch*

14:00–14:20   *Predicting Human Metaphor Paraphrase Judgments with Deep Neural Networks*
Yuri Bizzoni and Shalom Lappin

14:20–14:40   *A Report on the 2018 VUA Metaphor Detection Shared Task*
Chee Wee (Ben) Leong, Beata Beigman Klebanov and Ekaterina Shutova

14:40–15:40   Poster Session

An LSTM-CRF Based Approach to Token-Level Metaphor Detection
Malay Pramanick, Ashim Gupta and Pabitra Mitra

Unsupervised Detection of Metaphorical Adjective-Noun Pairs
Malay Pramanick and Pabitra Mitra

Phrase-Level Metaphor Identification Using Distributed Representations of Word Meaning
Omnia Zayed, John Philip McCrae and Paul Buitelaar

Bigrams and BiLSTMs Two Neural Networks for Sequential Metaphor Detection
Yuri Bizzoni and Mehdi Ghanimifard

Computationally Constructed Concepts: A Machine Learning Approach to Metaphor Interpretation Using Usage-Based Construction Grammatical Cues
Zachary Rosen

Neural Metaphor Detecting with CNN-LSTM Model
Chuhan Wu, Fangzhao Wu, Yubo Chen, Sixing Wu, Zhigang Yuan and Yongfeng Huang

Di-LSTM Contrast : A Deep Neural Network for Metaphor Detection
Krishnkant Swarnkar and Anil Kumar Singh

Conditional Random Fields for Metaphor Detection
Anna Mosolova, Ivan Bondarenko and Vadim Fomin

Challenges in Finding Metaphorical Connections

Katy Ilonka Gero
Columbia University
`katy@cs.columbia.edu`

Lydia Chilton
Columbia University
`chilton@cs.columbia.edu`

Abstract

Poetry is known for its novel expression using figurative language. We introduce a writing task that contains the essential challenges of generating meaningful figurative language and can be evaluated. We investigate how to find metaphorical connections between abstract themes and concrete domains by asking people to write four-line poems on a given metaphor, such as "death is a rose" or "anger is wood". We find that only 24% of poems successfully make a metaphorical connection. We present five alternate ways people respond to the prompt and release our dataset of 186 categorized poems. We suggest opportunities for computational approaches.

1 Introduction

Poetry expresses the feelings or emotions of an experience, often relying on figurative language to communicate an otherwise elusive idea. This makes poetry an exciting genre for those interested in generating figurative language.

Recently, researchers have made progress in computationally generating poetry (Ghazvininejad et al., 2016; Veale, 2013). However, in a survey of computer generated poetry, Oliviera (2017) notes that while poetic text must convey a conceptual message, this requirement is "often only softly satisfied".

We focus on creating intentionally meaningful lines of poetry. Poems generated from a single theme such as "love" can rely on language related to the theme, but are often ambiguous and have no clear meaning. Although ambiguity can be a desirable property in poetry, it makes it difficult to evaluate whether the meaning is intentional, or being attributed by the reader. We propose generating poetry from a metaphor such as "love is a rock". These poems can still have some ambiguity, but we can evaluate whether readers can detect

> Surrender is a book
> it's pages contain paragraphs of regret
> chapters of inaction
> an epilogue of defeat

Figure 1: Example poem for "surrender is a book".

their metaphorical meaning or not.

In this paper, we introduce a short poetry writing task that contains the essential challenges of generating meaningful figurative language. We establish a baseline for how well amateur writers perform and show that evaluators achieve high agreement.

The task is to write a four-line poem containing a given metaphor such as "love is a rock" or "death is a stream." Although these poems leave room for interpretation and novelty, we can evaluate whether or not they successfully express the given metaphor. An example poem from our dataset is shown in Figure 1.

Our study generates a dataset that includes successful poems, which generative computers systems may model or use as inspiration, as well as unsuccessful ones, which let us better understand the task and discover common failure points.

This paper makes the following contributions:

- Introducing a writing task that is short and contains the essential challenges of meaningful figurative language.
- A dataset of 186 poems, and their associated meta-data, annotated with their coherence to the prompt metaphor. [1]
- A categorization of common failure cases in how a poem relates to its prompt.

---

[1] http://github.com/kgero/metaphorical-connections

1

Proceedings of the Workshop on Figurative Language Processing, pages 1–6
New Orleans, Louisiana, June 6, 2018. ©2018 Association for Computational Linguistics

2 Related Work

Procedural poetry, in which poets use algorithmic processes to create their work, has a long history preceding the invention of modern computers and continues strong today (Parrish, 2018; Montfort, 2017). In computer science, the generation of poetry represents a challenge to generate emotional, creative, and meaningful text.

Some work analyzes the stylistic features of contemporary poetry (Kao and Jurafsky, 2012; Kaplan and Blei, 2007) and others build generative systems that output poems (Netzer et al., 2009; Colton et al., 2012; Manurung et al., 2000). A recent neural-network based system, Hafez (Ghazvininejad et al., 2016), produces rich sounding sonnets. This is a promising computational approach to achieve the stylistic aspects of poetry. However, it is an open problem whether computational approaches can produce the structural or meaningful aspects of poetry.

Generating metaphors is a challenge in artificial intelligence (Veale et al., 2016). Gagliano et al. (2016) use word embeddings to find connector words between two conceptual domains to aid in making metaphorical connections. Veale and Hao (2007) mine metaphorical relations using Google search results for adjectives that describe both terms. Later work (Veale, 2013) generates one line expressions from conceptual metaphors. It remains a challenge to expand a metaphor into a poem that expresses the feelings or emotions of an experience.

3 Experiment and Methodology

In this experiment, we ask 200 amateur writers to write four-line poems that use a given metaphor. Each writer is given one metaphorical prompt.

We base this poetry-writing task on expressing a metaphor because metaphors are a common but challenging aspect of poetry, and we can evaluate whether the poem expresses the given metaphor.

The metaphorical prompts are created by randomly combining one concrete noun and one poetic theme, a technique introduced by Gagliano et al. (2016). We use their lists of concrete nouns and poetic themes, a subset of which are shown in Table 1. Because the concrete and poetic words are paired randomly, we expect this task to be difficult—people may struggle to find a metaphorical connection between the words.

concrete nouns	poetic themes
bed	loss
horse	confusion
bell	faith
book	freedom
ship	grace
wing	hate
wood	jealousy
room	love

Table 1: Example words in the concrete noun and poetic theme lists, from (Gagliano et al., 2016). An example prompt metaphor, created by randomly drawing one word from each list, could be "faith is a horse".

We recruit 200 people from Amazon Mechanical Turk. Each writer is given one of the following 10 randomly generated metaphorical prompts:

- "Anger is wood"
- "Compassion is blood"
- "Death is a rose"
- "God is a breath"
- "Grace is a garden"
- "Hate is a mist"
- "Hope is a ship"
- "Immortality is a room"
- "Peace is a rock"
- "Surrender is a book"

We ask them each to write a four-line poem coherent with the prompt metaphor. They are told to not use the exact words of the metaphor as given but rather express the idea the metaphor represents. They are also told to use stylistic elements of poetry such as rhyme, alliteration, and line breaks. We collect 20 poems on each of the 10 metaphors. Workers are only allowed to write one poem and are paid $1 for the task.

The authors of the paper independently evaluate the poems. We analyze the success of the poems by indicating whether or not a poem contained its given metaphor. For poems that did not contain the given metaphor, we used grounded theory (Strauss and Corbin, 1990) to develop categories of how they failed. These categories include: not related at all, containing only one of the concepts, and three non-metaphorical connections. Example poems for each category are found in Figure 2.

A. No connection: just about **anger**
My **anger** is solid and vast
The ghosts of my present, the ghosts of my past
I can't break through the tunnel of time
My **anger is vicious**, my **anger** is mine

B. Attributional connection: <u>wood</u> is **angry**
The <u>bench of pine wood planks</u>
Held up peoples glutes
Till the people went home for the night
leaving the <u>bench</u>, **angry**, in abandonment

C. Offset connection: **anger** is a <u>fire</u>
<u>Wood</u> is a place where a **fire of anger**
   can be lit like a sparrow.
Both **anger** and <u>fire</u> work to light up a room.
Wood is the conductor of rage, the spite that turns heads.
Like ants marching through its hollow shell,
   <u>wood</u> is a **source of fury**.

D. Incoherent connection
Thoughts of breeze, my **anger is teaming**,
of rapture I freeze, my boiling pot is steaming,
tired of despair, my <u>wood is drying</u>,
once so full of **anger & rage**, now I feel like I am dying.

E. Metaphorical connection
the **anger grew**, like a tree
this **large, <u>immovable object had taken root**</u>
<u>casting shade on even the happiest parts of my life</u>
I could let it **consume me**, or **<u>cut it down</u>**

Figure 2: Example poems for the given metaphor "anger is wood". We show one example for each of the four failure cases and one for a successful metaphorical connection.

4 Results

On average people take 13.6 minutes on this writing task. 14 poems were plagiarized and removed from consideration, leaving 186 poems for the resulting analysis. The two evaluators had 97% observed agreement on whether the poem successfully made the given metaphorical connection. 24% of poems, or 45 poems, were found to be successful by at least one of the evaluators. 7% of poems were off-topic. Similarly the evaluators had 97% observed agreement on whether the poems were off-topic or not.

In the remaining poems, the poem used the words in the metaphor but did not make a metaphorical connection between the words. Our grounded theory found four alternate ways of relating the given concepts in the poem: *no connection*, *attributional connection*, *offset connection*, and *incoherent connection*.

Raters had a 69% agreement on these categories, indicating that it is sometimes ambiguous which error is made. Sometimes this is due to different interpretations of the poem and sometimes this is due to evaluators determining that a given poem didn't cleanly sit into a single category. For the remaining analysis, if evaluators disagreed on which category to place a poem in, a poem is considered to be in both categories.

The fraction of poems in each category is reported in Table 2. By looking at the other ways poems relate to the prompt, we learn the tactics people use when attempting to complete this task.

4.1 Categorization of Poems

We categorize six distinct ways poems relate to the prompt. We define and discuss the categories below. Figure 2 provides example poems for each category, while Table 2 reports the fraction of poems in each category.

4.1.1 Off-Topic

A poem is *off-topic* if it fails to include aspects of either word in the metaphor. For the prompt "surrender is a book" a poem might be about the loss of a lover, which has no relation to "surrender" or "book". 7% of poems are off topic. Although people write a poem, this is a case when the worker does not truly attempt to do the task.

4.1.2 No Connection

A poem has *no connection* if it explores the conceptual domain of only one word in the metaphor or does not relate the two conceptual domains. In Figure 1A, the poem talks only about feeling angry, "My anger is vicious", with no reference or connection to wood. There is only a vague attempt to connect anger with wood in the line "my anger is solid"; although wood is solid, many things are solid and this is not enough to establish a metaphorical connection.

This is the most common failure case for poems, with 41% of all poems placed in this category. Possibly these poems intended to express a connection, but the result was too vague and evaluators couldn't detect one. Alternatively, the writer couldn't find a metaphorical connection and simply wrote what they could about one of the words.

4.1.3 Attributional Connection

A poem has an *attributional connection* if it attributes the abstract concept directly to the concrete noun. In Figure 1B, the poem says the "[wooden] bench, [is] angry". Although this

prompt metaphor	off-topic	no connection	attributional	offset	incoherent	metaphorical
surrender is a book	0.11	**0.53**	0.47	0.11	0.05	0.05
death is a rose	0.00	0.30	**0.55**	0.40	0.20	0.10
god is a breath	0.00	0.26	0.21	0.11	**0.47**	0.11
grace is a garden	0.00	**0.67**	0.11	0.22	0.39	0.17
immortality is a room	0.05	**0.58**	0.05	0.11	0.47	0.21
compassion is blood	0.11	**0.37**	0.05	0.05	0.21	0.26
peace is a rock	0.10	**0.45**	0.10	0.10	0.05	0.35
hope is a ship	0.07	**0.36**	0.14	0.14	**0.36**	**0.36**
anger is wood	0.05	**0.37**	0.00	0.32	0.21	**0.37**
hate is a mist	0.11	0.26	0.05	0.00	0.26	**0.47**
all	0.07	**0.41**	0.17	0.15	0.26	0.24

Table 2: Success rates of the 10 metaphorical prompts. The fraction of successful poems is highlighted in blue. The bold number represents the most common connection for each prompt. Because poems can be placed in two categories if evaluators disagree, numbers do not add to 1 horizontally.

poem uses figurative language by personifying the bench, it is not coherent with the given metaphor.

This category is an especially common error for poems about the prompts "death is a rose" (55%) and "surrender is a book" (53%). Many poems said "the rose died" or "I surrender to the book". We posit that these connections are easier than metaphorical connections because they do not require a shared third aspect which writers have to generate themselves.

4.1.4 Offset Connection

A poem has an *offset connection* if it expresses a shared feature between one word in the metaphor and another word very related to the other word in the metaphor. In Figure 1C, the poem talks about the "fire of anger" for which "wood is a source of fury"; the poem is about the offset metaphor "anger is fire". "Death is a rose" had 40% of poems categorized as an offset connection; most commonly these poems talk about "life is a rose" and note that life, like roses, must end in death.

We suggest that writers make this error because they are looking for any connection they can find, even if the connections are not directly linked to the given metaphor. An offset connection increases the search space by allowing for connections within a broader set of domains.

4.1.5 Incoherent Connection

A poem has an *incoherent connection* if it relates the two words in the metaphor but in an unclear way. In Figure 1D, the poem says "anger is teaming, ... my wood is drying" with no supporting text to explain how these two concepts are related.

In this case writers acknowledge both words in the prompts but either do not attempt to connect them or connect them in an incoherent way.

4.1.6 Metaphorical Connection

A poem has a successful *metaphorical connection* if it relates the two words metaphorically in the way provided by the given metaphor and understood by the evaluators. In Figure 1E, the poem says that "anger grew, like a tree ... it had taken root". This poem takes several aspects of wood and coherently applies them to anger. Although this poem talks primarily about a tree, we do not consider this an offset connection because trees are the only source of wood.

Each of the given metaphors had at least one successful poem. All of our successful poems made creative connections, like "Immortality lies just down the hall / The path to it is not easy to find". Failed poems tended to repeat the same connections, like "I am surrounded by four walls indefinitely".

5 Discussion

The rate of success between different prompts varies greatly, from 5% for "surrender is a book" to 47% for "hate is a mist". Some prompts are more likely to result in different kinds of connections, like *offset connections*, than others. What explains these varying success rates?

We first explore whether word similarity between the two words in the prompt could account for this variability. In Figure 3, we plot WORD2VEC[2] word similarity against success rate for our 10 prompts. Based on these 10 data points, it seems that word similarity is not a strong predictor of users making a metaphorical connection. This suggests that people are not picking up on existing connections but finding new, creative ways to relate the words.

---

[2]https://code.google.com/archive/p/word2vec/

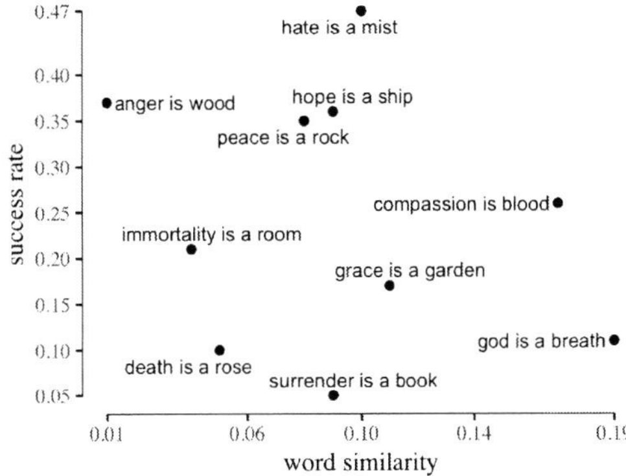

Figure 3: Fraction of successful poems as a function of the similarity between the words in the prompt.

Although we see no correlation between word similarity and success rate, it could be that WORD2VEC is not accurately modeling previous associations people may bring to the task. Other models of semantic relatedness may be able to better predict the success of people in the task.

Looking at the least successful prompts, we note that they use sensible but not metaphorical connections. The prompt "death is a rose" has many *attributional connections* saying "the rose died". Though sensible, it is not a metaphor. Similarly, the prompt "surrender is a book" often resulted in poems saying "I surrendered to the book" which is a connection, but does not express the target metaphor. In contrast, "anger is wood" had a high success rate. These words could also be connected by saying "the wood is angry" but this rarely happened, possibly because this phrase is not as sensible as "the rose died."

We hypothesize that if two words can be sensibly connected, people are likely to write a poem with this connection without checking whether the connection meets the target metaphor. If this does explain the varying success rates, it is likely that computational systems will have similar problems.

6 Future Work

We believe this task is a good candidate to test the ability of computers to automatically generate coherent poetry or to see how computational techniques could help novices better complete the task.

Further work could explore how computational techniques can aid in the evaluation of this task. This feedback could help people write successful poems, particularly if told which error they

are making. Can metaphor detection techniques, such as those based on conceptual metaphor theory (Shutova and Sun, 2013), evaluate whether a poem expresses its given metaphor? Can we detect what connections are being made?

Computer evaluation would also help further computer generation. Can the work of Veale (2013), which generates poetic metaphorical expressions, be extended to produce poems similar to the successful ones found in the paper? If we could express the target metaphor as a constraint, can computational techniques like those used in Hafez (2016) write poems based on metaphors, not just themes?

There is high potential for computational tools to aid people in this task. Given that only 24% of writers successfully wrote poems to a metaphorical prompt, there is an open problem of how to improve on this baseline. Future work could design computational aids, like those in (Gagliano et al., 2016), to suggest possible metaphorical connections that writers could accept or reject, similar to other creative writing aids (Clark et al., 2018).

Beyond poetry, helping people find connections between two domains has far-reaching applications from science education (Glynn, 1991) to product design (Hope et al., 2017). This is a hallmark of human intelligence that can be computationally supported.

7 Conclusion

In this paper we introduce a short poetry writing task that gets at the heart of meaningful figurative language. We collect 186 amateur examples and find that only 24% of poems successfully make the metaphorical connection, indicating that this task is hard but possible. The most common failure case is when poems make no connection between the words (41%). Other poems may fail by making a non-metaphorical connection or a connection with the wrong word.

We see potential in this task as a demonstration of computational creativity and figurative language generation. By analyzing the common errors we show ways in which improvements can be made. We believe that computational systems can improve upon this baseline.

Acknowledgements

This work is supported by NSF Graduate Research Fellowship Grant No. DGE 16-44869.

References

Elizabeth Clark, Anne Spencer Ross, Chenhao Tan, Yangfeng Ji, and Noah A Smith. 2018. Creative writing with a machine in the loop: Case studies on slogans and stories.

Simon Colton, Jacob Goodwin, and Tony Veale. 2012. Full-face poetry generation. In *ICCC*, pages 95–102.

Andrea Gagliano, Emily Paul, Kyle Booten, and Marti A Hearst. 2016. Intersecting word vectors to take figurative language to new heights. In *Proceedings of the Fifth Workshop on Computational Linguistics for Literature*, pages 20–31.

Marjan Ghazvininejad, Xing Shi, Yejin Choi, and Kevin Knight. 2016. Generating topical poetry. In *Proceedings of the 2016 Conference on Empirical Methods in Natural Language Processing*, pages 1183–1191.

Shawn M Glynn. 1991. Explaining science concepts: A teaching-with-analogies model. *The psychology of learning science*, pages 219–240.

Tom Hope, Joel Chan, Aniket Kittur, and Dafna Shahaf. 2017. Accelerating innovation through analogy mining. *CoRR*, abs/1706.05585.

Justine Kao and Dan Jurafsky. 2012. A computational analysis of style, affect, and imagery in contemporary poetry. In *Proceedings of the NAACL-HLT 2012 Workshop on Computational Linguistics for Literature*, pages 8–17.

David M Kaplan and David M Blei. 2007. A computational approach to style in american poetry. In *Data Mining, 2007. ICDM 2007. Seventh IEEE International Conference on*, pages 553–558. IEEE.

Hisar Manurung, Graeme Ritchie, and Henry Thompson. 2000. Towards a computational model of poetry generation. Technical report, The University of Edinburgh.

Nick Montfort. 2017. *The Truelist*. Counterpath.

Yael Netzer, David Gabay, Yoav Goldberg, and Michael Elhadad. 2009. Gaiku: Generating haiku with word associations norms. In *Proceedings of the Workshop on Computational Approaches to Linguistic Creativity*, pages 32–39. Association for Computational Linguistics.

Hugo Gonçalo Oliveira. 2017. A survey on intelligent poetry generation: Languages, features, techniques, reutilisation and evaluation. In *Proceedings of the 10th International Conference on Natural Language Generation*, pages 11–20.

Allison Parrish. 2018. *Articulations*. Counterpath.

Ekaterina Shutova and Lin Sun. 2013. Unsupervised metaphor identification using hierarchical graph factorization clustering. In *Proceedings of the 2013 Conference of the North American Chapter of the Association for Computational Linguistics: Human Language Technologies*, pages 978–988.

Anselm Strauss and Juliet M Corbin. 1990. *Basics of qualitative research: Grounded theory procedures and techniques*. Sage Publications, Inc.

Tony Veale. 2013. Less rhyme, more reason: Knowledge-based poetry generation with feeling, insight and wit. In *ICCC*, pages 152–159.

Tony Veale and Yanfen Hao. 2007. Comprehending and generating apt metaphors: a web-driven, case-based approach to figurative language. In *AAAI*, volume 2007, pages 1471–1476.

Tony Veale, Ekaterina Shutova, and Beata Beigman Klebanov. 2016. Metaphor: A computational perspective. *Synthesis Lectures on Human Language Technologies*, 9(1):33–54.

Linguistic Features of Sarcasm and Metaphor Production Quality

Stephen Skalicky and Scott A. Crossley

Department of Applied Linguistics
Georgia State University
scskalicky@gmail.com, scrossley@gsu.edu

Abstract

Using linguistic features to detect figurative language has provided a deeper insight into figurative language. The purpose of this study is to assess whether linguistic features can help explain differences in *quality* of figurative language. In this study a large corpus of metaphors and sarcastic responses are collected from human subjects and rated for figurative language quality based on theoretical components of metaphor, sarcasm, and creativity. Using natural language processing tools, specific linguistic features related to lexical sophistication and semantic cohesion were used to predict the human ratings of figurative language quality. Results demonstrate linguistic features were able to predict small amounts of variance in metaphor and sarcasm production quality.

1 Introduction

Computational approaches to figurative language identification and classification are becoming increasingly more sophisticated (e.g., Khodak et al., 2017). While these studies have produced computational models capable of predicting figurative from non-figurative language, these models typically have little to say regarding the *quality* of figurative language. However, it is important to consider the potential ways that linguistic features differ based on higher or lower quality examples of figurative language to better understand the linguistic nature of figurative language. Thus, the purpose of this study is to test whether linguistic features can be used to predict the quality of metaphor and sarcasm production, which are two types of figurative language. Specifically, this study investigates whether linguistic features related to lexical sophistication and semantic cohesion are predictive of human ratings of metaphor and sarcasm production quality. Because our purpose is not to develop models capable of differentiating between figurative and non-figurative language, we do not take a traditional classification approach that is commonly seen in computational figurative language research.

Creativity and Figurative Language. Creativity can be operationalized as an effective and original solution to a problem (Runco and Jaeger 2012), and figurative language is an example of linguistic creativity (Gerrig and Gibbs 1988). One method to operationalize the quality of figurative language is to consider the creativity of individual examples of figurative language. Because language associated with more creative ideas has been linked to greater conceptual distance via semantic network modeling (Acar and Runco 2014; Dumas and Dunbar 2014), as well as greater lexical sophistication via more diverse vocabulary and lower word frequency (Skalicky et al., 2017), it follows that figurative language (e.g., metaphors and sarcasm) quality may also be predicted using linguistic measures related to lexical sophistication and semantic cohesion.

Metaphor Quality. Although conceptual metaphors are defined as the mapping of one conceptual domain onto another, this mapping must also be apt and meaningful (Gibbs 1994; Glucksberg 2001). Moreover, metaphors do not need to include large gaps in conceptual domains in order to be defined as a metaphor. Indeed, the ability to create descriptive links between seemingly disparate concepts is fundamental to metaphor production (Kintsch 2008; Kintsch and Bowles 2002), and therefore metaphors with greater conceptual distance may also be more effective.

Sarcasm Quality. Sarcasm is best defined as specific instances of verbal irony which serve to provide ironic criticism or praise that is somehow contrary to reality (Colston 2017). Sarcasm naturally involves some sort of incongruity between what is said and the situation in which sarcasm is used.

Proceedings of the Workshop on Figurative Language Processing, pages 7–16
New Orleans, Louisiana, June 6, 2018. ©2018 Association for Computational Linguistics

Thus, one way to measure the effectiveness of sarcasm is to determine how incongruent a sarcastic statement is within a respective context.

Participants. A total of 61 participants were recruited for this study (46 females and 15 males). Participant age ranged from 17 to 63 ($M = 25.56$, $SD = 8.341$). The participants were recruited from the undergraduate and graduate student population at a large public university in the southeastern United States. Participants were compensated for their participation in the experiment.

We opted to recruit our own set of participants and create a new corpus of sarcasm and metaphor for several reasons. First, doing so allowed us to gather additional measures from the participants, including measures of individual differences, linguistic features, and language background. Secondly, we were also able to capture behavioral information, such as how long it took participants to produce their metaphorical and sarcastic answers. Finally, we were able to ensure the participants were aware that their task was to provide metaphor and sarcasm, and provided definitions for doing so, which in turn allowed us to focus on the main purpose of this investigation (i.e., measuring differences in figurative language quality).

Metaphor Production Items. Two different metaphor production tasks were developed from previously used metaphor stimuli (Beaty and Silvia 2013; Chiappe and Chiappe 2007). First, a conventional metaphor task was designed containing 22 different items. Each item consisted of a Topic and a Description. All of the Topics were nouns (e.g., *her family*), and all of the Descriptions were descriptions or properties of those nouns (e.g., *something that keeps her stable and prevents her from drifting into danger*). Participants were instructed to use the Description of the Topic to write a metaphor reflective of the same meaning in the Description, but without reusing any of the words from the Description. In addition, a novel metaphor task was used, where participants were presented with two scenarios: the most boring class they have attended, and the most disgusting item they have ever eaten or drunk. For each scenario, participants were instructed to produce a metaphor that described their feelings during that scenario and were also provided with an example of how to start their metaphors (e.g., *Being in that class was like _____*).

Sarcasm Production Items. Twelve different drawn cartoons were adapted or created to serve as sarcasm production prompts. Four of these items were black and white cartoons used by Huang et al. (2015) to prompt sarcastic responses, each taken from the Rosenzweig Picture Frustration Study, originally designed to assess patient responses to frustrating situations in order to diagnose aggression (Rosenzweig 1945). Each of the black and white cartoons is a single-panel cartoon which depicts a frustrating situation with more than one speaker (e.g., one person's car breaks down and thus two people missed their train). The person responsible for the frustration is shown saying something, whereas the victim of the frustration is presented with a blank speech bubble. Four additional items were created by revising four single-panel *Bizarro!* comics. *Bizarro!* is a single-panel comic strip created by Dan Piraro that is syndicated daily in print newspapers across the United States. *Bizarro!* comics typically depict absurd or otherwise unlikely situations for the purpose of humor, social commentary, or both (www.bizzaro.com). The specific *Bizarro!* comics used in this study were four desert island comics, which each depicted two people stranded on a small desert island in the middle of an ocean. The original cartoons all contained a single speech bubble for one of the speakers, which was made blank for the purposes of this study. Finally, an additional four sarcasm production items were developed by creating original comics each comprised of three panels with two speakers. In each comic, the first two panels set up an initial situation (e.g., a young man is recruited to join the army and is guaranteed to travel the world in an exciting manner by a military recruiter), while the final panel includes one of the speakers with an empty speech bubble in a situation designed to prompt a sarcastic response (e.g., the young man ends up peeling potatoes instead of traveling the world). For each of the twelve comics, participants were instructed to imagine they were the speaker with the empty speech bubble and to write something sarcastic they would say if they were in that situation.

1.1 Procedure

Participants were recruited to complete the metaphor and sarcasm production tasks in a single laboratory session. The researcher briefly described the procedure of the experiment. Participants then began the production test and were randomly assigned to take the metaphor or the sarcasm production task first.

Metaphor Production. During the metaphor production task session, participants were first provided with a definition of metaphor: *A metaphor is a comparison between two things in order to help describe something.* Then, during each trial, the screen displayed the Topic and Description in clearly marked areas, with a blank text box for the participants to type their metaphor using the keyboard. After completing all 22 conventional metaphor prompts, participants then completed the two novel metaphor situations in a randomized order.

Sarcasm Production. During the sarcasm production task, participants were provided with a definition of sarcasm: *Sarcasm is a form of indirect language. When someone is being sarcastic, they mean something different than what they literally said.* Each trial involved one of the 12 comics randomly displayed above a text box, with a reminder asking participants to supply a sarcastic comment for the situation depicted in the comic. After typing their sarcastic statement into the answer box, participants pressed the Enter key to move on to the next comic until they completed all 12 comics (in a random order).

Each participant completed all of the metaphor and all of the sarcasm prompts in a random order within each block. Any answers that were indicative of a lack of attention or were not direct responses to the prompt (e.g., the participant did not attempt to create a metaphor) were discarded, leaving a total of 1304 metaphors and 716 sarcastic responses.

Figure 1. Example sarcasm production item

Human Ratings. An analytic rubric was created in order to obtain measures of figurative language production quality for the metaphors and sarcastic responses provided by the participants. The rubric contained separate sections for metaphor and sarcasm, and was comprised of three separate subscales designed to capture metaphor or sarcasm quality based on participants' ability to develop accurate, effective, and original examples of metaphor and sarcasm. Accuracy was related to theoretical definitions of metaphor (conceptual distance) and sarcasm (incongruity), while effectiveness and originality were related to theoretical definitions of creativity (i.e., novelty and mirth). Accordingly, the metaphor section included the subscales *Conceptual Distance, Novelty,* and *Mirth,* and the sarcasm section included the subscales *Incongruity, Novelty,* and *Mirth.* Novelty refers to originality. Mirth is an emotional reaction typically associated with humor, wherein one can experience slight amusement to intense hilarity arising from humorous or playful stimuli (Martin 2007).

Each subscale was measured using a range of one through six, with a score of one meaning the example of figurative language did not meet the criterion in any way and a score of six meaning the answer met the criterion in every way. Two human raters were recruited to provide ratings of the participants' metaphor and sarcastic responses using this analytic rubric. After initial ratings, a third rater (i.e., the first author) adjudicated any disagreements of two points or greater for all of the subscales, resulting in the following adjudicated kappa levels of .872 for metaphor conceptual distance scores, .854 and .855 for metaphor novelty and metaphor mirth, .835 for sarcasm incongruity, and .783 and .777 for sarcasm novelty and sarcasm mirth. After adjudication, the raters' scores were averaged to provide a single score per subscale per item.

1.2 Linguistic Features

The metaphors and sarcastic responses produced by the participants were analyzed for lexical sophistication and semantic cohesion using two text analysis tools: The Tool for the Automatic Analysis of LExical Sophistication (TAALES; Kyle et al., 2017) and the Tool for the Automatic Analysis of Cohesion (TAACO; Crossley et al., 2016), respectively. These tools read in raw text files and use existing taggers (e.g. Stanford

CoreNLP) and dictionaries (e.g., Corpus of Contemporary American English frequency values, MRC Psycholinguistic Database, WordNet Lexical Database) to provide a comprehensive output for a broad range of NLP features. Details regarding the construction and validation of these tools can be found in their respective citations.

Lexical Sophistication. Lexical sophistication is a measure of how complex a text is. For instance, texts with more diverse vocabulary, lower frequency words, and words that take longer to process in the mental lexical all contribute to a text's level of lexical sophistication. To date, very few studies have investigated lexical sophistication in the context of figurative language, aside from one study reporting that satirical product reviews were less concrete than non-satirical product reviews (Skalicky and Crossley 2015). Thus, there is a need to perform more investigation into lexical sophistication and figurative language in order to better determine if these features interact with perceptions of figurative language quality. This study includes broad measures of lexical sophistication related to lexical frequency, psycholinguistic properties of words, and word exposure in order to investigate and report any initial links between figurative language production quality and lexical sophistication.

From TAALES, several indices representative of lexical sophistication were calculated. First, measures of psycholinguistic properties of words were gathered because these measures represent cognitive representations of lexical items and can be used to assess the relative sophistication of lexical items (Kyle and Crossley 2015). Specifically, these measures were word Familiarity, Concreteness, Imageability, and Meaningfulness. Word Familiarity represents how familiar one is with a specific word, with more familiar words being words that are also more commonly encountered, making familiarity similar to word frequency. Word Concreteness refers how perceptible an entity associated with a particular word is (Brysbaert et al., 2014). For example, the word *dog* is more concrete than the word *music*. Word Imageability represents the ease of conjuring a mental image of a word, with words like *tree* being more imageable than words such as *abatement* (Salsbury et al., 2011). Word Meaningfulness represents how many different associations to other words a particular word has. For example, a word such as *tree* has more associations (e.g., *branch,*

leaf, wood) than a word such as *savant*, which activates fewer associations (Salsbury et al., 2011). Measures of word Imageability, Familiarity, and Meaningfulness were all calculated based on the MRC Psycholinguistics Database norms (Coltheart 1981), which is a curated compilation of previous rating studies for these features. Word Concreteness values were calculated using the Brysbaert Concreteness norms (Brysbaert et al., 2014), which were derived from human ratings of word concreteness using online crowdsourcing.

In addition to those indices, linguistic features related to word exposure and use were also collected, as these represent the relative frequency of occurrence and use for certain words. These indices were spoken word frequency, semantic diversity, and age of acquisition. Spoken word frequency was calculated using counts from the spoken portion of the Corpus of Contemporary American English (COCA; Davies 2008). Semantic Diversity represents the number of different words contexts a particular word typically occurs in, and thus represents specificity of word meanings. Semantic Diversity was calculated for each word using the norms published by Hoffman et al. (2013). To calculate Semantic Diversity, Hoffman et al. (2013) separated the British National Corpus into chunks of 1,000 words, and then analyzed the total number of these 1,000 word contexts any particular word occurred in, as well as the semantic similarity of each word to all of the other words in those contexts. The end result is that words with higher Semantic Diversity can be used in more contexts and have more variable meanings than those with lower Semantic Diversity. Finally, Age of Acquisition (AoA) values represent human intuition regarding the age when they first learned a particular word. AoA values based on Kuperman et al., (2012) were used, which were collected using a large number of human raters via online crowdsourcing. All of these linguistic indices were calculated based on content words only.

Cohesion. TAACO was used in order to calculate semantic overlap between prompts and participant answers for the metaphors only. Distance between concepts used in metaphors has been accurately modeled using measures of semantic association, such as Latent Semantic Analysis (Kintsch 2008; Kintsch and Bowles 2002), and therefore a measure of semantic distance was included in this study in order to determine if distance between concepts influences human perceptions of metaphor production quality. To do so, the participants' metaphors were grouped by prompt and analyzed separately using the source text analysis option in TAACO. This option allows the user to load in a source text as a reference text for other texts to be compared against for semantic and cohesive similarity or differences. For each group of metaphors, the Description provided to the participants was loaded as the source text, and the participant's metaphor were analyzed to gather the amount of semantic overlap between participants' answers and the prompts using the word2vec measure in TAACO. Word2vec models the semantic direction and magnitude of words as they relate to other words (known as *vectors*). By modeling words as vectors, word2vec assumes words more closely grouped together are more semantically related than those that are further apart and employs predictive modeling in order to calculate the semantic relations among words in a text.

1.3 Statistical Analysis

The human ratings of figurative language production quality were first analyzed using Principle Component Analysis (PCA) in order to obtain weighted component scores of figurative language production quality for both the metaphors and the sarcastic responses. Afterwards, a series of linear mixed effects (LME) regression models were fit to determine if any of the linguistic features were predictive of figurative language production quality scores. For each LME model, the figurative language production quality score was entered as the dependent variable and the linguistic features were added as the independent predictor variables (also known as fixed effects). For metaphors, metaphor type (novel vs. conventional) was also added as a fixed effect, and for sarcastic responses, sarcasm prompt type was added as a fixed effect (black and white, desert island, or three-panel comics). Subjects and items were entered as crossed random effects, with a random slope of metaphor type or sarcasm prompt type fit on subjects where appropriate. Interactions were tested among the metaphor types and sarcasm prompt types and the linguistic features, with only significant interactions retained. The linguistic features were controlled for multicollinearity using Pearson correlations and variance inflation values (VIF), and were also z-scored before being entered into the models.

2 Results

2.1 Metaphor and Sarcasm Quality Ratings

The human ratings of metaphor and sarcasm for the three subscales (*Conceptual Distance/Incongruity, Novelty, and Mirth*) were analyzed using two separate PCAs for the remaining 1304 metaphors and 716 sarcastic responses after adjudication. Both of the PCAs reported that the Novelty and Mirth subscales loaded into a single component, which explained 71% of the variance in the PCA for metaphor production scores and 62% of the variance in the PCA for sarcastic response scores. For the metaphor PCA, the Conceptual Distance scores loaded into a separate component (from novelty/mirth) explaining 26% of the variance in ratings, and for the sarcastic responses PCA, the Incongruity subscale loaded into a separate component (from novelty/mirth) explaining 33% of the variance in ratings. Therefore, the ratings for Novelty and Mirth were averaged for both metaphors and sarcasms, and the ratings for Conceptual Distance and Incongruity were retained in their original manner, resulting in two dependent variables for the metaphors and sarcastic responses per item.

2.2 Predicting Metaphor Quality

Metaphor Conceptual Distance. An LME model with metaphor conceptual distance as the dependent variable and linguistic features related to lexical sophistication and source overlap (word2vec), along with metaphor type (conventional vs. novel) as predictor variables reported three linguistic indices as significant predictors of the conceptual distance ratings (Table 1).

First, metaphors containing words with higher average Age of Acquisition (AoA) scores received significantly lower conceptual distance ratings. Words with a higher AoA are those that are self-reported to be learned later in life based on human judgments, and therefore represent less frequent and more sophisticated vocabulary.

This suggests that more sophisticated language in terms of AoA scores was not necessary in order to construct metaphors with higher conceptual distance between the entities being described in the metaphors. For example, the following metaphor had an average AoA of 8.9 and a conceptual distance score of one: *Some professors are geniuses like a supercomputer.* The prompt for this metaphor was *Some professors are very smart.* The word *genius* has an AoA of 7.21 and the word *supercomputer* has an AoA of 12.44, and these two words contributed significantly to the higher AoA score. Moreover, the word *genius* is conceptually similar to the prompt (i.e., *very smart*), and does not allow for any alternative conceptual interpretations. Indeed, *genius* is essentially a synonym of *smart*, and thus represents the same concept, and the inclusion of *supercomputer* also contains concepts related to intelligence, further amplifying the notion of smartness evoked by the word *genius*. Conversely, the following metaphor has an average AoA of 3.5 and a conceptual distance score of five: *That book is worth my arm and leg* in response to the prompt *Some property is very valuable*. In this metaphor, the words *arm, leg,* and *book* all have AoA scores of less than four, and thus contribute to a relatively low AoA rating. Furthermore, there is greater conceptual distance between a variety of concepts in this metaphor, with the words *arm* and *leg* perhaps conceptualized as *high value currency*, but only if one is aware of the idiomatic use of the expression *costs an arm and a leg*. Unlike the *genius* metaphor with high AoA, the words *arm* and *leg* are also not more sophisticated synonyms of any words in the prompt.

In addition to AoA, metaphors with higher Semantic Diversity scores also received significantly lower conceptual distance scores. Words with higher Semantic Diversity are words with less specific and more ambiguous meanings, which may suggest that metaphors containing more semantically ambiguous words may not be directly referencing specific concepts to make an apt metaphorical comparison.

In a similar fashion, metaphors with higher average Word Concreteness received significantly higher conceptual distance scores. These findings suggest that the human raters' perceptions of conceptual distance in the metaphors were influenced by the use of specific words in the metaphors. This may be because metaphors with more specific word usage were better able to evoke conceptual comparisons that were more distantly related, making it easier for the raters to identify the size of the conceptual comparison in the metaphor. Conversely, metaphors with higher AoA scores may have tended to use conceptual synonyms with the same overall semantic meaning (e.g., the use of *genius* to describe a *smart* professor), lead-

ing to lowered perceptions of conceptual distance among the human raters.

The model explained a total of 4.1% of the variance in conceptual distance scores, suggesting that these linguistic features account for a relatively small amount of the variation in conceptual distance scores and that they did not play a strong role in the human raters' conceptual rating decisions.

Metaphor Novelty and Mirth. An LME model with the averaged metaphor novelty/mirth score of human ratings the dependent variable and the same linguistic features related to lexical sophistication and source overlap used in the previous model as predictor variables reported three linguistic indices as significant predictors of metaphor novelty/mirth ratings (Table 2).

First, MRC Imageability was a significant, negative predictor of the novelty/mirth ratings, suggesting that metaphors including more imageable words resulted in lower ratings of novelty/mirth. Second, word2vec source similarity was also a significant, negative predictor of novelty/mirth, suggesting that metaphors containing higher semantic overlap with the source text received lower ratings of novelty/mirth.

Third, COCA spoken word frequency was also a significant, negative predictor of novelty/mirth ratings, suggesting that metaphors containing words with higher spoken word frequency resulted in significantly lower ratings of novelty/mirth. There were no other significant main effects or interactions. These results cohere to suggest that metaphors received higher novelty/mirth ratings if they included more sophisticated language and also included less semantic overlap with the metaphor prompt.

From a lexical perspective, higher levels of both Spoken Word Frequency and Word Imageability resulted in significantly lower ratings of novelty/mirth for metaphors. The direction of their influence on the novelty/mirth ratings indicates that more lexically sophisticated metaphors received higher novelty/mirth scores.

In terms of cohesion, metaphors that contained greater semantic overlap with the metaphor prompt (as measured through word2vec) received significantly lower novelty/mirth scores. This finding makes intuitive sense because metaphors that were more closely related to the metaphor prompt were most likely those that were more cliché or did not make more distant comparisons.

The word2vec measure may also capture the extent to which participants relied on the language from the metaphor prompt. For example, the metaphor *Some relationships are like working in a research lab and having a project fail* received a novelty/mirth score of five and a semantic overlap score of -0.17. The only words repeated in this metaphor from the prompt are *some relationships*, while the rest of the metaphor includes words outside of the prompt.

Conversely, the metaphor *The earth is full of people working like bees* received a novelty/mirth score two and a semantic overlap score of 0.68.

Unlike the previous metaphor, this metaphor almost completely repeats the metaphor prompt word for word (i.e., *the earth is full of busy people*) and only includes three original words.

Much like the model predicting metaphor conceptual distance ratings, the linguistic features predicting the metaphor novelty/mirth scores explained a relatively small amount of variance in rater scores (7.5%), suggesting that linguistic features were just one small influence on the human ratings of novelty and mirth.

	Estimate	*SE*	*t*	*p*
(Intercept)	4.559	0.089	51.179	< .001
Metaphor Type: Novel	-0.228	0.399	-0.571	0.575
Source Similarity (word2vec)	0.010	0.032	0.324	0.746
MRC Familiarity	0.015	0.027	0.569	0.570
MRC Imageability	-0.011	0.039	-0.277	0.782
MRC Meaningfulness	-0.034	0.034	-0.999	0.318
Age of Acquisition*	-0.123	0.035	-3.533	< .001
Brysbaert Concreteness*	0.102	0.039	2.610	0.009
COCA Spoken Word Frequency	0.027	0.031	0.877	0.380
Semantic Diversity*	-0.106	0.035	-2.993	0.003
* = Significant predictor. SE = Standard Error. Baseline for Metaphor Type = Conventional.				

Table 1. LME predicting metaphor conceptual distance scores

	Estimate	*SE*	*t*	*p*
(Intercept)	3.292	0.101	32.604	< .001
Metaphor Type: Novel	0.165	0.388	0.425	0.676
Source Similarity (word2vec)*	-0.127	0.041	-3.127	0.002
MRC Familiarity	0.064	0.035	1.830	0.068
MRC Imageability*	-0.106	0.050	-2.120	0.034
MRC Meaningfulness	0.003	0.043	0.064	0.949
Age of Acquisition	-0.065	0.045	-1.451	0.147
Brysbaert Concreteness	-0.067	0.050	-1.347	0.178
COCA Spoken Word Frequency*	-0.314	0.041	-7.660	< .001
Semantic Diversity	-0.040	0.045	-0.895	0.371
* = Significant predictor. SE = Standard Error. Baseline for Metaphor Type = Conventional.				

Table 2. LME predicting metaphor novelty/mirth scores

2.3 Predicting Sarcasm Quality

Sarcasm Incongruity. An LME model predicting incongruity ratings of the sarcastic responses using linguistic features (MRC Familiarity, MRC Meaningfulness, Age of Acquisition, Brysbaert Concreteness, COCA Spoken Word Frequency, and Semantic Diversity) reported that MRC Meaningfulness was a significant, negative predictor of incongruity ratings, suggesting that sarcastic responses with more average associations to other words resulted in lower ratings of incongruity (Table 3). This model only accounted for 2% of the variance in incongruity scores, suggesting that this linguistic feature played a small role in raters' perceptions of incongruity in the sarcastic responses.

Sarcasm Novelty and Mirth. An LME model predicting novelty/mirth ratings of the sarcastic responses using the same linguistic features as the previous model included one significant main effect and two significant interactions (Table 4).

The main effect demonstrated that sarcastic responses containing higher levels of average AoA received significantly higher novelty/mirth ratings. This finding provide some evidence suggesting that sarcastic responses which are more lexically sophisticated are perceived as more creative, because higher amounts of AoA tend to suggest higher levels of lexical sophistication.

For example, the sarcastic reply of *at least we have water* for one of the desert island comics received a novelty/mirth score of 2.25 and had an average AoA score of 3.04, whereas the sarcastic reply *you have surgical precision behind the wheel* in response to the puddle splash comic received a novelty/mirth score of 4.75 and had an average AoA of 7.45. The second example's use of *surgical precision* represents less frequent words when compared to the first example, which in turn provides a higher likelihood that the author of the second sarcastic response coined an answer that was unique when compared to the other participants, subsequently increasing perceptions of novelty and perhaps mirth among the human raters. Thus, the AoA results suggest that using more lexically sophisticated language could be one strategy for producing more creative sarcastic responses.

	Estimate	*SE*	*t*	*p*
(Intercept)	4.396	0.099	44.278	< .001
Sarcasm Prompt: Black and White	0.216	0.129	1.676	0.128
Sarcasm Prompt: Desert Island	0.175	0.129	1.352	0.209
MRC Familiarity	0.063	0.035	1.806	0.071
MRC Meaningfulness*	-0.067	0.032	-2.079	0.038
Age of Acquisition	0.034	0.030	1.130	0.259
Brysbaert Concreteness	0.027	0.034	0.780	0.436
COCA Spoken Frequency	-0.003	0.033	-0.103	0.918
Semantic Diversity	-0.026	0.036	-0.729	0.466
* Significant effect. SE = Standard error. Baseline for Sarcasm Prompt = Three Panel Comic.				

Table 3. LME predicting sarcasm incongruity scores

	Estimate	*SE*	*t*	*p*
(Intercept)	2.965	0.125	23.661	< .001
MRC Familiarity	0.007	0.044	0.154	0.877
Sarcasm Prompt: Black and White	0.190	0.162	1.175	0.272
Sarcasm Prompt: Desert Island	0.377	0.162	2.328	0.046
Age of Acquisition*	0.114	0.038	3.013	0.003
Brysbaert Concreteness	0.038	0.063	0.607	0.544
COCA Spoken Frequency	0.030	0.039	0.763	0.446
Semantic Diversity	-0.065	0.043	-1.507	0.132
MRC Meaningfulness	0.001	0.039	0.018	0.985
Significant Interactions				
MRC Familiarity: Sarcasm Prompt: Black and White	0.196	0.120	1.638	0.102
MRC Familiarity: Sarcasm Prompt: Desert Island*	0.428	0.128	3.351	0.001
Concreteness: Sarcasm Prompt: Black and White	0.057	0.088	0.652	0.515
Concreteness: Sarcasm Prompt: Desert Island*	0.210	0.085	2.472	0.014
* Significant effect. SE = Standard error. Baseline for Sarcasm Prompt = Three Panel Comic.				

Table 4. LME predicting sarcasm novelty/mirth scores

Additionally, two lexical features interacted with prompt type in that there were significant differences between the desert island prompt and the three-panel comic prompt for both features. These interactions demonstrated that increasing levels of MRC Familiarity and Brysbaert Concreteness significantly increased perceptions of novelty/mirth for sarcastic replies made in response to the desert island prompts when compared to the three-panel comic prompts. Higher levels of both MRC Familiarity and Brysbaert Concreteness suggest less lexically sophisticated language, because words that are more familiar correlate with more frequently used words, and words that are and more concrete represent concepts that are more easily retrieved due to their encoding as both a lexical item (e.g., car) as well as the visual concept of that same item (e.g., a concept of a car). Because there was less contextual information available in the desert island prompts, it may be that sarcastic responses including less sophisticated language (i.e., more concrete concepts that are more familiar) were better able to index specific ideas indicative of sarcastic meaning for the desert island prompts when compared to the three-panel comic prompts, where contextual information could fill in semantic gaps for the raters. Much like the other models, these features accounted for a relatively small amount of variance in the raters' scores (6.8%), again suggesting that linguistic features played a small yet significant role in raters' perceptions of creativity among the sarcastic responses.

3 Discussion

The purpose of this study was to investigate whether differences in figurative language quality could be predicted using linguistic features related to lexical sophistication and semantic cohesion. Overall, the findings suggest that variables representative of lexical sophistication (and semantic cohesion for metaphors) played a small yet significant role in explaining variance among rater perceptions of figurative language quality, and also that perceptions of quality included both theoretical constructs related to metaphor and sarcasm (i.e., conceptual distance and incongruity) as well as to more generalized constructs of creative ability (i.e., novelty and mirth).

In regards to the theoretical components, greater conceptual distance scores were predicted by more sophisticated and specific language, perhaps because more specific words are better able to encode specific concepts, allowing for a more direct metaphorical comparison between two entities. For sarcastic responses, greater incongruity was marked by language with a lower number of word associations, which may have been a result of the use of more conversational language in sarcastic responses (e.g., *thank you*). As for the novelty and mirth scores, overall the results demonstrated that greater levels of lexical sophistication led to greater perceptions of novelty and mirth for both metaphors and sarcastic responses, although this effect was mediated by the different prompts for sarcastic responses.

Linguistic features were better able to predict variance in the novelty and mirth scores when compared to the conceptual distance or incongruity scores, suggesting that the raters may have attended more strongly to linguistic features when considering the creativity of the metaphors and sarcastic responses when compared to the concep-

tual distance or incongruity. This suggests that linguistic features related to lexical sophistication may be more suitable for measuring general measures of creativity, which are but one component of figurative language quality.

Finally, the linguistic features explained more variance in the metaphors when compared to the sarcastic responses, which is most likely a result of the linguistic context in which metaphors operate. Specifically, the understanding of a metaphor requires the possessing of conceptual information encoded in the metaphor. However, in order to understand a sarcastic reply, one must be more aware of the surrounding social and pragmatic context. Echoing contextual information linguistically is not necessary in many sarcastic responses, as it is known knowledge already available to those within the situation. For example, a simple *thank you* can be taken as sarcastic in the right contexts, which would be difficult to differentiate through linguistic means alone. Therefore, the contextual nature of sarcasm quality may make it more difficult to define using quantitative linguistic features when compared to other types of figurative language, such as metaphor.

4 Conclusion

One limitation present in this data is that the answers produced by the participants were generally short, which in turn could easily bias some of the lexical measurements used, as all of them reported average scores for all the content words in an answer. Nonetheless, this study has shed further light on linguistic features of figurative language by investigating connections between figurative language quality, lexical sophistication, and cohesion using theoretical definitions of creativity, metaphor, and sarcasm and demonstrating that linguistic features of figurative language quality may in part be related to generalized notions of creativity. Future work employing classifiers designed to discriminate figurative language from non-figurative language may want to consider the quality of figurative language, and one method for doing so may lie in linguistic features related to creativity in the examples under investigation.

Acknowledgments

We would like to thank Tori Morrison and Oni Nistor for the figurative language quality ratings.

References

Acar, Selcuk and Mark A. Runco. 2014. Assessing associative distance among ideas elicited by tests of divergent thinking. *Creativity Research Journal* 26(2). 229–238.

Beaty, Roger E. and Paul J. Silvia. 2013. Metaphorically speaking: cognitive abilities and the production of figurative language. *Memory & Cognition* 41(2). 255–267.

Brysbaert, Marc, Amy Beth Warriner, and Victor Kuperman. 2014. Concreteness ratings for 40 thousand generally known English word lemmas. *Behavior Research Methods* 46(3). 904–911.

Chiappe, Dan L. and Penny Chiappe. 2007. The role of working memory in metaphor production and comprehension. *Journal of Memory and Language* 56(2). 172–188.

Colston, Herbert L. 2017. Irony and sarcasm. In Salvatore Attardo (ed.), *The Routledge handbook of language and humor*, 234–249. New York, NY: Routledge.

Coltheart, Max. 1981. The MRC psycholinguistic database. *The Quarterly Journal of Experimental Psychology* 33(4). 497–505.

Crossley, Scott A., Kristopher Kyle, and Danielle S. McNamara. 2016. The tool for the automatic analysis of text cohesion (TAACO): Automatic assessment of local, global, and text cohesion. *Behavior Research Methods* 48. 1227–1237.

Davies, Mark. 2008. *The corpus of contemporary American English*. BYE, Brigham Young University.

Dumas, Denis and Kevin N. Dunbar. 2014. Understanding fluency and originality: A latent variable perspective. *Thinking Skills and Creativity* 14. 56–67.

Gerrig, Richard J. and Raymond W. Gibbs. 1988. Beyond the lexicon: Creativity in language production. *Metaphor and Symbol* 3(3). 1–19.

Gibbs, Raymond W. 1994. *The poetics of mind: Figurative thought, language, and understanding*. Cambridge, MA: Cambridge University Press.

Glucksberg, Sam. 2001. *Understanding figurative language: From metaphor to idioms*. Oxford University Press.

Hoffman, Paul, Matthew A. Lambon Ralph, and Timothy T. Rogers. 2013. Semantic diversity: A measure of semantic ambiguity based on variability in the contextual usage of words. *Behavior Research Methods* 45(3). 718–730.

Huang, Li, Francesca Gino, and Adam D. Galinsky. 2015. The highest form of intelligence: Sarcasm increases creativity for both expressers and recipients. *Organizational Behavior and Human Decision Processes* 131. 162–177.

Khodak, Mikhail, Nikunj Saunshi, and Kiran Vodrahalli. 2017. A large self-annotated corpus for sarcasm. *arXiv preprint arXiv:1704.05579*. https://arxiv.org/abs/1704.05579 (15 June, 2017).

Kintsch, Walter. 2008. How the mind computes the meaning of metaphor. In Raymond W. Gibbs Jr (ed.), *The Cambridge handbook of metaphor and thought*, 129–142. Cambridge, MA: Cambridge University Press.

Kintsch, Walter and Anita R. Bowles. 2002. Metaphor comprehension: What makes a metaphor difficult to understand? *Metaphor and Symbol* 17(4). 249–262.

Kuperman, Victor, Hans Stadthagen-Gonzalez, and Marc Brysbaert. 2012. Age-of-acquisition ratings for 30,000 English words. *Behavior Research Methods* 44(4). 978–990.

Kyle, Kristopher and Scott A. Crossley. 2015. Automatically assessing lexical sophistication: Indices, tools, findings, and application. *TESOL Quarterly* 49(4). 757–786.

Kyle, Kristopher, Scott Crossley, and Cynthia Berger. 2017. The tool for the automatic analysis of lexical sophistication (TAALES): version 2.0. *Behavior Research Methods*.

Martin, Rod A. 2007. *The psychology of humor: An integrative approach*. Burlington, MA: Elsevier Academic Press.

Rosenzweig, Saul. 1945. The picture-association method and its application in a study of reactions to frustration. *Journal of personality* 14(1). 3–23.

Runco, Mark A. and Garrett J. Jaeger. 2012. The standard definition of creativity. *Creativity Research Journal* 24(1). 92–96.

Salsbury, Tom, Scott A. Crossley, and Danielle S. McNamara. 2011. Psycholinguistic word information in second language oral discourse. *Second Language Research* 27(3). 343–360.

Skalicky, Stephen and Scott Crossley. 2015. A statistical analysis of satirical Amazon.com product reviews. *The European Journal of Humour Research* 2(3). 66–85.

Skalicky, Stephen, Scott A. Crossley, Danielle S. McNamara, and Kasia Muldner. 2017. Identifying creativity during problem solving using linguistic features. *Creativity Research Journal* 29(4). 343–353.

Leveraging Syntactic Constructions for Metaphor Identification

Kevin Stowe
University of Colorado, Boulder
kevin.stowe@colorado.edu

Martha Palmer
University of Colorado, Boulder
martha.palmer@colorado.edu

Abstract

Identification of metaphoric language in text is critical for generating effective semantic representations for natural language understanding. Computational approaches to metaphor identification have largely relied on heuristic based models or feature-based machine learning, using hand-crafted lexical resources coupled with basic syntactic information. However, recent work has shown the predictive power of syntactic constructions in determining metaphoric source and target domains (Sullivan, 2013). Our work intends to explore syntactic constructions and their relation to metaphoric language. We undertake a corpus-based analysis of predicate-argument constructions and their metaphoric properties, and attempt to effectively represent syntactic constructions as features for metaphor processing, both in identifying source and target domains and in distinguishing metaphoric words from non-metaphoric.

1 Metaphor Background

Metaphor can be understood as the conceptualization of one entity using another. Lakoff and Johnson's seminal work shows that metaphors are present at the cognitive level and expressed linguistically (Lakoff and Johnson, 1980). A typical conceptual metaphor mapping is ARGUMENT IS WAR, in which ARGUMENT is structured through the domain of WAR:

1. He *defended* his position through his publications.

2. Her speech *attacked* his viewpoint.

The term "linguistic metaphor" is used to indicate these types of words and phrases. We will focus on linguistic metaphor, as identifying these utterances as metaphoric is critical for generating correct semantic interpretations. For instance, in the examples above, literal semantic interpretations of 'defend' and 'attack' will yield nonsensical utterances: a physical position cannot reasonably be defended by a publication, nor can a speech physically attack any kind of entity.

Automatic metaphor processing tends to involve two main tasks: identifying which words are being used metaphorically (here called metaphor *identification*), and attempting to provide an accurate semantic interpretation for an utterance (here called metaphor *interpretation*). The first has largely been approached as a supervised machine learning problem, typically using lexical semantic features and their interaction with context to learn the kinds of situations where lexical metaphors appear. The problem of metaphor interpretation is more complex, with approaches including the implementation of full metaphoric interpretation systems (Martin, 1990), (Ovchinnikova et al., 2014), identification of source and target domains (Dodge et al., 2015), developing knowledge bases (Gordon et al., 2015), and providing literal paraphrases to metaphoric phrases (Shutova, 2010), (Shutova, 2013).

In both identification and interpretation systems, syntax tends to play a limited role. Many systems rely only on lexical semantics of target words, or use only minimal context or dependency relations to help disambiguate in context (Gargett and Barnden, 2015), (Rai et al., 2016). Others rely on topic modeling and other document and sentence level features to provide general semantics, and compare the lexical semantics to that, ignoring the more "middle"-level syntactic interactions (Heintz et al., 2013). While these approaches have been effective in many areas, there is evidence that figurative language is significantly influenced by syntactic constructions, and thus if they can be represented more effectively, metaphor processing

Proceedings of the Workshop on Figurative Language Processing, pages 17–26
New Orleans, Louisiana, June 6, 2018. ©2018 Association for Computational Linguistics

capabilities can be improved.

We will examine five kinds of predicate-argument constructions in corpus data to assess their metaphoric distributions and usefulness as features for classification. Our contribution is twofold. First, we examine the LCC metaphor corpus, which includes source and target annotations, to determine their use in predicate-argument constructions (Mohler et al., 2016), and employ syntactic representations as features to improve source/target classification. Second, we investigate predicate-argument constructions in the VUAMC corpus of metaphor annotation (Pragglejaz Group, 2007), and employ syntactic features to predict metaphoric vs non-metaphoric words.

2 Metaphor and Constructions

Recent metaphor research has indicated that construction grammar can be employed to determine the source and target domains of linguistic metaphors (Sullivan, 2013). In many cases, certain constructions can determine what syntactic components are allowable as source and target domains. For example, verbs tend to evoke source domains. The target domain is then evoked by one or more of the verb's arguments (from Sullivan pg 88):

1. the **cinema** *beckoned* (intransitive)

2. the **criticism** *stung* him (transitive)

3. Meredith *flung* him **an eager glance** (ditransitive)

In these instances, the verb is from the source domain and at least one of the objects is from the target. However, arguments can also be neutral and don't necessarily evoke the target domain. Pronouns like 'him' in (2) and (3) don't evoke any domain. The optionality of domain evocation makes it harder to predict which elements of the construction participate in the metaphor. Despite this limitation, this analysis shows that syntactic structures beyond the lexical level can be indicative of source and target domains. To better understand how these structures determine metaphor, we explored metaphor-annotated corpus data for predicate-argument constructions.

3 Computational Approaches

While metaphor processing has largely been focused on capturing lexical semantics, there have been a variety of approaches that incorporate syntactic information. Many computational approaches focus on specific constructions, perhaps indicating the need to classify different metaphoric constructions through different means. The dataset of (Tsvetkov et al., 2014) provides adjective-noun annotation which has been extensively studied (Rei et al., 2017), (Bulat et al., 2017). A particularly promising approach is that of (Gutierrez et al., 2016), who use compositional distributional semantic models (CDSMs) to represent metaphors as transformations in vector space, specifically for adjective-noun constructions. Another relevant approach is that of (Haagsma and Bjerva, 2016) who use clustering and selectional preference information to detect metaphors in predicate argument constructions, including verbs with objects, subjects, and both. Their highest F1 is 57.8 for verbs with both arguments.

Many systems that rely heavily on lexical resources also include some dependency information. (Rai et al., 2016) and (Gargett and Barnden, 2015) use a variety of syntactic features including lemma, part of speech, and dependency relations. However, both systems are feature-rich and these syntactic elements' contribution is unclear. (**?**) use lexical features along with contrasting those features between the target word and its head. (Dodge et al., 2015) employ a variety of constructions in identifying metaphoric source and target domains. They identify a broad range of constructions and use these as templates that metaphoric expressions can fill. Our work expands on this idea by formalizing the constructions into features for statistical metaphor identification.

Perhaps the most syntactically oriented metaphor identification system is that of (Hovy et al., 2013), who uses syntactic tree kernels to identify metaphor. They use combinations of syntactic features via tree kernels and semantics via WordNet supersenses and target word embeddings. Our approach expands on this by exploring different syntactic representations and incorporating semantics through word embeddings into the syntactic structures.

4 Corpus Analysis

Sullivan identifies a large number of constructions and the possible configurations of their arguments with regard to source and target domains. While some corpus examples are provided that show the variety of source-target patterns in each construction's argument structure, an in-depth analysis of how these constructions and their metaphoric properties are distributed is still needed. We examined the predicate argument constructions they analyze by using hand-annotated metaphor corpora to better understand the distributional patterns that occur. This allows us to make predictions about what kind of constructions and arguments are useful for metaphor identification and interpretation and what might be a computationally feasible way to implement them.

While they examine many kinds of constructions, most of them seem based almost entirely on the lexical semantics of the words involved, and thus can be captured simply by effectively representing the meaning of individual words. Domain and predicative adjective constructions fall into this category: the construction is identified by the type of adjective, which needs to be represented at the lexical level. The more interesting cases are argument structure constructions, which take many forms. Sullivan identifies nine different argument structure constructions that each have their own source and target properties:

1. **Intransitive**
2. **Transitive**
3. Intrasitive Resultative
4. Transitive Resultative
5. **Ditransitive**
6. **Equation**
7. Predicative AP
8. Predicative PP
9. **Simile**

To identify the use of metaphor in these constructions, we will rely on two resources: the LCC metaphor corpus and the VUAMC corpus. The freely available portion of the LCC corpus contains approximately 7,500 source/target pairs, allowing for a more in-depth look at metaphoric semantics. The VUAMC contains approximately 200,000 words of text with each word tagged as metaphoric or non-metaphoric. This allows for large scale analysis of metaphoricity versus non-metaphoricity at the word level.

4.1 Identifying Constructions

To examine metaphors in these corpora, we need a method for automatically identifying predicate-argument constructions. The VUAMC corpus, as a subsection of the BNC baby, comes with gold-standard dependency parses. For the LCC dataset, we used the dependency parser from Stanford Core NLP tools (Manning et al., 2014). These parses are sufficient to identify intransitives, transitives, and ditransitive constructions. Verb instances that have an indirect object are ditransitive, those that lack an indirect object but have a direct object are transitive, and those that lack either but have a subject are intransitive. Copulas are marked in the dependency parses, so we can easily identify equative constructions. While similes can take many forms, Sullivan's work focuses on simile constructions that consist of a copular verb and the word 'like'. This oversimplifies to some degree, as many similes don't need a copula ('she fretted like a mother hen', 'they flew like bats'), but it allows us to create a subset of equative constructions that represent copular similes.

This analysis is necessarily limited, as the we cannot automatically capture more complex constructions via dependency parses, and many of these are often metaphorically rich. While we understand this limitation, we believe that we can utilize syntactic features of these basic constructions as a starting point, with a future goal of expanding to more complex examples.

Also note that we only identify the surface realization of these constructions - any dropped arguments or missing elements that aren't in the dependency parse aren't considered a part of the construction. Thus we see examples of typically ditransitive verbs (like 'give') that occur intransitively and transitively, as they lack overt direct and indirect objects.

5 LCC Analysis

To explore source and target domains, we employ the free portion of the LCC corpus from Mohler et al, which contains approximately 7,500 source/target metaphor pairs in sentential context, rated from 0 to 3 on their degree of metaphoricity. For our research, we included only those instances that were rated above 1.5, yielding approximately 3,000 metaphoric sentences. These annotations also include the source and target domains of the metaphors, and the lexical trigger phrases that engender the source and target domains. This allows us to quantify Sullivan's analysis of source and target domains in different constructions, and shows the actual distribution of source and target domain items in each construction.

In order to identify constructions in the LCC data, we extracted syntactic relations from the dependency parses, using the basic patterns previously defined to identify predicate argument constructions. This allows us to identify the five different constructions: intransitives, transitives, ditransitives, equatives (copulas), and similes (analyzed as a subset of equative constructions). For each construction found, we can identify the predicate and the predicate's arguments, and determine for each whether they are identified as metaphoric and whether they belong to the source or target domain.

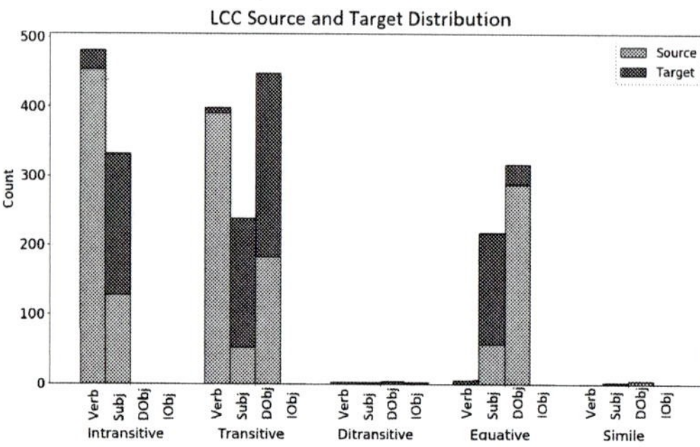

Figure 1: Counts of metaphoric items in the LCC. Each bar represents the total instances of argument in each construction, as well as the percentage of items that belong to source and target domains.

The vast majority of constructions in the LCC are intransitive, transitive, and equative. Ditransitives (.4%) and similes (.1%) are exceedingly rare. This may be because the similes found are only the verbal type: instances of a copula with the word 'like'. Other similes are likely missed by this automatic approach.

The majority of metaphoric verbs (92%) are source domain items, supporting Sullivan's claims. Subjects and objects tend to be from the target domain (61% each). Ditransitive verb constructions are relatively rare, with only 43 found, and only 3 of those containing a metaphoric verb.

Figure 1 shows the counts of source and target items in the LCC data, based on construction and argument of the construction. Note that in equative constructions, direct objects are almost always source domain items, showing a parallel between copular arguments and verbs. This is likely due to the predicative nature of the direct objects of copular verbs.

5.1 Source and Target Identification

Given that verbs and their argument structures have varying distributions of source and target domain items, we believe that these syntactic structures can be effectively employed in the classification of source and target domain words. While identifying source and target domains at the sentence level requires lexical and sentential semantics and may not require syntactic information, identifying lexical triggers can be improved by using better syntactic representations. To this end we set up a classification task for identifying source and target elements.

The LCC contains phrase-level annotations for source and target elements. We split each sentence into words, projecting the source and target annotations to the word level. From this, we developed three classification tasks: (1) identifying source words, (2) identifying target words, and (3) identifying any metaphoric word (either source or target). Our classification scheme focuses on verbs and nouns, as these are the elements that compose the syntactic structures in question.

We developed a set of different representations designed to capture construction-like structures, and employ them for source/target classification. This approach follows the intuition of (Hovy et al., 2013): "metaphorical use differs from literal use in certain syntactic patterns". We implemented this theory by developing various representations of constructional syntax and pairing them with lexical semantic features.

For our lexical semantics component, we experimented with the word embeddings from word2vec (Mikolov et al., 2013), using the pretrained Google News data, as well as the Glove embeddings (Pennington et al., 2014). We found in validation that the Google News vectors yielded slightly better performance, and so those were used in further experiments.

5.2 Syntactic Representations

Hovy et al use tree kernels to represent the semantic structure of instances, providing information from dependency parses, part of speech tags, and WordNet supersenses. Our approach follows this work by experimenting with a variety of different ways of meshing syntactic and semantic components. This involves creating a computationally feasible syntactic representation and combining it with semantics (in our case, word embeddings)

Construction		Verb			Subject			Direct Object			Indirect Object		
	%	SRC	TRG	-MET	SRC	TRG	-MET	SRC	TRG	-MET	SRC	TRG	-MET
Intransitive	66.5	454	24	6329	128	204	2385	-	-	-	-	-	-
Transitive	20.0	391	8	1648	53	186	1808	183	265	1599	-	-	-
Ditransitive	.4	3	0	40	0	3	40	3	1	39	1	2	40
Equation	13.0	0	6	1323	57	161	909	288	29	1012	-	-	-
-Simile	.1	0	0	13	1	2	10	8	5	0	-	-	-

Table 1: % Metaphor by Construction (LCC). For each predicate, the count of source (SRC), target (TRG), and non-metaphoric (-MET) instances are counted, as well as those for all of each construction's defining arguments.

from relevant contexts.

5.2.1 Predicate Argument Construction

For a basic integration of syntax, we used the above corpus analysis technique to identify which predicate-argument construction the verb token belongs to. This results in a one-hot vector representing either an intransitive, transitive, ditransitive, equative, or simile construction. This provides basic, purely syntactic knowledge of how many arguments this particular instance of a verb currently has. For nouns, we extend this to include which slot in the construction the noun is filling (subject, direct object, indirect object) in addition to the type of predicate-argument construction.

5.2.2 Head and Dependent Features

Including representations of the head word and dependent words of the word to be classified is a straightforward way to include basic syntactic information. For verbs, this mainly involves the dependents, although many verbs also have head words. We include a concatenation of the average embedding over the word's dependents and the embedding of the word's head.

5.2.3 Dependency Relations

A more general and perhaps more powerful way of converting dependency relations into syntactically relevant features is to include the specific dependency relations for each dependent of the target. For verbs, these include things like subjects, direct objects, adverbial modifiers, nominal modifiers, passive subjects, and more. Capturing the fine-grained dependencies for each verb is analogous to determining the exact syntactic construction it is being realized in. Combining this feature with the embeddings of dependents and heads is a promising avenue for linking syntax and semantics.

5.2.4 VerbNet Class

VerbNet is a lexical semantic resource that groups verbs into classes based on their syntactic behavior (Kipper-Schuler, 2005). It categorizes over 6,000 verbs into classes, each of which contains syntactic frames that the verbs in the class can appear in. It also contains distinct senses, allowing it to distinguish between different verb uses in context. Previous approaches have employed VerbNet as a lexical resource (Beigman Klebanov et al., 2016), but aggregated the senses of each verb, removing the syntactic distinctions that VerbNet makes for different word senses.

We ran word-sense disambiguation to determine the VerbNet class for each verb token (Palmer et al., 2017). We included one-hot vectors representing verb senses for each token, and combining this with knowledge of the particular constructions and the lexical semantics provided by embeddings for each token gives syntactically motivated information about the semantics of the utterance. For noun identification, we include the VerbNet class of the head of that noun.

5.3 Experiments

As a baseline, we began with using the embedding of the word to be classified. We concatenated this with the embeddings of the single previous and following words, as this proved the best context in our validation. This creates a representation of lexical semantics and a word's context, without any specific knowledge of the syntactic relations the word is involved in. We then added each syntactic representation. These experiments were done using a training-validation-test split of 76/12/12. We experimented with Maximum Entropy, Naive Bayes, Random Forest and Support Vector Machine classifiers, and through validation chose a SVM with a linear kernel, L2 regularization and squared hinge loss. We then ran the classifier using our baseline, and added each feature separately. Finally, we combined the best feature set for each classification task, judged by the improved performance of each feature over the baseline. The classification was split into three tasks: identifying source items, identifying target items, and identifying metaphoric (either source or target) from non-metaphoric. The results of these experiments are in table 2.

From these results we can see that classifying source-domain words in the LCC data is harder than classifying target-domain words. This may be because of the broad range of domains, as the corpus contains 114 possible source domains. Target items are much easier to classify, likely because the dataset contains only a limited number (32) of target domains. Embeddings are effective at representing semantics, and they can accurately determine the domain of lexical items, allowing for easy classification of target items.

Our syntactic features show mixed results. Adding sentential context is consistently effective, showing that naive contextual approaches are helpful. Adding dependency embeddings is also consistently effective, supporting our hypothesis that knowledge of syntactic properties can be helpful in metaphor classification. Other syntactic features are inconsistent, especially in predicting the metaphoricity of verbs. Selecting only the feature sets that showed improvement over the baseline yields the best results for most categories.

6 VUAMC Analysis

The LCC allows for an in-depth examination of source and target domains, but is relatively small compared to the VUAMC. We can use the VUAMC data to inspect the distribution of word metaphoricity with regard to argument structure constructions. While Sullivan's work focuses on source and target domain elements and not whether or not words are used metaphorically, we can examine the binary classifications in the VUAMC to provide insight into the distribution of metaphoric verbs and the predicate-argument constructions they participate in. Counts of argument structure verbs and arguments and their metaphoricity are shown in table 3.

From the data in table 3, we can see clear distinctions between different constructions and the metaphoricity of their arguments. Verbs in instransitive constructions are much less likely to be metaphoric than those used in transitives, and both less so than those in ditransitive constructions.

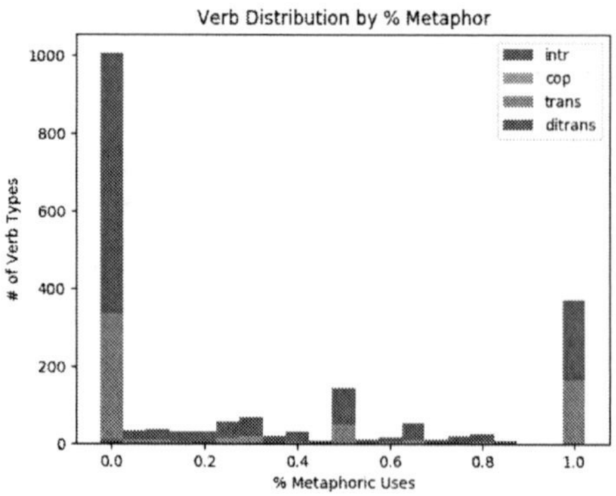

Figure 2: Verb types by percent of metaphoric use in each construction. Each bar represents the number of verb types that match the X axis for percentage of metaphoric usages.

The VUAMC chooses not to mark copular verbs as metaphoric, and only one instance was found of equative constructions having a metaphoric verb.

We might expect that different constructions would also impact the distribution of the predicates' arguments. However, from the data we see that verb arguments are fairly consistent. Indirect objects in ditransitive constructions were never observed to be metaphoric, but direct objects are between 11% and 16% metaphoric throughout. Subjects vary from 2.8% in ditransitives to 11.7% in equative constructions. One distinctive feature is that subjects are much less likely than objects to be metaphoric.

The overall distribution of metaphoric uses by verb construction shows that the more arguments that are present in the construction, the more likely the verb is being used metaphorically. For further evidence, we can examine the distribution of metaphoric usages on a verb-specific basis.

We calculated the average metaphoricity of each verb found in the VUAMC, and sorted them by the type of construction they are found in. We performed this analysis on a type and token basis, shown in figures 2 and 3. From the data, we see that the majority of verbs in all constructions are used exclusively non metaphorically. While a large number of verb types only occur metaphorically, this accounts for a much smaller number of verb tokens. Verb types that occur only metaphorically are relatively rare. We can also see that ditransitive and copula verb types are exceedingly

	Verbs			Nouns		
Features	Src	Trg	Met	Src	Trg	Met
Baseline (Embedding,1-word context)	.467	.316	.483	.440	.701	.597
+Context	**.494**	**.545**	.436	**.487**	**.705**	**.593**
+Dependent Embeddings	**.482**	**.421**	.444	**.570**	**.717**	**.631**
+Dependency Relations	**.488**	**.384**	.482	**.486**	**.718**	**.601**
+Argument Construction	.459	**.461**	.457	.456	.661	**.598**
+VerbNet Class	.467	**.555**	.473	.433	.684	.589
Best Combination	.551	.600	.505	.519	.705	.630

Table 2: Classification of Source and Target elements in the LCC Corpus. Metaphor (MET) is the classification of a word as either Source or Target against non-metaphoric words.

Verb		Predicate			Subject			Direct Object			Indirect Object		
	%	+M	-M	%Met	+M	-M	%Met	+M	-M	%Met	+M	-M	%Met
Intransitive	75.1	5118	24301	17.4	284	4627	5.8	-	-	-	-	-	-
Transitive	13.1	1517	3612	29.6	119	3125	3.7	654	4475	12.8	-	-	-
Ditransitive	.2	24	35	40.7	1	35	2.8	9	50	15.2	59	0	0
Equation	11.6	1	4548	.02	449	3376	11.7	468	3736	11.1	-	-	-
-Simile	.1	0	35	0.0	2	28	6.7	7	26	21.2	-	-	-

Table 3: % Metaphor by Construction (VUAMC). For each predicate, the count of metaphoric (+M) and non-metaphoric (-M) instances are counted, as well as those for all of each construction's defining arguments.

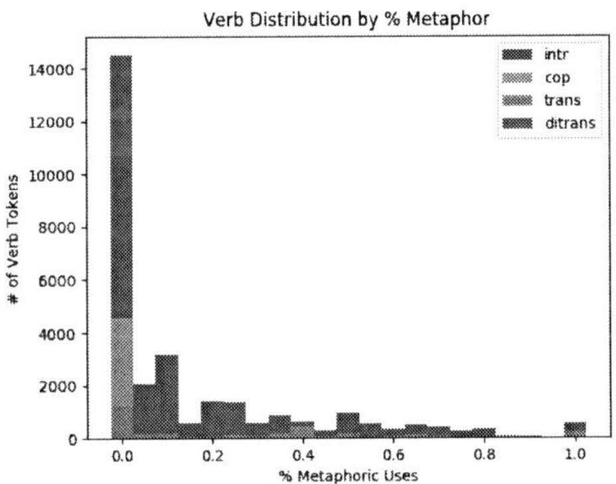

Figure 3: Verb tokens by percent of metaphoric use in each construction. Each bar represents the number of verb tokens that belong to verb types that match the X axis for percentage of metaphoric usages.

rare, but copula tokens are very common and almost always literal.

We extended this analysis by examining the distribution of the verb types that can appear intransitively, transitively, and ditransitively. Our hypothesis in studying these verbs is that the type of construction the verb appears in is predictive of that verb's metaphoric use, independent of the verb's overall behavior. Eleven verbs appeared in all three constructions, and the analysis of their metaphoricity is presented in figure 4.

From the distribution in the VUAMC corpus, the data indicates that the type of argument structure construction does not significantly change the distribution of metaphoricity. The verbs generally have the same percentage of metaphoric usages regardless of which construction they appear in. Only 'give' appears in more than 2 instances of the ditransitive, and its distribution mirrors that of its use in other constructions.

Two components from our corpus analysis stand relevant for automatic metaphor processing. First, in broad scope over all verb tokens, predicates' metaphor distributions are dependent on the kind of construction they occur in. Second, the verb itself is critical, as each verb tends to follow the same pattern of metaphoricity throughout its constructions. This supports our belief that identification of metaphor requires modeling of the interaction of syntactic and semantic information.

6.1 Metaphor Identification (VUAMC)

We employ the same experimental set up of the previous classification task using the VUAMC. The VUAMC doesn't contain source or target annotations, so the classification problem is limited to identifying metaphoric words from non-metaphoric words. We employ the same baseline and syntactic representation features. Again, we

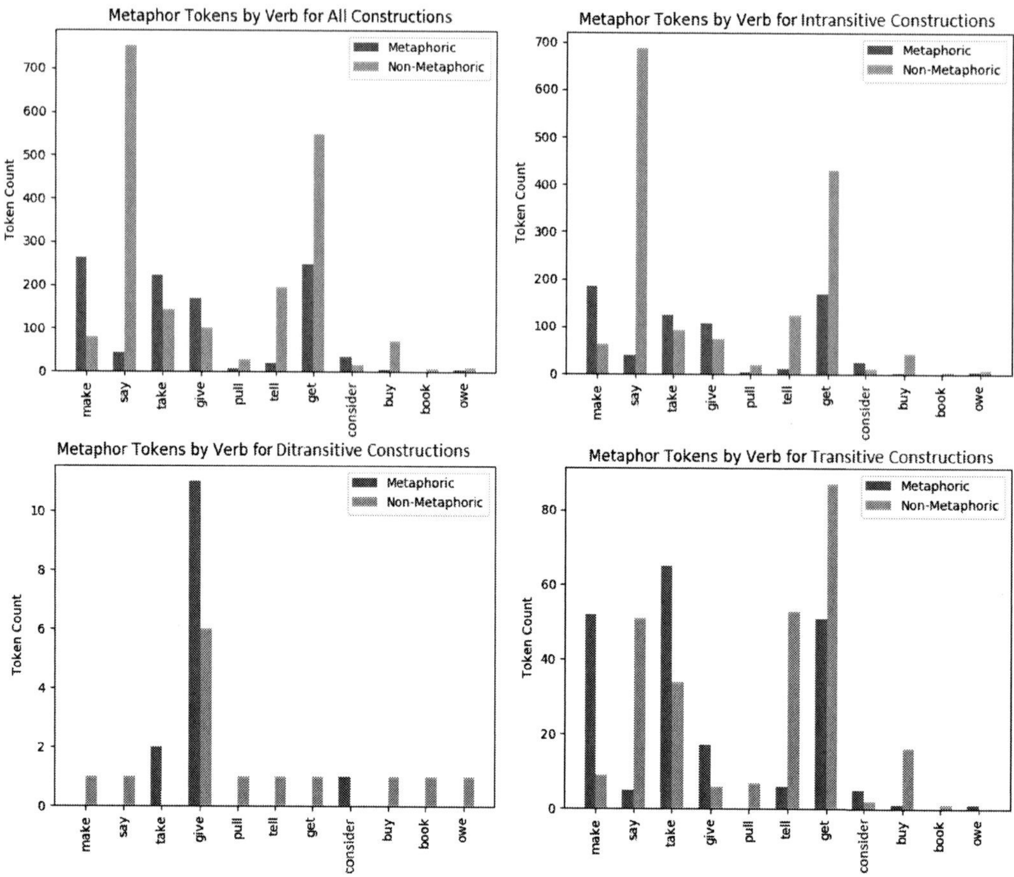

Figure 4: Counts of metaphoric uses by verb and construction for those verbs that occur in intransitive, transitive, and ditransitive constructions

used a split of 76/12/12, using a linear SVM.

For metaphoric identification in the VUAMC, all of the syntactic features improved classification over the baseline for verbs. For nouns, the dependency embeddings and VerbNet class of the noun's head were effective. For both, combining all of the syntactic representations yields the best performance. While this classification based on syntactic is slightly lower than some recent experiments (Beigman Klebanov et al., 2016), it shows improvement over using purely lexical semantics, and we believe the incorporation of better syntactic representations can be used to improve metaphor identification systems.

7 Conclusions

The type of syntactic construction a verb is present in provides unique evidence of how it is being used metaphorically. It is important to effectively integrate syntax and semantics to detect and interpret metaphor, and because there are so many types of metaphors and they occur in such a wide array of contexts, it may be helpful to use separate methods of representing metaphoric semantics depending on the syntactic constructions involved. While our results indicate that these integrations of syntactic representations do not yet achieve state of the

Model	Verbs	Nouns
Baseline (Embedding, 1-Word context)	339	303
+Context	**.488**	.224
+Dependency Embeddings	**.425**	**.349**
+Dependency Relations	**.466**	**.393**
+Argument Construction	**.471**	.289
+VerbNet Class	**.418**	**.330**
+All	.531	.505

Table 4: Results of adding different syntactic models for VUAMC verb classification.

art performance, we believe that improving representations of syntactic constructions can provide some benefit to metaphor processing.

To that end, our future goals include exploring better representations of the interaction between syntax and semantics. Models like syntactic tree kernels, compositional distributional semantic models, and other syntactically driven methods are likely to improve classification if they can properly combine syntactic and semantic representations. Additionally, as different constructions are likely to yield different types of metaphoricity, we aim to employ ensemble methods that incorporate construction-based knowledge to select the most effective classifier, and extending our approach to identifying source and target domains in addition to lexical triggers.

Acknowledgements

We gratefully acknowledge the support of the Defense Threat Reduction Agency, HDTRA1-16-1-0002/Project #1553695, eTASC - Empirical Evidence for a Theoretical Approach to Semantic Components and a grant from the Defense Advanced Research Projects Agency 15-18-CwC-FP-032 Communicating with Computers, a subcontract from UIUC. Any opinions, findings, and conclusions or recommendations expressed in this material are those of the authors and do not necessarily reflect the views of any government agency.

References

Beata Beigman Klebanov, Chee Wee Leong, E. Dario Gutierrez, Ekaterina Shutova, and Michael Flor. 2016. Semantic classifications for detection of verb metaphors. In *Proceedings of the 54th Annual Meeting of the Association for Computational Linguistics (Volume 2: Short Papers)*, pages 101–106, Berlin, Germany. Association for Computational Linguistics.

Luana Bulat, Stephen Clark, and Ekaterina Shutova. 2017. Modelling metaphor with attribute-based semantics. In *Proceedings of the 15th Conference of the European Chapter of the Association for Computational Linguistics: Volume 2, Short Papers*, pages 523–528, Valencia, Spain. Association for Computational Linguistics.

Ellen Dodge, Jisup Hong, and Elise Stickles. 2015. Metanet: Deep semantic automatic metaphor analysis. In *Proceedings of the Third Workshop on Metaphor in NLP*, pages 40–49, Denver, Colorado. Association for Computational Linguistics.

Andrew Gargett and John Barnden. 2015. Modeling the interaction between sensory and affective meanings for detecting metaphor. In *Third Workshop on Metaphor in NLP*, pages 21–30, Denver, CO.

Jonathan Gordon, Jerry Hobbs, Jonathan May, and Fabrizio Morbini. 2015. High-precision abductive mapping of multilingual metaphors. In *Proceedings of the Third Workshop on Metaphor in NLP*, pages 50–55, Denver, Colorado. Association for Computational Linguistics.

E.Dario Gutierrez, Ekaterina Shutova, Tyler Marghetis, and Benjamin Bergen. 2016. Literal and metaphorical senses in compositional distributional semantic models. In *Proceedings of the 54th Annual Meeting of the Association for Computational Linguistics (Volume 1: Long Papers)*, pages 183–193, Berlin, Germany. Association for Computational Linguistics.

Hessel Haagsma and Johannes Bjerva. 2016. Detecting novel metaphor using selectional preference information. In *Proceedings of the Fourth Workshop on Metaphor in NLP*, pages 10–17, San Diego, California. Association for Computational Linguistics.

Ilana Heintz, Ryan Gabbard, Mahesh Srivastava, Dave Barner, Donald Black, Majorie Friedman, and Ralph Weischedel. 2013. Automatic extraction of linguistic metaphors with lda topic modeling. In *Proceedings of the First Workshop on Metaphor in NLP*, pages 58–66, Atlanta, Georgia. Association for Computational Linguistics.

Dirk Hovy, Shashank Shrivastava, Sujay Kumar Jauhar, Mrinmaya Sachan, Kartik Goyal, Huying Li, Whitney Sanders, and Eduard Hovy. 2013. Identifying metaphorical word use with tree kernels. In *Proceedings of the First Workshop on Metaphor in NLP*, pages 52–57, Atlanta, Georgia. Association for Computational Linguistics.

Karen Kipper-Schuler. 2005. *VerbNet: A broad-coverage, comprehensive verb lexicon*. Ph.D. thesis, University of Pennsylvania.

George Lakoff and Mark Johnson. 1980. *Metaphors We Live By*. University of Chicago Press, Chicago and London.

Christopher D. Manning, Mihai Surdeanu, John Bauer, Jenny Finkel, Steven J. Bethard, and David McClosky. 2014. The Stanford CoreNLP natural language processing toolkit. In *Association for Computational Linguistics (ACL) System Demonstrations*, pages 55–60.

James H. Martin. 1990. *A Computational Model of Metaphor Interpretation*. Academic Press, Inc.

Tomas Mikolov, Ilya Sutskever, Kai Chen, Greg Corrado, and Jeffrey Dean. 2013. Distributed representations of words and phrases and their compositionality. *CoRR*, abs/1310.4546.

Michael Mohler, Mary Brunson, Bryan Rink, and Marc Tomlinson. 2016. Introducing the lcc metaphor datasets. In *Proceedings of the Tenth International Conference on Language Resources and Evaluation (LREC 2016)*, Paris, France. European Language Resources Association (ELRA).

Ekaterina Ovchinnikova, Ross Israel, Suzanne Wertheim, Vladimir Zaytsev, Niloofar Montazeri, and Jerry Hobbs. 2014. Abductive inference for interpretation of metaphors. In *Proceedings of the Second Workshop on Metaphor in NLP*, pages 33–41, Baltimore, MD. Association for Computational Linguistics.

Martha Palmer, James Gung, Claire Bonial, Jinho Choi, Orin Hargraves, Derek Palmer, and Kevin Stowe. 2017. The pitfalls of shortcuts: Tales from the word sense tagging trenches. *Essays in Lexical Semantics and Computational Lexicography - In Honor of Adam Kilgariff.*

Jeffrey Pennington, Richard Socher, and Christopher D. Manning. 2014. Glove: Global vectors for word representation. In *Empirical Methods in Natural Language Processing (EMNLP)*, pages 1532–1543.

Pragglejaz Group. 2007. MIP: A method for identifying metaphorically used words in discourse. *Metaphor and Symbol*, 22(1):1–39.

Sunny Rai, Shampa Chakraverty, and Devendra K. Tayal. 2016. Supervised metaphor detection using conditional random fields. In *Proceedings of the Fourth Workshop on Metaphor in NLP*, pages 18–27, San Diego, California. Association for Computational Linguistics.

Marek Rei, Luana Bulat, Douwe Kiela, and Ekaterina Shutova. 2017. Grasping the finer point: A supervised similarity network for metaphor detection. In *Proceedings of the 2017 Conference on Empirical Methods in Natural Language Processing*, pages 1537–1546, Copenhagen, Denmark. Association for Computational Linguistics.

Ekaterina Shutova. 2010. Automatic metaphor interpretation as a paraphrasing task. In *Human Language Technologies: The 2010 Annual Conference of the North American Chapter of the Association for Computational Linguistics*, pages 1029–1037, Los Angeles, California. Association for Computational Linguistics.

Ekaterina Shutova. 2013. Metaphor identification a interpretation. In *Second Joint Conference on Lexical and Computational Semantics (*SEM), Volume 1: Proceedings of the Main Conference and the Shared Task: Semantic Textual Similarity*, pages 276–285, Atlanta, Georgia, USA. Association for Computational Linguistics.

Karen Sullivan. 2013. *Frames and Constructions in Metaphoric Language*. John Benjamins.

Yulia Tsvetkov, Leonid Boytsov, Anatole Gershman, Eric Nyberg, and Chris Dyer. 2014. Metaphor detection with cross-lingual model transfer. In *Proceedings of the 52nd Annual Meeting of the Association for Computational Linguistics (Volume 1: Long Papers)*, pages 248–258, Baltimore, Maryland. Association for Computational Linguistics.

Literal, Metphorical or Both? Detecting Metaphoricity in Isolated Adjective-Noun Phrases

Agnieszka Mykowiecka
ICS PAS
Jana Kazimierza 5
Warsaw, Poland
agn@ipipan.waw.pl

Małgorzata Marciniak
ICS PAS
Jana Kazimierza 5
Warsaw, Poland
mm@ipipan.waw.pl

Aleksander Wawer
ICS PAS
Jana Kazimierza 5
Warsaw, Poland
axw@ipipan.waw.pl

Abstract

The paper addresses the classification of isolated Polish adjective-noun phrases according to their metaphoricity. We tested neural networks to predict if a phrase has a literal or metaphorical sense or can have both senses depending on usage. The input to the neural network consists of word embeddings, but we also tested the impact of information about the domain of the adjective and about the abstractness of the noun. We applied our solution to English data available on the Internet and compared it to results published in papers. We found that the solution based on word embeddings only can achieve results comparable with complex solutions requiring additional information.

1 Introduction

One of the essential features of every natural language is its ambiguity. And apart from the homonymy and polysemy of words, the phenomenon which makes automatic text understanding difficult is the possible metaphorical usage of both simple and more complex phrases. Identification of potentially figurative usage is crucial for language processing efficiency and may improve the performance of many NLP applications. It is crucial for information extraction tasks, as the lack of figurative meaning detection may lead to false identification of a particular object or event (Patwardhan and Riloff, 2007). For example, we do not want to extract a mention of some kind of pastry in the phrase *These vegan recipes are a piece of cake*. In machine translation (Shutova, 2011) and textual entailment (Agerri, 2008) tasks, similar examples can easily be given as well. Tasks which can potentially be solved better when metaphors are correctly recognized are numerous. In particular, (Thibodeau and Boroditsky, 2011) even analyze the role of metaphor in reasoning about social policy on crime.

Our research problem results directly from the very well-known fact that language expressions can be interpreted literally i.e. their meaning can be a composition of the meaning of their parts; or metaphorically, when either the meaning of some words or combination of them is not interpreted literally.

Let us illustrate this in the Polish language on multiple phrases with an adjective *żelazny* '(to be made of) iron'. The expression e.g. *żelazny uchwyt* 'iron grip' can denote just a grip/handle which is made of iron, but it can also describe a feeling of fear and intimidation. The chances of these two interpretations are not equal for all expressions. With some of them, e.g. *żelazna krata* 'iron grille' it is hard to imagine when they get a figurative, non-literal meaning – they are strictly compositional – while others, e.g. *żelazne nerwy* 'iron nerves' are only used in the figurative, non-literal meaning. Identification of potentially figurative usages may improve the performance of many NLP applications. Although the ultimate goal is to decide whether each phrase occurrence could be interpreted compositionally (literally) or not, such task requires annotated data which is quite hard to prepare. In this work, we concentrate on the initial classification of isolated adjective-noun (AN) phrases – we try to categorize Polish phrases built up from a noun and a modifying adjective into these three categories, i.e. phrases which are almost certainly interpreted literally (L), phrases which only have a metaphorical meaning (M) and phrases which occur in both interpretations (B).

Although we apply this categorization in Polish, it may as well be used for other languages. For example, in English the phrases 'dirty hands' may be used literally and figuratively and qualify as B.

27

Proceedings of the Workshop on Figurative Language Processing, pages 27–33
New Orleans, Louisiana, June 6, 2018. ©2018 Association for Computational Linguistics

2   Related Work

The problem of recognizing the metaphoricity of isolated phrases has been considered as a research topic in several papers. Almost all authors focus on phrases which are only literal or metaphorical and neglect phrases that represent both senses.

Gutierrez et al. (2016) address recognition of the metaphorical and literal meaning of adjective-noun phrases on the basis of metaphorical or literal senses of the adjective. Their approach was based on the model proposed in (Baroni and Zamparelli, 2010) to represent the vector of an unseen adjective-noun phrase $\mathbf{p}$ as a linear transformation given by a matrix $\mathbf{A}_{(a)}$ of an adjective a over a noun vector $\mathbf{n}$:

$$\mathbf{A}_{(a)}\,\mathbf{n} = \mathbf{p}$$

They represent various (literal or metaphorical) senses of an adjective as two different matrixes: $\mathbf{A}_{LIT(a)}$ and $\mathbf{A}_{MET(a)}$, as in (Kartsaklis and Sadrzadeh, 2013). Gutierrez et al. (2016) assume that the literal or metaphorical meaning of the adjective, that is part of an AN phrase, makes the phrase literal or metaphorical, so they represent each literal adjective-noun phrase p_i containing adjective a as:

$$\mathbf{A}_{LIT(a)}\,\mathbf{n}_i = \mathbf{p}_i$$

and each metaphorical phrase i as:

$$\mathbf{A}_{MET(a)}\,\mathbf{n}_i = \mathbf{p}_i$$

The vectors of whole phrases and nouns can be extracted from a corpus, so the goal is to learn adjective matrices: literal ($\hat{\mathbf{A}}_{LIT(a)}$) and metaphorical ($\hat{\mathbf{A}}_{MET(a)}$) separately. To test the method, they prepared a very peculiar dataset consisting of 3991 literal and 4601 metaphorical AN phrases for only 23 adjectives, so it contained an average 370 phrases per each adjective. The requirement of many examples per adjective is crucial in this method and simultaneously difficult to obtain — at least if we want to take phrases with more than a dozen occurrences in texts used for creating vector representation into account. The best result reported by the authors was 0.809 accuracy (ACC).

Tsvetkov et al. (2014) applied a random forest classifier to detect metaphorical and literal AN phrases. Classifiers included in the ensemble were trained on the basis of three features, abstractness and imageability of nouns, supersenses, and vector-space word representation. Information about abstractness and imageability originated from the MRC psycholinguistic database

(Wilson, 1988); as the database is not big, they propagated this information to other words based on vector representation. Supersenses for a noun were obtained from the WordNet as a combination of the supersenses of all synsets to which the noun belongs. Adjectives are classified into 13 supersenses adapted from GermaNet, but the information necessary for it was taken from the WordNet. To prepare vector space representation the authors used a variation of latent semantic analysis. To evaluate the method, they prepared training data consisting of 884 metaphorical AN phrases and the same number of literal phrases. The data contains phrases with 654 adjectives, so an average of 2.7 phrases per adjective. Furthermore, they collected a test set consisting of 200 phrases (100 phrases per each type) with 167 adjectives from the train set and 33 new ones. The data does not include weak metaphors and phrases which can have both interpretations. The method achieved ACC = 0.86.

Shutova et al. (2016) used word and visual embeddings to represent phrases and their components in order to detect metaphorical usage. They adopted the cosine similarity of embedding vectors as the measure of metaphoricity and postulated that the similarity is lower for metaphorical expressions. A threshold needed for classification was fixed on the basis of development data. For data from (Tsvetkov et al., 2014), the authors reported F1-measure equal to 0.79 (an accuracy is not given). A similar approach is described in the paper (Rei et al., 2017), where the authors improved the idea of Shutova et al. (2016) applying deep learning to establish the threshold. The evaluation performed on the same data indicated an accuracy of 0.829 and the F1-measure equal to 0.811, which is better than the original solution.

Bizzoni et al. (2017) proposed detecting the metaphoricity of AN phrases on the basis of word vectors only. They tested several configurations of single-layered neural networks to classify AN phrases into two groups: metaphorical and literal. They didn't use any additional knowledge except Word2Vec trained on Google News (Mikolov et al., 2013). The different configuration of neural networks was tested on the data from (Gutierrez et al., 2016), described above. The method achieved an accuracy of 0.915 when trained on 500 phrases and 0.985 when trained on 8000 phrases. Simultaneously, Wawer and Mykowiecka

(2017) proposed a similar approach to the problem of metaphoricity detection for Polish data. The authors noticed that detection of metaphorical and literal senses of phrases is not enough, and proposed classification into three types of AN phrases: literal metaphorical and phrases which occur in both interpretations (B). For this task, they reported an accuracy of 0.7, but the task is more difficult.

3 Polish Data

We prepared data containing Polish adjective-noun phrases divided into three classes. We distinguished literal (L) and metaphorical (M) phrases as in the English experiments mentioned in Section 2. Similar datasets for English excluded weak metaphors and phrases with both literal and metaphorical senses like *drowning students* (Tsvetkov et al., 2014). In our data, phrases with both meaning (B) made up the third class, we excluded only phrases that may have both senses but a literal (or metaphorical) one is not represented in NKJP (National Corpus of Polish, (Przepiórkowski et al., 2012)). An example of such phrase is *dobry pasterz* 'good shepherd' for which we were not able to find literal meaning in the corpus.

We collected 2380 adjective-noun phrases containing 259 different adjectives, so, an average 9.18 phrases per adjective. The adjectives were manually assigned to 55 classes (typology designed for this experiment) which represent such notions as: emotions, quantity, dimension, shape, colour, etc. Among the nouns we distinguished only two classes: abstract and concrete. We did not follow WordNet typology here (e.g. hyperonymy) as too elaborate and difficult to apply.

The dataset is an extension of the resource described in (Wawer and Mykowiecka, 2017). The process of data collecting was carried out in several steps. First, we prepared a list of 440 metaphorical phrases and collected literal and more metaphorical phrases containing the same adjectives from the frequent phrases in NKJP (National Corpus of Polish, (Przepiórkowski et al., 2012)). It resulted in the collection of many phrases for each adjective. The most numerous group, 79 phrases, was collected for the adjective *czarny* 'black', it consists of 45 literal, 27 metaphorical phrases and only 7 phrases of both types (phrases of B type are rarer then literal and

phrase type	adjectives	M	L	B
all phrases	259	1034	1018	328
physical feature	21	185	115	36
dimension	11	147	131	38
color	12	61	182	36
material	16	42	79	15
luminosity	5	48	42	15
sense	18	71	20	13
temperature	4	40	49	13
tidiness	4	56	21	7
empty/full	2	58	22	2
animal	22	32	27	23
emotion	13	28	25	11
good/bad	2	17	24	15
society	24	23	23	8
sequence	2	1	41	11
body/mind f.	7	32	12	0
space orientation	5	0	29	12
sound	5	22	10	4
life/death	4	20	8	1
strength/weakness	2	18	9	1
civilization	8	10	17	1
weather	5	18	3	6
truth false	2	4	20	3
condition	4	2	9	14
easy/difficult	1	6	16	1
freedom	2	11	8	3
terrain stability	3	10	6	5
...				
other 29 domains	55	72	70	34

Table 1: Number of phrases

metaphorical ones). In order to improve the participation of B phrases in our data we looked for them in dictionaries and added them if they occurred a dozen times in our texts. Moreover we added literal and metaphorical phrases for adjectives included in the new B phrases. The obtained list of phrases was evaluated by two annotators and inconsistencies were discussed in a larger group of annotators. Table 1 contains detailed information about numbers of different types of phrases for adjective domains for which more than 20 examples were collected.

In order to implement experiments, we used distributional semantic models (DSM) created by Word2vec from the gensim package (Řehůřek and Sojka, 2010) and described in (Mykowiecka et al., 2017) and avilable from `http://zil.ipipan.waw.pl/CoDeS`. As Polish is a highly inflectional language, we decided to use models based on lemmas. We used the Continuous Bag of Words (CBOW) architecture. As a learning strategy, we selected negative sampling in the standard configuration of 5 positive examples and 1 negative. Models were prepared on the basis of NKJP (general corpus of Polish) and a dump of Polish Wikipedia from 2016. Two models based on 300 or 100 dimensions were used in our experiments; one consisted of all data, while the second was limited to words occurring no fewer than 50 times for NKJP data or no fewer than 30 times for Wikipedia data.

4 Experiments Description

In our experiments, we adopted the method described in (Wawer and Mykowiecka, 2017) as a starting point. The authors applied neural networks to predict if a phrase has a literal or metaphorical sense or can have both senses depending on its usage. Word embeddings of phrase components are the input to the network. The task consists in classifying of the input phrases into three groups: L, M, and B types. Our aim was to test the method on bigger and better balanced data. We also tested not only dense neural architecture but also a sequential one, namely LSTM. The sequence in our case is a short one, consisting of two words.

Moreover, we wanted to test the impact of the type of adjective and noun on the results. To compare the results for Polish with similar experiments for English, we also performed experiments on the literal and metaphorical phrases alone. In the latter case, we eliminated B type phrases from the input data. The architecture of the network is given in Figure 1. In the task of classification into L, M, B types, the output layer consists of three instances referring to three labels.

The impact of the type of adjectives and nouns was tested by extending appropriate word embeddings with additional features.

5 Results for Polish

In this section, we describe the results obtained for Polish phrases for different parameters. In all experiments, we performed 10-fold cross-validation (shuffling each time the entire set, the standard sklearn procedure resulted in a slightly different total number of phrases tested). The results were collected and the average results are given for precision, recall, F1-measure and accuracy.

Although the classification of adjective-noun phrases into M, L, B types is consistent with the linguistics reality, similar studies relating to English neglect phrases which may have both literal and metaphorical meanings. So, initially, we removed phrases annotated as B types from the data and performed the experiments with classification

into two types only.

	2 dense layers, vec. size 100				
	nb	ep.	P	R	F1	acc.
M	1030	10	0.88	0.88	0.88	
		20	0.89	0.87	0.88	
L	1017	10	0.88	0.88	0.88	
		20	0.87	0.89	0.88	
avg.	2047	10	0.88	0.88	0.88	0.879
		20	0.88	0.88	0.88	0.878
	3 dense layers, vec. size 100				
	nb	ep.	P	R	F1	acc.
M	1030	10	0.89	0.86	0.87	
		20	0.90	0.87	0.88	
L	1017	10	0.86	0.89	0.88	
		20	0.87	0.90	0.89	
avg.	2047	10	0.88	0.88	0.88	0.876
		20	0.88	0.88	0.88	0.884

Table 2: Input: only embeddings, vectors 100

In Tables 2 and 3, we can see that the size of vectors, the tested number of epochs and choosing either 2 or 3 dense layers do not seem to have a great influence on the results. Thus, we tested the influence of a separate addition of domain of adjectives and type of noun only for models with a vector of size 300 and 3 dense layers (Table 4). Next, we tested adding both noun type and adjective domain again on all the variants as used in experiments reported in Tables 2 and 3, the results are given in Tables 5 and 6. In all these cases, we see only very small differences in F1 and accuracy. It turned out that on average, the simplest model with embeddings of size 100, 2 dense layers and no additional information is almost identically good as the model with embeddings of size 300, 3 dense layers and additional information consisting of adjective domain and binary noun type. Training nets for an additional 10 epochs did not im-

	2 dense layers, vec. size 300				
	nb	ep.	P	R	F1	acc.
M	1030	10	0.90	0.85	0.87	
		20	0.90	0.87	0.88	
L	1017	10	0.85	0.91	0.88	
		20	0.87	0.90	0.88	
avg.	2047	10	0.88	0.88	0.88	0.888
		20	0.88	0.88	0.88	0.884
	3 dense layers, vec. size 300				
	nb	ep.	P	R	F1	acc.
M	1030	10	0.90	0.85	0.87	
		20	0.90	0.87	0.89	
L	1017	10	0.85	0.91	0.88	
		20	0.88	0.91	0.89	
avg.	2047	10	0.88	0.88	0.88	0.876
		20	0.89	0.89	0.89	0.889

Table 3: Input: only embeddings, size of vectors 300

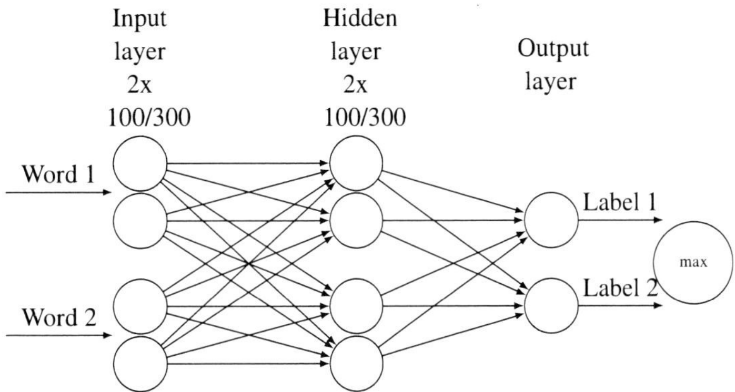

Figure 1: Net architecture for L and M phrases classification

prove the results significantly.

	3 dense layers, vec. 300, 20 epochs			
	nb	P	R	F1	acc.
	adjective domains				
M	1030	0.90	0.88	0.89	
L	1017	0.88	0.89	0.89	
avg.	2047	0.89	0.89	0.89	0.885
	noun type				
M	1030	0.91	0.87	0.89	
L	1017	0.87	0.91	0.89	
avg.	2047	0.89	0.89	0.89	0.889

Table 4: Input: word embeddings, type of noun or adjective domain

	2 dense layers, vec. size 100				
	nb	ep.	P	R	F1	acc.
M	1030	10	0.90	0.87	0.88	
		20	0.89	0.87	0.88	
L	1017	10	0.87	0.91	0.89	
		20	0.87	0.89	0.88	
avg.	2047	10	0.89	0.89	0.89	0.886
		20	0.88	0.88	0.88	0.880

	3 dense layers, vec. size 100				
	nb	ep.	P	R	F1	acc.
M	1030	10	0.88	0.87	0.88	
		20	0.90	0.87	0.88	
L	1017	10	0.87	0.88	0.88	
		20	0.87	0.90	0.89	
avg.	2047	10	0.88	0.88	0.88	0.876
		20	0.89	0.89	0.89	0.886

Table 5: Input: word embeddings, adjective domain, type of noun (abstract/concrete)

The same architecture was used to classify phrases into three groups. Table 7 shows the results for classification of all the data into literal, metaphorical and both type phrases; the input data consists of word embeddings of 300 dimensions

	2 dense layers, vec. size 300				
	nb	ep.	P	R	F1	acc.
M	1030	10	0.90	0.90	0.89	
		20	0.89	0.89	0.89	
L	1017	10	0.87	0.90	0.89	
		20	0.89	0.89	0.89	
avg.	2047	10	0.88	0.88	0.88	0.883
		20	0.89	0.89	0.89	0.890

	3 dense layers, vec. size 300				
	nb	ep.	P	R	F1	acc.
M	1030	10	0.90	0.88	0.89	
		20	0.89	0.88	0.88	
L	1017	10	0.89	0.90	0.89	
		20	0.88	0.89	0.88	
avg.	2047	10	0.89	0.89	0.89	0.890
		20	0.88	0.88	0.88	0.884

Table 6: Input: word embeddings, adjective domain and type of noun (abstract/concrete), vectors 300

(the results for 100 vectors are slightly lower – F1 for B class is equal to 0.48). The results for the B phrases are much lower than for L and M phrases. Adjective domains and abstractness do not improve the results, see Table 8.

6 Results for English Data

As it is difficult to compare methods applied on different data, we decided to use our method on data available on the Internet and compare it with the results reported in papers. The available resources contain only literal and metaphorical phrases. We tested two sets of such data. The first one was originally used in (Tsvetkov et al., 2014) – the solution described in Section 2 and the data is available from `https://github.com/ytsvetko/metaphor`. The train set consists of 884 metaphorical phrases and 884 literal ones, and

	nb	P	R	F1	acc.
		3 dense layers, 20 epochs			
M	1030	0.82	0.86	0.84	
L	1017	0.80	0.78	0.79	
B	328	0.52	0.47	0.49	
avg.	2374	0.77	0.77	0.77	0.773
		LSTM, 2 layers, 10 epochs			
M	1030	0.84	0.86	0.85	
L	1017	0.81	0.82	0.82	
B	328	0.52	0.46	0.49	
avg.	2374	0.78	0.79	0.79	0.789

Table 7: Polish phrases classification into M, L and B; 300 dimennsions vectors

	nb	P	R	F1	acc.
		LSTM, 2 layers, 10 epochs			
M	1030	0.83	0.85	0.84	
L	1017	0.80	0.82	0.81	
B	328	0.48	0.40	0.44	
avg.	2374	0.77	0.78	0.77	0.778

Table 8: Polish phrases classification into M, L and B. Input: 300 dimensions word embeddings, adjective domain and type of noun

the test set has 100 phrases of each type. In our experiment, we used 300 element pre-trained GLoVe vectors trained on Wikipedia 2014 and Gigaword 5 (Pennington et al., 2014). We neglected to add information on adjective domains to directly test the solution based only on distributed word representation. Our results for both dense and LSTM architectures are given in Table 9. Tsvetkov et al. (2014) reported in their paper an accuracy of 0.86, which is a little higher than our result – 0.84. The same data was used in (Rei et al., 2017) where the authors reported an accuracy of 0.829 and for metaphor detection precision: 0.903, recall: 0.730 and F1-measure: 0.811. Our overall slightly better result (in comparison to (Rei et al., 2017)) is due to better recall for metaphorical phrases.

The second data set chosen was that prepared by (Gutierrez et al., 2016). The results of our experiments are reported in Table 10. In this case, the accuracy obtained by the network with one hidden dense layer was equal to 0.969 (between the results given in (Bizzoni et al., 2017)). This significant increase is due to the much smaller number of different adjectives and the larger number of phrases with the same adjective in this data set.

7 Conclusions

Information included in standard word embeddings makes it possible to differentiate between literal and metaphorical adjective-noun phrases,

	nb	P	R	F1	acc.
Dense, 20 epochs, 10-times cross validation					
M	882	0.87	0.86	0.86	
L	871	0.86	0.87	0.86	
avg.	1753	0.86	0.86	0.86	0.864
LSTM, 20 epochs, 10-times cross validation					
M	882	0.86	0.86	0.85	
L	871	0.86	0.85	0.85	
avg.	0.86	0.86	0.86	0.855	
Dense, 20 epochs, test data					
M	100	0.90	0.72	0.80	
L	100	0.77	0.92	0.84	
avg.	200	0.83	0.82	0.82	0.819
GRU, 2 hidden layers, 20 epochs, test data					
M	100	0.90	0.78	0.83	
L	100	0.81	0.91	0.85	
avg.	200	0.85	0.84	0.84	0.845
LSTM, 2 hidden layers, 20 epochs, test data					
M	100	0.90	0.76	0.83	
L	100	0.79	0.92	0.85	
avg.	200	0.85	0.84	0.84	0.84

Table 9: Our results for Tsvetkov et al. (2014) data

	nb	P	R	F1	acc.
Dense, 20 epochs, 10-times cross validation					
M	4596	0.96	0.97	0.97	
L	3991	0.96	0.97	0.97	
avg.	8587	0.97	0.97	0.97	0.969

Table 10: Our results for (Gutierrez et al., 2016) data

both in Polish and English. It seems that not using the cosine measure of vector similarity for metaphors detection (as discussed in Section 2), but applying a neural network to this problem is a good solution.

For the tested network architectures the accuracy varies between 0.81 and 0.97 depending on the character and size of the training set. The effect of using sequential architecture (GRU or LSTM units) is not straightforward: it improves results on the training/test set scenario, but not in the case of cross-validation setting.

Surprisingly, the adjective domain and the information on noun concreteness do not seem to have any significant influence on the results.

Recognizing phrases which can have either literal or metaphorical meaning (depending on the context) is much harder. The best F1 result for these phrases is at a level of 0.49. The overall results for recognition of the three labels (L, M and B) are lower by 0.11 than the results for recognition of just L and M cases. Still the result of 0.77 could be of practical use.

In the future, we plan to focus on phrases that have both literal and metaphorical usages (B) and recognize their usage on sentence level. Although the recognition of a type of phrase considered in isolation cannot be fully reliable, we think that the obtained results can be used as the additional source of information for phrases which are less frequent in text.

Acknowledgments

This work was supported by the Polish National Science Centre project 2014/15/B/ST6/05186.

References

Rodrigo Agerri. 2008. Metaphor in textual entailment. In *Coling 2008: Companion volume – Posters and Demonstrations*, pages 3–6.

Marco Baroni and Roberto Zamparelli. 2010. Nouns are vectors, adjectives are matrices: Representing adjective-noun constructions in semantic space. In *Proceedings of the 2010 Conference on Empirical Methods in Natural Language Processing*, EMNLP '10, pages 1183–1193, Stroudsburg, PA, USA. Association for Computational Linguistics.

Yuri Bizzoni, Stergios Chatzikyriakidis, and Mehdi Ghanimifard. 2017. "deep" learning : Detecting metaphoricity in adjective-noun pairs. In *Proceedings of the Workshop on Stylistic Variation*, pages 43–52. Association for Computational Linguistics.

Dario Gutierrez, Ekaterina Shutova, Tyler Marghetis, and Benjamin Bergen. 2016. Literal and metaphorical senses in compositional distributional semantic models. In *Proceedings of ACL 2016 (short papers)*.

Dimitri Kartsaklis and Mehrnoosh Sadrzadeh. 2013. Prior Disambiguation of Word Tensors for Constructing Sentence Vectors. In *Proceedings of the 2013 Conference on Empirical Methods in Natural Language Processing*, pages 1590–1601. Association for Computational Linguistics.

Tomas Mikolov, Ilya Sutskever, Kai Chen, Greg S Corrado, and Jeff Dean. 2013. Distributed representations of words and phrases and their compositionality. In C.J.C. Burges, L. Bottou, M. Welling, Z. Ghahramani, and K.Q. Weinberger, editors, *Advances in Neural Information Processing Systems 26*, pages 3111–3119.

Agnieszka Mykowiecka, Małgorzata Marciniak, and Piotr Rychlik. 2017. Testing word embeddings for Polish. *Cognitive Studies / Études Cognitives*, 17:1–19.

Siddharth Patwardhan and Ellen Riloff. 2007. Effective information extraction with semantic affinity patterns and relevant regions. In *Proceedings of the 2007 Joint Conference on Empirical Methods in Natural Language Processing and Computational Natural Language Learning (EMNLP-CoNLL)*, pages 717–727, Prague, Czech Republic. Association for Computational Linguistics.

Jeffrey Pennington, Richard Socher, and Christopher D. Manning. 2014. Glove: Global vectors for word representation. In *Empirical Methods in Natural Language Processing (EMNLP)*, pages 1532–1543.

Adam Przepiórkowski, Mirosław Bańko, Rafał L. Górski, and Barbara Lewandowska-Tomaszczyk, editors. 2012. *Narodowy Korpus Języka Polskiego*. Wydawnictwo Naukowe PWN, Warsaw.

Radim Řehůřek and Petr Sojka. 2010. Software framework for topic modelling with large corpora. In *Proceedings of the LREC 2010 Workshop on New Challenges for NLP Frameworks*, pages 45–50, Valletta, Malta. ELRA.

Marek Rei, Luana Bulat, Douwe Kiela, and Ekaterina Shutova. 2017. Grasping the finer point: A supervised similarity network for metaphor detection. In *Proceedings of the 2017 Conference on Empirical Methods in Natural Language Processing*, pages 1537–1546. Association for Computational Linguistics.

Ekaterina Shutova. 2011. *Computational Approaches to Figurative Language*. Ph.D. thesis.

Ekaterina Shutova, Douwe Kiela, and Jean Maillard. 2016. Black holes and white rabbits: Metaphor identification with visual features. In *HLT-NAACL*. The Association for Computational Linguistics.

Paul H. Thibodeau and Lera Boroditsky. 2011. Metaphors we think with: The role of metaphor in reasoning. *PLOSone*, 6(2).

Yulia Tsvetkov, Leonid Boytsov, Anatole Gershman, Eric Nyberg, and Chris Dyer. 2014. Metaphor detection with cross-lingual model transfer. In *Proceedings of the 52nd Annual Meeting of the Association for Computational Linguistics*, pages 248–258. Association of Computational Linguistics.

Aleksander Wawer and Agnieszka Mykowiecka. 2017. Detecting metaphorical phrases in the Polish language. In *Proceedings of the International Conference Recent Advances in Natural Language Processing, RANLP 2017*, pages 772–777, Varna, Bulgaria. INCOMA Ltd.

Michael Wilson. 1988. Mrc psycholinguistic database: Machine-usable dictionary, version 2.00. *Behavior Research Methods, Instruments, and Computers*, 20(1):6–10.

Catching Idiomatic Expressions in EFL essays

Michael Flor
Educational Testing Service
660 Rosedale Road
Princeton, NJ 08541, USA
`mflor@ets.org`

Beata Beigman Klebanov
Educational Testing Service
660 Rosedale Road
Princeton, NJ 08541, USA
`bbeigmanklebanov@ets.org`

Abstract

This paper presents an exploratory study on large-scale detection of idiomatic expressions in essays written by non-native speakers of English. We describe a computational search procedure for automatic detection of idiom-candidate phrases in essay texts. The study used a corpus of essays written during a standardized examination of English language proficiency. Automatically-flagged candidate expressions were manually annotated for idiomaticity. The study found that idioms are widely used in EFL essays. The study also showed that a search algorithm that accommodates the syntactic and lexical flexibility of idioms can increase the recall of idiom instances by 30%, but it also increases the amount of false positives.

1 Introduction

An idiom is an expression whose meaning cannot be derived from the usual meaning of its constituents. As such, idioms present a special learning problem for non-native speakers of English (Cooper, 1998), especially learners of English as foreign language (EFL). Understanding of idiomatic expressions can be important, for example, in academic settings, where presentation of ideas often involves figurative language (Littlemore et al., 2011). Even more encompassing is the notion that "natural use of idioms can overtly demonstrate participation in a realm of shared cultural knowledge and interests, and so help a learner gain social acceptance" (Boers and Lindstromberg, 2009). Indeed, it has been claimed that accurate and appropriate use of idioms is a strong distinguishing mark of the native-like command of the language and might be a reliable measure of the proficiency of foreign learners (Cowie et al., 1984).

The present research is informed by the idea that estimation of the use of idiomatic expressions in student essays might be utilized as yet another indicator of proficiency in English. For practical text-analysis applications (e.g. web-based services), and for use in large-scale assessments, such estimation would require automatic tools. Such tools might use a two-step approach: find candidate expressions in text and then verify that they are indeed idiomatic. We have conducted a large-scale study to examine the feasibility of the first step – finding a variety of idiom-candidate expressions in student essays. A wide-coverage extended search algorithm was used to flag candidate expressions and manual annotation was used for verification.

Prior computational work on detection of idioms concentrated on methods of discrimination – is a given expression compositional/idiomatic or not (or to what degree). For purposes of evaluation, such research always relied on manually curated sets of candidate expressions. Our current work is complementary, our question is: how can we automatically obtain a great variety of idiom-candidate expressions, in unrestricted context.

The rest of this paper is structured as follows. Section 2 presents related work on idioms and EFL. Section 3 outlines the complexities of idiom detection. Section 4 describes our approach to detecting candidate idioms in essays. Section 5 describes the corpus and the annotation study. Results and additional experiments are presented in section 6.

2 Idioms and EFL

Applied linguistic research has focused on EFL students' knowledge, comprehension and pro-

Proceedings of the Workshop on Figurative Language Processing, pages 34–44
New Orleans, Louisiana, June 6, 2018. ©2018 Association for Computational Linguistics

duction of idioms. Cooper (1999) investigated idiom comprehension with non-native English speakers from diverse backgrounds, and found that subjects used a variety of strategies for comprehension. Laufer (2000) investigated avoidance of English idioms by EFL university students, using a fill-in translation test, and found that lower English proficiency was associated with greater avoidance of English idioms. Tran (2013) investigated knowledge of 50 idioms collected from the lists of frequently used English idioms and found poor idiomatic competence among EFL students in Vietnam. Multiple factors contribute to *figurative competency*, such as learners' proficiency levels, types of idioms, learners' vocabulary knowledge, and similarity of idioms between foreign and native language (Alhaysony, 2017; Na Ranong, 2014; de Caro, 2009; Irujo, 1986).

Researchers have also looked at figurative language that EFL learners encounter in their educational environments and materials (e.g. textbooks, lectures, etc.). Liu (2003) conducted a corpus-based study of the spoken American English idioms encountered most frequently by college students and provided suggestions for improving the development of idiom teaching and reference materials, including improving the coverage of idiom variants. Littlemore et al. (2011; 2001) investigated the range of difficulties that non-native speakers of English experience when encountering metaphors[1] in British university lectures, including non-understanding (failure to interpret) and misunderstanding (incorrect interpretation).

A complementary line of research focuses on the EFL students' use of metaphors in language production. Littlemore et al. (2014) analyzed the use of metaphors in 200 exam essays written by EFL students, at different levels of English proficiency. They found that metaphor use increases with proficiency level, and even suggested that descriptors for metaphor use could be integrated in the rating scales for writing. Beigman Klebanov and Flor (2013) investigated the use of metaphors in 116 argumentative essays and found moderate-to-strong correlation between the percentage of metaphorically used words in an essay and the writing quality score. Notably, both studies used a small number of essays and conducted an exhaustive manual analysis of metaphoric expressions.

3 Idiom identification

Syntactic and lexical flexibility are two of the issues dealt with at length in the linguistic and psycholinguistic literature on idioms (Glucksberg, 2001; Nunberg et al., 1994). Idioms can vary from being fully syntactically flexible to not at all. Although, traditionally, idiomatic expressions had been considered as 'fixed expressions' (Alexander, 1978), researchers have demonstrated that idioms allow a lot of variation, including adjectival and adverbial modification, quantification, negation, substitution, passivization and topicalization. Glucksberg (2001) illustrates the flexibility of idiomatic expressions, using the idiom *"don't give up the ship"*, which has a wide range of variations:

1. Tense inflection: *He gave up the ship.*

2. Number inflection: *Cowardly? You wont believe it: They gave up all the ships!*

3. Passivization: *The ship was given up by the city council.*

4. Adverbial and adjectival modification: *After holding out as long as possible, he finally gave up the last ship.*

5. Word substitution: *Give up the ship? Hell, he gave up the whole fleet!*

It has been long noted that many idioms allow for application of various kinds of modifiers, which often insert words and phrases around or even into the core idiomatic phrase (Ernst, 1981). Linguists have proposed different theories and taxonomies for idiom modification (McClure, 2011; Glucksberg, 2001; Nicolas, 1995), while psycholinguistic experiments demonstrated the flexibility of idiom recognition mechanisms (Hamblin and Gibbs, 1999; McGlone et al., 1994; Gibbs and Nayak, 1989; Gibbs et al., 1989). Researchers who focused on computer-aided identification of idiomatic expressions in texts have noted the need to account for idiom flexibility (Bond et al., 2015; Minugh, 2006; Moon, 1998).

---

[1]On the close relation between idioms and metaphors, see Gibbs et al. (1997)

In this respect, it is important to mention one very common sub-type of idiomatic expressions: idioms that are not fully lexically specified. Such idioms, e.g. *"be the apple of one's eye"*, include slots that must be filled in context, thus involving modification and discontinuity of the lexical components of the idiom, posing an additional challenge for automatic detection.

3.1 Automated detection of idioms

In computational linguistics, idiom detection systems fall into one of two paradigms (Muzny and Zettlemoyer, 2013): type classification, where a decision is made whether an expression (out of any context) is always/usually idiomatic or literal (Shutova et al., 2010; Gedigian et al., 2006; Widdows and Dorow, 2005), and token classification, where each occurrence of a phrase, in a specific context, can be idiomatic or literal (Peng et al., 2014; Li and Sporleder, 2009; Sporleder and Li, 2009; Fazly et al., 2009; Katz and Giesbrecht, 2006).

Early work on idiom detection involved small sets of expressions (Fazly and Stevenson, 2006), and focused on specific types of syntactic constructions (such as verb + complement, e.g. *"stir excitement"*,*"play with fire"*) (Shutova et al., 2010; Li and Sporleder, 2009; Diab and Bhutada, 2009; Diab and Krishna, 2009). More recent research on detection of non-compositional word combinations has shown a proliferation of approaches, but much work still focuses on acontextual classification (Hashimoto and Tsuruoka, 2016; Cordeiro et al., 2016; Ramisch et al., 2016; Yazdani et al., 2015; Salehi et al., 2014; Salehi and Cook, 2013; Kiela and Clark, 2013; Reddy et al., 2011). Recent work on detection of idiom instances in context (Gharbieh et al., 2016; Salton et al., 2016; Peng et al., 2014) focused only on Verb+Noun constructions, using the same dataset (Cook et al., 2008). A notable exception is the work of Feldman and Peng (2013), which is not limited by the type of syntactic construction.

4 Procedure for identifying idiom-candidates in essays

Our approach to identifying idiomatic expressions in texts is motivated by three factors.

First, we aim for broad coverage, so as to identify as many different idioms as possible. Second, we aim at identifying idiomatic expressions in context, in real-life texts. Third, our focus is on learner language, in essays written by non-native learners of English. We assume that most of the idioms that might be found in such texts are very well known idioms that are listed in various dictionaries. Our approach to idiom detection proposes two phases: candidate detection followed by verification. We compiled a large listing of idiomatic expressions that we want to detect. The idea is to automatically identify such expressions in texts, as candidate-idioms, and then apply verification algorithms that would confirm/reject the candidate expressions as being an idiom in the given context. In this paper we report on our initial results with the first part of this approach - detecting candidate-idiom expressions in student essays.

4.1 A collection of idioms

For our collection, we use Wiktionary as a resource. Wiktionary has a facility for contributors to tag definitions as idiomatic. The English Wiktionary was used in some previous computational work on idioms (Salehi et al., 2014), as it has rather broad coverage for idioms (although it is far from being complete (Muzny and Zettlemoyer, 2013)). We collected all English expressions that were tagged as idiomatic, from the English Wiktionary of October 2015. That initial list totaled about 8,000 entries. From that list, we eliminated several classes of expressions. First, we eliminated all single-word expressions, (e.g. *backwater*), since we are interested in idiomatic phrases. Next, we eliminated verb-particle constructions and prepositional verbs (such as *whisk away* and *yell at*). Finally, we eliminated expressions that are common greetings (e.g. *good evening*) or conventional dialogic expressions (e.g. *how do you do*). The resulting list contains 5,075 English idiomatic expressions. The list is of course extensible and more idioms can be added in the future.

4.2 The algorithm

Our algorithm for detecting candidate idiom expressions involves checking whether any of the listed idioms occur in a text. Since idiomatic expressions can exhibit considerable flexibility with inflectional and syntactic-form variations, a broad-coverage search algorithm must take such variation into account. This is achieved by enriched representation and flexible algorithmic matching.

Our initial Wiktionary-based list of 5,075 expressions contains only canonical forms of idioms. Using an in-house morphological toolkit, we automatically enrich the representation of an idiom entry by including all inflectional variants to the idiom's content words. The automatic expansion is not part-of-speech sensitive. For example *"melting pot"* is expanded to "{*melting, melt, molten, melts, melted, meltings*} {*pots, pot, potted, potting*}".

The next step is to mark optional elements in the idiom representation: determiners, prepositions and a set of other common function words (see appendix for the full list), as well as possessive "'s", and punctuation like commas and hyphens. An idiom should be matched even if such elements are missing in the text. For example, with inflectional expansion and with marking of optional elements, the idiom *"give the royal treatment"* becomes "{*give, given, gave, giving, gives*} *[the,a,an]* {*royal, royals*} {*treatment, treatments*}". The need for optional elements stems from the notion that writers, especially EFL writers, often omit articles and prepositions, or use erroneous ones (Dale et al., 2012).

The third step is the treatment of idioms that are not fully lexicalized, for example *"pour one's heart out"* or *"knock someone's socks off"*. We pre-fill the slots with a set of pronouns that might occur in such position. For idioms that include a possessive slot, we substitute the canonical *"someone's"* with possessive pronouns. For example, *"knock someone's socks off"* becomes "{*knocked, knock, knocking, knocks*} *[my, your, his, her, our, their, one, someone]* *['s]* {*sock, socked, socking, socks*} *off*". For other idioms, the substitution list uses non-possessive pronouns. For example, in canonical expressions like *"bite off more than one can chew"*, *"one"* is substituted with "{*i, you, he, she, we, they, one, someone,somebody, me, him, her, us, them*}". Reflexive pronouns in canonical idiom forms (e.g. *"let oneself go"*)

are expanded to a set of reflexives "{*myself, oneself, yourself, yourselves, himself, herself, itself, ourselves, themselves*}". All automatically added pronouns are treated as optional elements. This treatment does not fill the slots with non-pronominal material (names and full noun phrases), but that is compensated with the skip-words-algorithm (see below).

The automated enrichment described above is performed only once, when we transform the list of canonical idioms into an enriched search-specification format. Some idioms allow insertion of various modifiers over the core components, for example *"kick the proverbial bucket"*, *"pay little attention"*. To detect such variant instances, we provide some flexibility to the search algorithm. Essentially, the search algorithm must match all the non-optional elements of an idiom, in sequence. Flexibility is achieved when the algorithm is allowed to match the core components, in order (as specified by the enriched representation), but they don't have to be consecutive. The algorithm may allow up to k unmatched words between the first and last elements of an idiom. This enables detection of idioms with unspecified modifiers and intervening insertions. The value of k is a settable parameter.

Note that the algorithm has two separate skip strategies. On the one hand, there are optional elements in the idiom search-specification, such as determiners or pronouns. This means that not all components of an idiom have to be matched in order to spot a potential idiom-instance. On the other hand, the algorithm can skip over tokens in the text, to allow for intervening material. The combination of these two approaches allows to find instances of lexically underspecified idioms. For example, the idiom *"change one's mind"* is expanded to "{*changes, changing, change, changed*} *[my, your, his, her, our, their, one, someone]* *['s]* {*minds, mind, minding, minded*}", and the algorithm can identify *"changed the people's minds"* in a text, because the pronouns are optional and *'the'* and *'people'* are skippable.

The approach outlined above was implemented with a tokenizer, a sentence-boundary detection module and an indexing module. Since we are using a tokenizer, the idiom-

Annotation category	Explanation
Idiomatic use	choose this option if you think that the sentence indeed contains an instance of the idiom
Literal Use	choose this option if you think that the expression is correct, but it is used in a literal and not idiomatic sense
Wrong Expression	choose this option if you think that the system picked up a wrong expression, not an intended one
Need More Context	choose this option if you feel that you need more context to decide

Table 1: Classification categories for the idiom annotation study.

search specifications are token-oriented, which allows for very simple specification of patterns (e.g. all the examples above). The sentence detector allows restricting the search only within sentences (and never across sentences). For each sentence in each text under consideration, we need to check whether any of our 5,075 enriched expressions is present in the sentence. Naive search would amount to matching against 5,075 expressions. Indexing allows for a faster solution. The enriched dictionary of idioms is indexed by keywords (non-optional idiom components) when it is loaded to memory. Each text (essay) is also indexed, on-the-fly, when loaded for processing. The indices are cross-compared, and the algorithm attempts to find only those idioms whose keywords appear in the index of the current text.

One limitation of the above approach is the constraint of sequential matching (even with skips). Some idioms are flexible enough to allow for passivization or topicalization (Glucksberg, 2001), variations that invert the word order (especially for idioms involving a verb + direct object, e.g. *the ship was given up by the city council*). Extending our algorithm to handle such cases is left for future work.

It should be stressed that the approach outlined above identifies idiom-candidates, i.e. it finds, in texts, expressions that are likely to be instantiations of stock idioms. However, the current algorithm does not perform any verification - it does not attempt to confirm that the detected expressions are actually idioms in context. Adding such capabilities is subject of continuing research.

5 Data and annotation

We conducted a study in which our flexible algorithm was applied to a large set of essays written by EFL students. Candidate-idioms were automatically marked and later manually annotated.

5.1 Data

We used the publicly available corpus of essays, the ETS Corpus of Non-Native Written English (Blanchard et al., 2014, 2013). This corpus consists of essays written for the TOEFL® iBT test. The test is used internationally as a measure of academic English proficiency, among other purposes, to inform admissions decisions for students seeking to study at institutions of higher learning where English is the language of instruction. The corpus contains about 12,000 essays, sampled from eight prompts (i.e. eight different discussion topics), along with score levels (low/medium/high) for each essay. Each prompt poses a proposition and asks examinees to write an argumentative essay, stating their arguments for or against the proposition.

For our present work, we sampled 3,305 essays from this corpus, selecting (a) only among essays that received medium or high score; and (b) only among essays that had at least one candidate idiom match (using the algorithm with maximum skip $k = 4$). The sampled data set has 1,111,618 words; essay length varies from 143 to 801 words, with an average of 336.

5.2 The annotation study

In total, our algorithm identified 5,704 expressions as candidate-idiom instances, in the 3,305 essays. All those expressions were then annotated, using the following setup. For each candidate-idiom expression, the whole sentence in which that expression occurred was automatically extracted from the essay, and all such sentences were collected in a spreadsheet file. For each extract, we provided the full sentence, what idiom (canonical form) was tentatively detected, and what were the first and last words of the detected instance. For each candidate-expression, the annotator had to pick one out of four classification options (see Table 1).

All annotation was performed by a single annotator, a native speaker of American English, contracted through a commercial linguistic service provider. The annotator was given an explanation of how the data was pre-processed, and was encouraged to consult the Wiktionary entries for the canonical stock expressions. Upon completion of a training session with 100 instances, the annotator was given 300 new candidate instances. This set of 300 items was also annotated by the first author. We had exact agreement in 285 cases out of 300, which is 95% (Cohen's kappa 0.92). The annotator then proceeded to annotate the rest of the 5K+ candidate instances. The first author also adjudicated the disagreed cases from the 300-items set, and twenty-one instances that the annotator marked as 'Need More Context' in the rest of the data.

6 Results

Out of 5,704 instances marked by our algorithm, the annotation study confirmed 1,302 cases as idiomatic uses, 693 cases were found to be literal uses, and 3,709 cases were classified as wrong expressions.

It should be noted that since the annotation was performed only on the automatically flagged candidate instances, it is quite possible that essays in our data set contain even more idioms: a) undetected instances (e.g. due to word order inversions, insertions larger than $k = 4$, etc.), and b) instances of idioms that are not on our current list.

The 1,302 attested idiom instances in our data belong to 294 types (canonical forms). Table 2 lists some of the most common idioms found in the essays. Thus, out of 5,075 idioms types in our dictionary, we found attested instances for $294/5,075 = 5.8\%$. This demonstrates that argumentative essays written to TOEFL prompts have quite a rich variety of idiomatic expressions. Notably, the idioms were not concentrated in just a few es-

says. Out of 3,305 essays, 1,017 essays (30%) had at least one verified idiom instance.

Idiom (canonical form)	Count
pay attention	112
matter of fact	84
other than	54
long run	46
find oneself	37
come to mind	36
side effect	35
day-to-day	34
change one's mind	32
again and again	30
great deal	28
jack of all trades	23
rush hour	22
open doors	21

Table 2: Instance counts for fourteen most frequent idioms found in student essays in the corpus.

The majority (65%) of the automatically marked candidates were classified as 'Wrong Expression' (WE). Such instances are misdetected by our algorithm when the mandatory content words of an idiom-specification do occur in text, but are not part of the sought-for expression, or are even parts of unrelated expressions. See examples in Table 3.

Ideally, we would like our algorithm to mark as candidates only expressions that might be idioms or literal uses, so that some verification algorithm might then distinguish among them. The proliferation of wrong expressions complicates this outlook. In order to check how the quality of marked candidate instances is affected by our skip algorithm, we conducted two additional experiments.

6.1 Additional experiments

We applied the candidate-idiom detection algorithm to the 3,305 essays, using different values of the max-skip-tokens parameter k, from 0 to 4. With $k = 0$, no intervening words are allowed within an idiom. Notably, $k = 4$ was used in the annotation study, so all candidate expressions marked in runs with smaller values of k are proper subsets of the annotated data. The results are presented in Figure 1A.

Predictably, increasing the value of k allows to detect more idioms, but it also leads to the

Canonical form	Sentence with candidate	Status
long run	Because, such advertisements are neither wise and profitable options for firms in the *long run* nor legal in many countries.	Idiom
grass roots	we have to understand the content from the *grass root* level of that matter.	Idiom
try one's hand	Thereby we have stories of some 60-70 year old *trying their hands* at trekking or a cross-country run.	Idiom
draw a line	When do we *draw the line* to where we should stop gaining any new knowledge?	Idiom
draw a line	Suppose if a student is thought in class to *draw lines*, boxes...	Literal
great deal	Some people even offer a *great deal*, but you have to pay in advance, and in the end you do not even get a product.	Literal
leave home	And also the most of us *leave home* eary in the morning and come back home late in the night.	Literal
well-oiled	People already realize *well the oil* will be run out in a short time.	WE
come to life	So can you disagree with above statement after *coming across Faradays life*?	WE
any more for any more	The *more you do, the more* you learn, and life become more interesting.	WE

Table 3: Examples of candidate-idiom expressions in context and their annotations.

increase in the number of candidates that are literal uses, and an increase in the number of wrongly-marked expressions (false positives). The largest increase is observed in transition from zero to just one allowed intervening word. The number of detected idioms increases by 222 instances (22%), while the number of literal uses increases by 79 instances (13%). At the same time, the number of wrong expressions increases dramatically from 153 to 2214 (more than a 1300%).

As we raise the value of k further, the amount of added idiomatic instances decreases (3.7% added at $k = 2$, 2% at $k = 3$ and 0.7% at $k = 4$). The amount of added literal uses also decreases (1.3%, 0.7%, 0.4%). The amount of added WE instances decreases slowly (25%, 17%, 14.8%), hundreds of WE instances are added for each increment of k. This suggests that $k = 4$ might be a practical limit for our current approach, since wrong expressions become increasingly dominant in the output.

The largest number of wrong expressions is produced by the idiom "*any more for any more*": 683 at $k = 1$, rising to 998 when $k = 4$. Since 'any' and 'for' are optional, the algorithm flags any sequence of 'more ... more' with up to k intervening words. Other idioms that generated more than 100 WE instances

(at $k = 4$) are "*day of days*" (157), "*well and good*" (134), "*more like it*" (124). No literal or idiomatic use of those expressions was found.

Overall the skip-enabled search shows considerable promise. With no skip, the algorithm found 1,000 idiom instances in texts. With skip $k = 4$, the algorithm found 1,302 instances, an increase of 30%. To illustrate the usefulness of the skip-enabled search, we list some extended forms of idioms that were detected. For "*pay attention*": *researchers should pay their attention on the specific subject; if Einstein had not paid specific attention to...; pay particular attention.* For "*change one's mind*": *...people change their mind; you might change your mind; the customer change his mind after...; advertisements can change consumer's mind about products.*

In a second experiment we also varied the values of k, but this time we switched all the optional (function) words in idiom specifications to being mandatory. Thus, for example, for "*draw a line*", a determiner in the middle is now mandatory – one of {*the*, *a*, *an*} should be matched for an instance to be flagged. (Punctuation and "*'s*" remain optional.) The results are presented in Figure 1B.

The general trends observed in the previous experiment are still present: as the number of allowable insertions rises, more idiom instances are detected, but also more literal uses and more misdetected expressions; the increment decays with larger k.

Next we compare between the results of the two experiments (each bar in Figure 1A vs. a corresponding bar in Figure 1B). When function words in the patterns are mandatory, the number of detected idioms is reduced by 0.6% at $k = 0$, 3.6% at $k = 1$, 5.4% at $k = 2$, 6.5% at $k = 3$ and 6.7% at $k = 4$ (from 1,302 to 1,214). There is also some reduction in the number of detected literal-use instances (6.2% at $k = 4$). The strongest reduction is in the number of misdetected expressions: 70% at $k = 4$ (3,709 to 1,090) and 74% at $k = 1$. Some such reduction might have been expected: with all mandatory components, the idiom patterns are stricter, and so less irrelevant material fits into them. However, the magnitude of the reduction is impressive, as it demonstrates that function words in idioms can be very useful for filtering out irrelevant material.

Still, with function words being non-optional, we loose about 6.7% of idioms. Here are some corpus examples of idiom instances that are detected when optional components are allowed, but are not detected otherwise. For *'pain in the neck'*: *"... but it's always a pain of neck to decide whether going with a tour guide or by themselves"*; here the student used a wrong preposition *of*. For *'seize the day'*: *"... young people tend to seize each day because even in his early age an human being is fully aware..."*; here the student used the unexpected determiner *each*, but not any from the 'mandatory' set.

7 Conclusions

We presented a large-scale investigation of the use of idiomatic expressions in argumentative essays written by non-native English speakers.

We described a search procedure for automatic detection of candidate phrases in essay texts. The procedure was developed to address multiple demands - provide wide coverage (with an extensible dictionary with thousands of idioms) and address the flexibility of idiomatic expressions (via lexical enrichment and skip-steps in the search algorithm).

In an annotation study, candidate-idiom instances were automatically marked and then manually classified as idiomatic, literal, or wrong (misidentified) expressions. The study revealed that stock idiomatic expressions are quite common in EFL student essays and that a rather rich variety of English idioms is used.

Our study has confirmed the importance of tending to the syntactic and lexical flexibility of English idiomatic expressions. Allowing optional components in idioms and lexical insertions in text, increases recall of idiom instances by 30% relative to a baseline.

The flexible candidate-detection algorithm also flags a lot of irrelevant material, especially when more intervening words are allowed within an idiom. We have shown that consideration of function words in idioms can

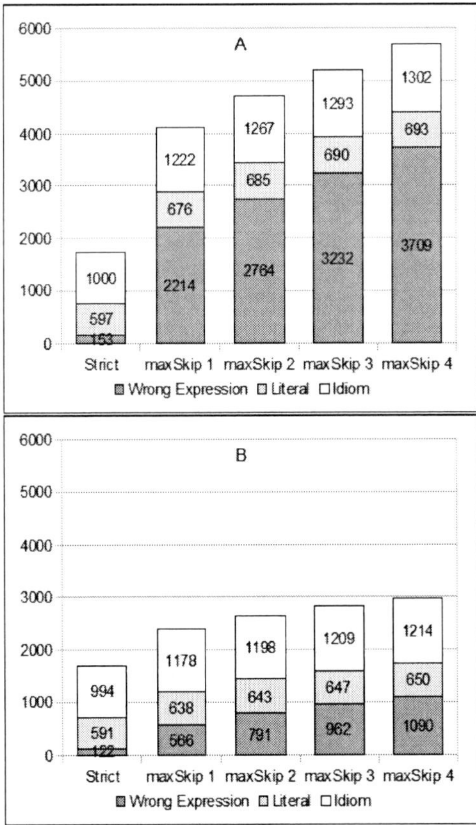

Figure 1: Counts of Idiom, Literal Use and Wrong Expression instances marked in essays, as a function of the number of allowable intervening words in candidate detection. Panel A: with optional words in idioms; Panel B: all words in idioms are mandatory.

help reduce the amount of false positives. We are working on integrating those findings towards an improved algorithm.

References

Richard Alexander. 1978. Fixed expressions in English: a linguistic, psycholinguistic, sociolinguistic and didactic study. *Lingustic Agency, University of Trier*, 26:171–188.

Maha Alhaysony. 2017. Strategies and difficulties of understanding English idioms: A case study of Saudi university efl students. *International Journal of English Linguistics*, 7(3):70–84.

Beata Beigman Klebanov and Michael Flor. 2013. Argumentation-relevant metaphors in test-taker essays. In *Proceedings of the First Workshop on Metaphor in NLP*, pages 11–20, Atlanta, Georgia. Association for Computational Linguistics.

Daniel Blanchard, Joel Tetreault, Derrick Higgins, Aoife Cahill, and Martin Chodorow. 2013. *TOEFL11: A Corpus of Non-Native English. Research Report ETS RR13-24*. Educational Testing Service, Princeton, NJ, USA.

Daniel Blanchard, Joel Tetreault, Derrick Higgins, Aoife Cahill, and Martin Chodorow. 2014. *ETS Corpus of Non-Native Written English, Catalog No. LDC2014T06*. Linguistic Data Consortium, Philadelphia, PA, USA.

Frank Boers and Seth Lindstromberg. 2009. *Optimizing a Lexical Approach to Instructed Second Language Acquisition*. Palgrave MacMillan, UK.

Francis Bond, Jia Qian Ho, and Dan Flickinger. 2015. Feeling our way to an analysis of English possessed idioms. In *Proceedings of the 22nd International Conference on Head-Driven Phrase Structure Grammar*, pages 61–74, Stanford, CA, USA. CSLI Publications.

Edith Eliana Roberto de Caro. 2009. The advantages and importance of learning and using idioms in English. *Cuadernos de Lingstica Hispnica*, 14:121–136.

Paul Cook, Afsaneh Fazly, and Suzanne Stevenson. 2008. The VNC-Tokens Dataset. In *Proceedings of the LREC Workshop Towards a Shared Task for Multiword Expressions (MWE 2008)*, pages 19–22. European Language Resources Association (ELRA).

Thomas C. Cooper. 1998. Teaching idioms. *Foreign Language Annals*, 31(2):255–266.

Thomas C. Cooper. 1999. Processing of idioms by L2 learners of English. *TESOL Quarterly*, 33(2):233–262.

Silvio Cordeiro, Carlos Ramisch, Marco Idiart, and Aline Villavicencio. 2016. Predicting the compositionality of nominal compounds: Giving word embeddings a hard time. In *Proceedings of the 54th Annual Meeting of the Association for Computational Linguistics (Volume 1: Long Papers)*, pages 1986–1997, Berlin, Germany. Association for Computational Linguistics.

Anthony Paul Cowie, Ronald Mackin, and Isabel R. McCaig. 1984. *Oxford Dictionary of Current Idiomatic English, vol. I-II. General Introduction*. Oxford University Press, Oxford, UK.

Robert Dale, Ilya Anisimoff, and George Narroway. 2012. Hoo 2012: A report on the preposition and determiner error correction shared task. In *Proceedings of the Seventh Workshop on Building Educational Applications Using NLP*, pages 54–62, Montréal, Canada. Association for Computational Linguistics.

Mona Diab and Pravin Bhutada. 2009. Verb noun construction mwe token classification. In *Proceedings of the Workshop on Multiword Expressions: Identification, Interpretation, Disambiguation and Applications*, pages 17–22, Singapore. Association for Computational Linguistics.

Mona Diab and Madhav Krishna. 2009. Handling sparsity for verb noun MWE token classification. In *Proceedings of the Workshop on Geometrical Models of Natural Language Semantics*, pages 96–103, Athens, Greece. Association for Computational Linguistics.

Thomas Ernst. 1981. Grist for the linguistic mill: Idioms and extra adjectives. *Journal of Linguistic Research*, 113(5):51–68.

Afsaneh Fazly, Paul Cook, and Suzanne Stevenson. 2009. Unsupervised type and token identification of idiomatic expressions. *Computational Linguistics*, 35(1):61–103.

Afsaneh Fazly and Suzanne Stevenson. 2006. Automatically constructing a lexicon of verb phrase idiomatic combinations. In *Proceedings of the 11th Conference of the European Chapter of the Association for Computational Linguistics*, pages 337–344. Association for Computational Linguistics.

Anna Feldman and Jing Peng. 2013. Automatic detection of idiomatic clauses. In *Computational Linguistics and Intelligent Text Processing*, pages 435–446. Springer.

Matt Gedigian, John Bryant, Srini Narayanan, and Branimir Ciric. 2006. Catching metaphors. In *Proceedings of the Third Workshop on Scalable Natural Language Understanding*, pages 41–48, New York City, New York. Association for Computational Linguistics.

Waseem Gharbieh, Virendra C. Bhavsar, and Paul Cook. 2016. A Word Embedding Approach to Identifying Verb-Noun Idiomatic Combinations. In *Proceedings of the 12th Workshop on Multiword Expression*, pages 112–118. Association for Computational Linguistics.

Raymond W. Gibbs, Josephine M. Bogdanovich, Jeffrey R. Sykes, and Dale J. Barr. 1997. Metaphor in idiom comprehension. *Journal of Memory and Language*, 37:141–154.

Raymond W. Gibbs and Nandini P. Nayak. 1989. Psycholinguistic studies on the syntactic behavior of idioms. *Cognitive Psychology*, 21(1):100–138.

Raymond W. Gibbs, Nandini P. Nayak, and Cooper Cutting. 1989. How to kick the bucket and not decompose: Analyzability and idiom processing. *Journal of Memory and Language*, 28(5):576–593.

Sam Glucksberg. 2001. *Understanding Figurative Language: from metaphors to idioms*. Oxford University Press, New York, NY.

Jennifer L. Hamblin and W. Gibbs, Raymond. 1999. Why you cant kick the bucket as you slowly die: Verbs in idiom comprehension. *Journal of Psycholinguistic Research*, 28(1):25–39.

Kazuma Hashimoto and Yoshimasa Tsuruoka. 2016. Adaptive joint learning of compositional and non-compositional phrase embeddings. In *Proceedings of the 54th Annual Meeting of the Association for Computational Linguistics (Volume 1: Long Papers)*, pages 205–215, Berlin, Germany. Association for Computational Linguistics.

Suzanne Irujo. 1986. A piece of cake: Learning and teaching idioms. *ELT Journal*, 40(3):236–242.

Graham Katz and Eugenie Giesbrecht. 2006. Automatic identification of non-compositional multi-word expressions using latent semantic analysis. In *Proceedings of the Workshop on Multiword Expressions: Identifying and Exploiting Underlying Properties*, pages 12–19, Sydney, Australia. Association for Computational Linguistics.

Douwe Kiela and Stephen Clark. 2013. Detecting compositionality of multi-word expressions using nearest neighbours in vector space models. In *Proceedings of the 2013 Conference on Empirical Methods in Natural Language Processing*, pages 1427–1432, Seattle, Washington, USA. Association for Computational Linguistics.

Batia Laufer. 2000. Avoidance of idioms in a second language: the effect of l1-l2 degree of similarity. *Studia Linguistica*, 54(2):186–196.

Linlin Li and Caroline Sporleder. 2009. A cohesion graph based approach for unsupervised recognition of literal and non-literal use of multiword expressions. In *Proceedings of the 2009 Workshop on Graph-based Methods for Natural Language Processing (TextGraphs-4)*, pages 75–83, Suntec, Singapore. Association for Computational Linguistics.

Jeannette Littlemore. 2001. Metaphor as a source of misunderstanding for overseas students in academic lectures. *Teaching in Higher Education*, 6(3):333–351.

Jeannette Littlemore, Tina Krennmayr, James Turner, and Sarah Turner. 2014. An investigation into metaphor use at different levels of second language writing. *Applied Linguistics*, 35(2):117–144.

Jeannette. Littlemore, Phyllis Trautman Chen, Almut Koester, and John Barnden. 2011. Difficulties in metaphor comprehension faced by international students whose first language is not English. *Applied Linguistics*, 32(4):408–429.

Dilin Liu. 2003. The most frequently used spoken American English idioms: A corpus analysis and its implications. *TESOL Quarterly*, 37(4):671–700.

Scott McClure. 2011. Modification in noncombining idioms. *Semantics and Pragmatics*, 4(7):1–7.

Matthew S. McGlone, Sam Glucksberg, and Cristina Cacciari. 1994. Semantic productivity and idiom comprehension. *Discourse Processes*, 17(2):167–190.

David Minugh. 2006 The filling in the sandwich: Internal expansion of idiomatic expressions. In Roberta Facchinetti, editor, *Corpus Linguistics 25 Years on*, pages 205–224. Rodopi, Amsterdam, NL.

Rosamund Moon. 1998. *Fixed Expressions and Idioms in English: A Corpus-Based Approach*. Clarendon Press, Oxford, UK.

Grace Muzny and Luke Zettlemoyer. 2013. Automatic idiom identification in Wiktionary. In *Proceedings of the 2013 Conference on Empirical Methods in Natural Language Processing*, pages 1417–1421, Seattle, Washington, USA. Association for Computational Linguistics.

Sirirat Na Ranong. 2014. Idiom comprehension and processing: The case of Thai EFL learners. *Journal of English Studies*, 9:51–97.

Tim Nicolas. 1995. Semantics of idiom modification. In Martin Everaert, Erik-Jan van der Linden, Andrew Schenk, and Robert Schreuder, editors, *Idioms: Structural and Psychological Perspectives*, pages 233–254. Lawrence Erlbaum, Hillsdale, NJ, USA.

Geoffrey Nunberg, Ivan A. Sag, and Thomas Wasow. 1994. Idioms. *Language*, 70(3):491–538.

Jing Peng, Anna Feldman, and Ekaterina Vylomova. 2014. Classifying idiomatic and literal expressions using topic models and intensity of emotions. In *Proceedings of the 2014 Conference on Empirical Methods in Natural Language Processing (EMNLP)*, pages 2019–2027, Doha, Qatar. Association for Computational Linguistics.

Carlos Ramisch, Silvio Cordeiro, Leonardo Zilio, Marco Idiart, and Aline Villavicencio. 2016. How naked is the naked truth? a multilingual lexicon of nominal compound compositionality. In *Proceedings of the 54th Annual Meeting of the Association for Computational Linguistics (Volume 2: Short Papers)*, pages 156–161, Berlin, Germany. Association for Computational Linguistics.

Siva Reddy, Diana McCarthy, and Suresh Manandhar. 2011. An empirical study on compositionality in compound nouns. In *Proceedings of 5th International Joint Conference on Natural Language Processing*, pages 210–218, Chiang Mai, Thailand. Asian Federation of Natural Language Processing.

Bahar Salehi and Paul Cook. 2013. Predicting the compositionality of multiword expressions using translations in multiple languages. In *Second Joint Conference on Lexical and Computational Semantics (*SEM), Volume 1: Proceedings of the Main Conference and the Shared Task: Semantic Textual Similarity*, pages 266–275, Atlanta, Georgia, USA. Association for Computational Linguistics.

Bahar Salehi, Paul Cook, and Timothy Baldwin. 2014. Detecting non-compositional mwe components using wiktionary. In *Proceedings of the 2014 Conference on Empirical Methods in Natural Language Processing (EMNLP)*, pages 1792–1797, Doha, Qatar. Association for Computational Linguistics.

Giancarlo Salton, Robert Ross, and John Kelleher. 2016. Idiom token classification using sentential distributed semantics. In *Proceedings of the 54th Annual Meeting of the Association of Computational Linguistics*, pages 194–204, Berlin, Germany. Association for Computational Linguistics.

Ekaterina Shutova, Lin Sun, and Anna Korhonen. 2010. Metaphor identification using verb and noun clustering. In *Proceedings of the 23rd International Conference on Computational Linguistics (Coling 2010)*, pages 1002–1010, Beijing, China. Coling 2010 Organizing Committee.

Caroline Sporleder and Linlin Li. 2009. Unsupervised recognition of literal and non-literal use of idiomatic expressions. In *Proceedings of the 12th Conference of the European Chapter of the ACL (EACL 2009)*, pages 754–762, Athens, Greece. Association for Computational Linguistics.

Huong Quynh Tran. 2013. Figurative idiomatic competence: An analysis of EFL learners in Vietnam. *Language Education in Asia*, 4(1):23–38.

Dominic Widdows and Beate Dorow. 2005. Automatic extraction of idioms using graph analysis and asymmetric lexicosyntactic patterns. In *Proceedings of the ACL-SIGLEX Workshop on Deep Lexical Acquisition*, pages 48–56, Ann Arbor, Michigan. Association for Computational Linguistics.

Majid Yazdani, Meghdad Farahmand, and James Henderson. 2015. Learning semantic composition to detect non-compositionality of multiword expressions. In *Proceedings of the 2015 Conference on Empirical Methods in Natural Language Processing*, pages 1733–1742, Lisbon, Portugal. Association for Computational Linguistics.

Appendix

The list of words that were defined as optional in idiom specifications: Determiners: *a, an, the, any, some*; Wh-words: *what, who, whom, whose, how, when, why, where*; Auxiliary verbs: *can, can't, cannot, could, couldn't, may, might, should, do, does, did, done, don't, doesn't, didn't*; Be forms: *be, been, was, wasn't, were, weren't, ain't, am , is, are, isn't, aren't*; Common prepositions: *in, on, of, off, at, as, to, for, from, down, up, it, and, or, with*; Pronouns: *i, me, my, you, your, he, his, him, she, her, hers, we, our, ours, us, they, them, their, theirs*; Demonstratives: *there, here, this, that, these, those*; Other: *but, yet, and, or, so, s, 's, one, someone, somebody, thus, such, ever, never, no, not, none*.

Predicting Human Metaphor Paraphrase Judgments with Deep Neural Networks

Yuri Bizzoni and **Shalom Lappin**
University of Gothenburg
`firstname.lastname@gu.se`

Abstract

We propose a new annotated corpus for metaphor interpretation by paraphrase, and a novel DNN model for performing this task. Our corpus consists of 200 sets of 5 sentences, with each set containing one reference metaphorical sentence, and four ranked candidate paraphrases. Our model is trained for a binary classification of paraphrase candidates, and then used to predict graded paraphrase acceptability. It reaches an encouraging 75% accuracy on the binary classification task, and high Pearson (.75) and Spearman (.68) correlations on the gradient judgment prediction task.

1 Introduction

Metaphor is an increasingly studied phenomenon in computational linguistics. But while metaphor detection has received considerable attention in the NLP literature (Dunn et al., 2014; Veale et al., 2016) and in corpus linguistics (Krennmayr, 2015) in recent years, not much work has focused on the task of metaphor paraphrasing - assigning an appropriate interpretation to a metaphorical expression. Moreover, there are few (if any) annotated corpora of metaphor paraphrases (Shutova and Teufel, 2010). The main papers in this area are Shutova (2010), and Bollegala and Shutova (2013). The first applies a supervised method combining WordNet and distributional word vectors to produce the best paraphrase of a single verb used metaphorically in a sentence. The second approach, conceptually related to the first, builds an unsupervised system that, given a sentence with a single metaphorical verb and a set of potential paraphrases, selects the most accurate candidate through a combination of mutual information scores and distributional similarity.

Despite the computational and linguistic interest of this task, little research has been devoted to it.

Some quantitative analyses of figurative language have involved metaphor interpretation and paraphrasing. These focus on integrating paraphrase into automatic Textual Entailment frames (Agerri, 2008), to explore the properties of distributional semantics in larger-than-word structures (Turney, 2013). Alternatively, they study the sentiment features of metaphor usage (Mohammad et al., 2016; Kozareva, 2015). This last aspect of figurative interpretation is considered a particularly hard task and has generated several approaches

The task of metaphor interpretation is a particular case of paraphrase detection, although this characterization is not unproblematic, as we will see in Section 6.

In Bollegala and Shutova (2013), metaphor paraphrase is treated as a ranking problem. Given a metaphorical usage of a verb in a short sentence, several candidate literal sentences are retrieved from the Web and ranked. This approach requires the authors to create a gradient score to label their paraphrases, a perspective that is now gaining currency in broader semantic similarity tasks (Xu et al., 2015; Agirre et al., 2016).

Mohammad et al. (2016) resort to metaphor paraphrasing in order to perform a quantitative study on the emotions associated with the usage of metaphors. They create a small corpus of paraphrase pairs formed from a metaphorical expression and a literal equivalent. They ask candidates to judge the degree of "emotionality" conveyed by the metaphorical and the literal expressions. While the study has shown that metaphorical paraphrases are generally perceived as more emotionally charged than their literal equivalents, a corpus of this kind has not been used to train a computational model for metaphor paraphrase scoring.

In this paper we present a new dataset for

Proceedings of the Workshop on Figurative Language Processing, pages 45–55
New Orleans, Louisiana, June 6, 2018. ©2018 Association for Computational Linguistics

metaphor paraphrase identification and ranking. In our corpus, paraphrase recognition is treated as an ordering problem, where sets of sentences are ranked with respect to a reference metaphor sentence.

The main difference with respect to existing work in this field consists in the syntactic and semantic diversity covered by our dataset. The metaphors in our corpus are not confined to a single part of speech. We introduce metaphorical examples of nouns, adjectives, verbs and a number of multi-word metaphors.

Our corpus is, to the best of our knowledge, the largest existing dataset for metaphor paraphrase detection and ranking.

As we describe in Section 2, it is composed of groups of five sentences: one metaphor, and four candidates that can be ranked as its literal paraphrases.

The inspiration for the structure of our dataset comes from a recent work on paraphrase (Bizzoni and Lappin, 2017), where a similarly organized dataset was introduced to deal with paraphrase detection.

In our work, we use an analogous structure to model metaphor paraphrase. Also, while Bizzoni and Lappin (2017) present a corpus annotated by a single human, each paraphrase set in our corpus was judged by 20 different Amazon Mechanical Turk (AMT) annotators, making the grading of our sentences more robust and reliable (see Section 2.1).

We use this corpus to test a neural network model formed by a combination of Convolutional Neural Networks (CNNs) and Long Short Term Memory Recurrent Neural Networks (LSTM RNNs). We test this model on two classification problems: (i) binary paraphrase classification and (ii) paraphrase ranking. We show that our system can achieve significant correlation with human judgments on the ranking task as a by-product of supervised binary learning. To the best of our knowledge, this is the first work in metaphor paraphrasing to use supervised gradient representations.

2 A New Corpus for Metaphor Paraphrase Evaluation

We present a dataset for metaphor paraphrase designed to allow users to rank non-metaphorical candidates as paraphrases of a metaphorical sentence or expression. Our corpus is formed of 200 sets of five sentence paraphrase candidates for a metaphorical sentence or expression.[1]

In each set, the first sentence contains a metaphor, and it provides the reference sentence to be paraphrased. The remaining four sentences are labeled on a 1-4 scale based on the degree to which they paraphrase the reference sentence. This is on analogy with the annotation frame used for SemEval Semantic Similarity tasks (Agirre et al., 2016). Broadly, our labels represent the following categories:

1 Two sentences cannot be considered paraphrases.

2 Two sentences cannot be considered paraphrase, but they show a degree of semantic similarity.

3 Two sentences could be considered paraphrases, although they present some important difference in style or content (they are not strong paraphrases).

4 Two sentences are strong paraphrases.

On average, every group of five sentences contains a strong paraphrase, a loose paraphrase and two non-paraphrases, one of which may use some relevant words from the metaphor in question.[2]

The following examples illustrate these ranking labels.

- Metaphor: *The crowd was a river in the street*

    - The crowd was large and impetuous in the street. *Score: 4*
    - There were a lot of people in the street. *Score: 3*
    - There were few people in the street. *Score: 2*
    - We reached a river at the end of the street. *Score: 1*

We believe that this annotation scheme is useful. While it sustains graded semantic similarity labels, it also provides sets of semantically related

---

[1] Our annotated data set and the code for our model is available at `https://github.com/yuri-bizzoni/Metaphor-Paraphrase`.

[2] Some of the problems raised by the concept of paraphrase in figurative language are discussed in Section 6.

elements, each one of which can be scored or ordered independently of the others. Therefore, the metaphorical sentence can be tested separately for each literal candidate in the set in a binary classification task.

In the test phase, the annotation scheme allows us to observe how a system represents the similarity between a metaphorical and a literal sentence by taking the scores of two candidates as points of relative proximity to the metaphor.

It can be argued that a good literal paraphrase of a metaphor needs to compensate to some extent for the expressive or sentimental bias that a metaphor usually supplies, as argued in Mohammad et al. (2016). In general a binary classification can be misleading because it conceals the different levels of similarity between competing candidates.

For example, the literal sentence *Republican candidates during the convention were terrible* can be considered to be a loose paraphrase of the metaphor **The Republican convention was a horror show**, or alternatively, as a semantically related non-paraphrase. Which of these conclusions we adopt depends on our decision concerning how much interpretative content a literal sentence needs to provide in order to qualify as a valid paraphrase of a metaphor. The question whether the two sentences are acceptable paraphrases or not can be hard to answer. By contrast, it would be far fetched to suggest that *The Republican convention was a joy to follow* is a better or even equally strong literal paraphrase for **The Republican convention was a horror show**.

In this sense, the sentences **Her new occupation was a dream come true** and *She liked her new occupation* can be considered to be loose paraphrases, in that the term *liked* can be judged an acceptable, but not ideal interpretation of the more intense metaphorical expression **a dream come true**. By contrast, *She hated her new occupation* cannot be plausibly regarded as more similar in meaning than *She liked her new occupation* to **Her new occupation was a dream come true**.

Our training dataset is divided into four main sections:

1. Noun phrase Metaphors : *My lawyer is an angel.*

2. Adjective Metaphors : *The rich man had a cold heart.*

3. Verb Metaphors : *She cut him down with her words.*

4. Multi-word Metaphors : *The seeds of change were planted in 1943.*

All these sentences and their candidates were manually produced to insure that for each group we have a strong literal paraphrase, a loose literal paraphrase and two semantically related non-paraphrases. Here "semantically related" can indicate either a re-use of the metaphorical words to express a different meaning, or an unacceptable interpretation of the reference metaphor.

Although the paraphrases were generated freely and cover a number of possible (mis)interpretations, we did take several issues into account. For example, for sentiment related metaphors two opposite interpretations are often proposed, forcing the system to make a choice between two sentiment poles when ranking the paraphrases (*I love my job – I hate my job* for *My job is a dream*). In general, antonymous interpretations (*Time passes very fast – Time is slow* for *Time flies*) are listed, when possible, among the four competing choices.

Our corpus has the advantage of being suitable for both binary classification and gradient paraphrase judgment prediction. For the former, we map every score over a given gradient threshold label to 1, and scores below that threshold to 0. For gradient classification, we use all the scoring labels to test the correlation between the system's ordered predictions and human judgments. We will show how, once a model has been trained for a binary detection task, we can evaluate its performance on the gradient ordering task.

We stress that our corpus is under development. As far as we know it is unique for the kind of task we are discussing. The main difficulty in building this corpus is that there is no obvious way to collect the data automatically. Even if there were a procedure to extract pairs of paraphrases containing a metaphoric element semi-automatically, it does not seem possible to generate alternative paraphrase candidates automatically.

The reference sentences we chose were either selected from published sources or created manually by the authors. In all cases, the paraphrase candidates had to be crafted manually. We tried to keep a balanced diversity inside the corpus. The dataset is divided among metaphorically used Nouns, Adjectives and Verbs, plus a section of

Multi Word metaphors. The corpus is an attempt to represent metaphor in different parts of speech.

A native speaker of English independently checked all the sentences for acceptability.

2.1 Collecting judgments through AMT

Originally, one author individually annotated the entire corpus. The difference between strong and loose literal paraphrases can be a matter of individual sensibility.

While such annotations could be used as the basis for a preliminary study, we needed more judgments to build a statistically reliable annotated dataset. Therefore we used crowd sourcing to solicit judgments from large numbers of annotators. We collected human judgments on the degree of paraphrasehood for each pair of sentences in a set (with the reference metaphor sentence in the pair) through Amazon Mechanical Turk (AMT).

Annotators were presented with four *metaphor - candidate paraphrase* pairs, all relating to the same metaphor. They were asked to express a judgment between 1 and 4, according to the scheme given above.

We collected 20 human judgments for each pair *metaphor - candidate paraphrase*. Analyzing individual annotators' response patterns, we were able to filter out a small number of "rogue" annotators (less than 10%). This filtering process was based on annotators' answers to some control elements inserted in the corpus, and evaluation of their overall performance. For example, an annotator who consistently assigned the same score to all sentences is classified as "rogue".

We then computed the mean judgment for each sentence pair and compared it with the original judgments expressed by one of the authors. We found a high Pearson correlation between the annotators' mean judgments and the author's judgment of close to 0.93.

The annotators' understanding of the problem and their evaluation of the sentence pairs seem, on average, to correspond very closely to that of our original single annotator. The high correlation also suggests a small level of variation from the mean across AMT annotators. Finally, a similar correlation strengthens the hypothesis that paraphrase detection is better modeled as an ordering, rather than a binary, task. If this had not been the case, we would expect more polarized judgments tending towards the highest and lowest scores, instead of the more evenly distributed judgment patterns that we observed.

These mean judgments appear to provide reliable data for supervision of a machine learning model. We thus set the upper bound for the performance of a machine learning algorithm trained on this data to be around .9, on the basis of the Pearson correlation with the original single annotator scores. In what follows, we refer to the mean judgments of AMT annotators as our gold standard when evaluating our results, unless otherwise indicated.

3 A DNN for Metaphor Paraphrase Classification

For classification and gradient judgment prediction we constructed a deep neural network. Its architecture consists of three main components:

1. Two encoders that learn the representation of two sentences separately

2. A unified layer that merges the output of the encoders

3. A final set of fully connected layers that operate on the merged representation of the two sentences to generate a judgment.

The encoder for each pair of sentences taken as input is composed of two parallel Convolutional Neural Networks (CNNs) and LSTM RNNs, feeding two sequenced fully connected layers. We use an "Atrous" CNN (Chen et al., 2016). Interestingly, classical CNNs only decrease our accuracy by approximately two points and reach a good F1 score, as Table 1 indicates.

Using a CNN (we apply 25 filters of length 5) as a first layer proved to be an efficient strategy. While CNNs were originally introduced in the field of computer vision, they have been successfully applied to problems in computational semantics, such as text classification and sentiment analysis (Lai et al., 2015), as well as to paraphrase recognition (Socher et al., 2011). In NLP applications, CNNs usually abstract over a series of word- or character-level embeddings, instead of pixels. In this part of our model, the encoder learns a more compact representation of the sentence, with reduced vector space dimensions and features. This permits the entire DNN to focus on the information most relevant to paraphrase identification.

The output of each CNN is passed through a max pooling layer to an LSTM RNN. Since the CNN and the max pooling layer perform discriminative reduction of the input's dimensions, we can run a relatively small LSTM RNN model (20 hidden units). In this phase, the vector dimensions of the sentence representation are further reduced, with relevant information conserved and highlighted, particularly for the sequential structure of the data. Each encoder is completed by two successive fully connected layers, of dimensions 15 and 10 respectively, the first one having a 0.5 dropout rate.

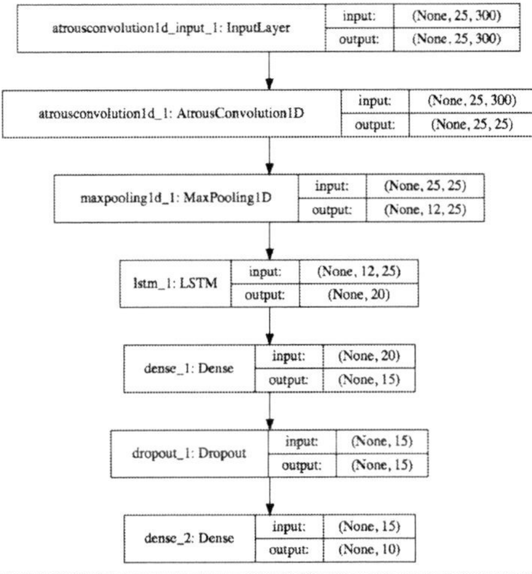

Figure 1: Example of an encoder. Input is passed to a CNN, a max pooling layer, an LSTM RNN, and finally two fully connected layers, the first having a dropout rate of .5. The input's and output's shape is indicated in brackets for each layer

Each sentence is thus transformed to a 10 dimensional vector. To perform the final comparison, these two low dimensional vectors are passed to a layer that merges them into a single vector. We tried several ways of merging the encoders' outputs, and we found that simple vector concatenation was the best option. We produce a 20 dimensional two-sentence vector as the final output of the DNN.

We do not apply any special mechanism for "comparison" or "alignment" in this phase. To measure the similarity of two sequences our model makes use only of the information contained in the merged vector that the encoders produce. We did not use a device in the merging phase to assess similarity between the two sequences. This allows a high degree of freedom in the interpretation patterns we are trying to model, but it also involves a fair amount of noise, which increases the risk of error.

The merging layer feeds the concatenated input to a final fully connected layer. The last layer applies a sigmoid function to produce the judgments. The advantage of using a sigmoid function in this case is that, while it performs well for binary classification, it returns a gradient over its input, thus generating an ordering of values appropriate for the ranking task. The combination of these three kinds of Neural Networks in this order (CNN, LSTM RNN and fully connected layers) has been explored in other works, with interesting results (Sainath et al., 2015). This research has indicated that these architectures can complement each other in complex semantic tasks, such as sentiment analysis (Wang et al., 2016) and text representation (Vosoughi et al., 2016).

The fundamental idea here is that these three kinds of Neural Network capture information in different ways that can be combined to achieve a better global representation of sentence input. While a CNN can reduce the spectral variance of input, an LSTM RNN is designed to model its sequential temporal dimension. At the same time, an LSTM RNN's performance can be strongly improved by providing it with better features (Pascanu et al., 2014), such as the ones produced by a CNN, as happens in our case. The densely connected layers contribute a clearer, more separable final vector representation of one sentence.

To encode the original sentences we used Word2Vec embeddings pre-trained on the very large Google News dataset (Mikolov et al., 2013). We used these embeddings to create the input sequences for our model.

We take as a baseline for evaluating our model the cosine similarity of the sentence vectors, obtained through combining their respective pre-trained lexical embeddings. This baseline gives very low accuracy and F1 scores.

4   Binary Classification Task

As discussed above, our corpus can be applied to model two sub-problems: binary classification and paraphrase ordering.

To use our corpus for a binary classification task

Model	Accuracy	F1
Baseline (cosine similarity)	50.8	10.1
Our model	**75.2**	74.6
Encoders without LSTM	64.4	64.9
Encoders without ACNN	62.6	61.5
Using CNN instead of ACNN	61.0	61.6
ACNN with 10 filters	73.4	71.7
LSTM with 10 filters	72.3	70.6
Merging via multiplication	53.4	69.6
Aligner	49.4	61.6
Aligner + our model	73.4	75.

Table 1: Accuracy for different versions of the model, and the baseline. Each version ran on our standard train and test data, without performing cross-validation. We use as a baseline the cosine similarity between the mean of the word vectors composing each sentence.

we map each set of five sentences into a series of pairs, where the first element is the metaphor we want to interpret and the second element is one of its four literal candidates.

Gradient labels are then replaced by binary ones. We consider all labels higher than *2* as positive judgments (Paraphrase) and all labels less than or equal to *2* as negative judgments (Non-Paraphrase), reflecting the ranking discussed in Section 2. We train our model with these labels for a binary metaphor paraphrase detection task.

Keeping the order of the input fixed (we will discuss this issue below), we ran the training phase for 15 epochs.

We reached an average accuracy of 67% for 12 fold cross-validation.

Interestingly, when trained on the pre-defined training set only, our model reaches the higher accuracy of 75%.

We strongly suspect that this discrepancy in performance is due to the small training and test sets created by the partitions of the 12 fold cross validation process.

In general, this task is particularly hard, both because of the complexity of the semantic properties involved in accurate paraphrase (see 4.1), and the limited size of the training set. It seems to us that an average accuracy of 67% on a 12 fold partitioning of training and test sets is a reasonable result, given the size of our corpus.

We observe that our architecture learned to recognize different semantic phenomena related to metaphor interpretation with a promising level of accuracy, but such phenomena need to be represented in the training set.

In light of the fact that previous work in this field is concerned with single verb paraphrase ranking (Bollegala and Shutova, 2013), where the metaphorical element is explicitly identified, and the candidates don't contain any syntactic-semantic expansion, our results are encouraging.[3]

Although a small corpus may cause instability in results, our DNN seems able to generalize with relative consistency on the following patterns:

- **Sentiment**. *My life in California was a nightmare – My life in California was terrible*. Our system seems able to discriminate the right sentiment polarity of a metaphor by picking the right paraphrase, even when some candidates contain sentiment words of opposite polarity, which are usually very similar in a distributional space

- **Non metaphorical word re-use**. Our system seems able, in several cases, to discriminate the correct paraphrase for a metaphor, even when some candidates re-use the words of the metaphor to convey a (wrong) literal meaning. *My life in California was a dream – I lived in California and had a dream*

- **Cases of multi-word metaphor** Although well represented in our corpus, multi-word metaphors are in some respects the most difficult to correctly paraphrase, since the interpretation has to be extended to a number of words. Nonetheless, our model was able to correctly handle these in a number of situations. *You can plant the seeds of anger – You can act in a way that will engender rage*

However, our model had trouble with several others cases.

It seems to have particular difficulty in discriminating sentiment intensity, with assignment of higher scores to paraphrases that value the sentiment intensity of the metaphor, which creates problems in several instances. Also, cases of metaphoric exaggeration (*My roommate is a sport maniac – My roommate is a sport person*), negation (*My roommate was not an eagle – My roommate was dumb.*) and syntactic inversions pose difficulties for our models.

We found that our model is able to abstract over specific patterns, but, predictably, it has difficulty in learning when the semantic focus of an interpretation consists in a phrase that is under represented in the training data.

---

[3]It should be noted that Bollegala and Shutova (2013) employ an unsupervised approach.

In some cases, the effect of data scarcity can be observed in an "overfit weighting" of specific terms. Some words that were seen in the data only once are associated with a high or low score independently of their context, degrading the overall performance of the model. We believe that these idiosyncrasies, can be overcome through training on a larger data set.

4.1 The gray areas of interpretation

We observe that, on occasion, the model's errors fall into a gray area between clear paraphrase and clear non-paraphrase. Here the correctness of a label is not obvious.

These cases are particularly important in metaphor paraphrasing, since this task requires an interpretative leap from the metaphor to its literal equivalent. For example, the pair *I was home watching the days slip by from my window – I was home thinking about the time I was wasting* can be considered as a loose paraphrase pair. Alternatively, it can be regarded as a case of non-paraphrase, since the second element introduces some interpretative elements (*I was thinking about the time*) that are not in the original.

In our test set we labeled it as 3 (loose paraphrase), but if our system fails to label it correctly in a binary task, it is not entirely clear that it is making an error. For these cases, the approach presented in the next section is particularly useful.

5 Paraphrase Ordering Task

The high degree of correlation we found between the AMT annotations and our single annotator's judgments indicate that we can use this dataset for an ordering task as well. Since the human judgments we collected about the "degree of paraphrasehood" are quite consistent, it is reasonable to pursue a non-binary approach.

Once the DNN has learned representations for binary classification, we can apply it to rank the sentences of the test set in order of similarity.

We apply the sigmoid value distribution for the candidate sentences in a set of five (the reference and four candidates) to determine the ranking.

To do this we use the original structure of our dataset, composed of sets of five sentences. First, we assign a similarity score to all pairs of sentences (reference sentence and candidate para-

phrase) in a set. This is the similarity score learned in the binary task, so it is determined by the sigmoid function applied on the output.

The following is an example of an ordered set with strong correlation between the model's predictions (marked in bold) and our annotations (given in italics)

- The candidate is a fox

    - **0.13** *1* The candidate owns a fox
    - **0.30** *2* The candidate is stupid
    - **0.41** *3* The candidate is intelligent
    - **0.64** *4* The candidate is a cunning person

We compute the average Pearson and Spearman correlations on all sets of the test corpus, to check the extent to which the ranking that our DNN produces matches our mean crowd source human annotations.

While Pearson correlation measures the relationship between two continuous variables, Spearman correlation evaluates the monotonic relation between two variables, continuous or ordinal.

Since the first of our variables, the model's judgment, is continuous, while the second one, the human labels, is ordinal, both measures are of interest.

We found comparable and meaningful correlations between mean AMT rankings and the ordering that our model predicts, on both metrics. On the balanced training and test set, we achieve an average Pearson correlation of 0.75 and an average Spearman correlation of 0.68. On a twelve fold cross-validation frame, we achieve an average Pearson correlation of 0.55 and an average Spearman correlation of 0.54. We chose a twelve fold cross-validation because it is the smallest partition we can use to get meaningful results. We conjecture that the average cross fold validation performance is lower because of the small size of the training data in each fold. These results are displayed in Table 2.[4]

These correlations indicate that our model achieves an encouraging level of accuracy in predicting our gradient annotations for the candidate sentences in a set when trained for a binary classification task.

This task differs from the binary classification task in several important respects. In one way,

---

[4]As discussed above, the upper bound for our model's performance can be set at 0.9, the correlation between our single annotator's and the mean crowd sourced judgments.

it is easier. A non-paraphrase can be misjudged as a paraphrase and still appear in the right order within a ranking. In another sense, it is more difficult. Strict paraphrases, loose paraphrases, and various kinds of semantically similar non-paraphrases have to be ordered in accord with human judgment patterns, which is a more complex task than simple binary classification.

We should consider to what extent this task is different from a multi-class categorization problem. Broadly, multi-class categorization requires a system for linking a pair of sentences to a specific class of similarity. This is dependent upon the classes defined by the annotator and presented in the training phase. In several cases determining these ranked categories might be problematic. A class corresponding to our label "3", for example, could contain many different phenomena related to metaphor paraphrase: expansions, reformulations, reduction in the expressivity of the sentence, or particular interpretations of the metaphor's meaning. Our way of formulating the ordering task allows us to overcome this problem. A paraphrase containing an expansion and a paraphrase involving some information loss, both labeled as "3", might have quite different scoring, but they still fall between all "2" elements and all "4" elements in a ranking.

We can see that our gradient ranking system provides a more nuanced view of the paraphrase relation than a binary classification.

Consider the following example:

- My life in California was a dream

    - **0.03** *1* I had a dream once
    - **0.05** *2* While living in California I had a dream
    - **0.11** *3* My life in California was nice, I enjoyed it
    - **0.58** *4* My life in California was absolutely great

The human annotators consider the pair **My life in California was a dream** – *My life in California was nice, I enjoyed it* as loose paraphrases, while the model scored it very low. But the difference in sentiment intensity between the metaphor and the literal candidate renders the semantic relation between the two sentences less than perspicuous. Such intensity is instead present in **My life in California was absolutely great**, marked as a more valid paraphrase (score 4).

Measure	12-fold value	Baseline
Accuracy	67	51
Pearson correlation	0.553	0.151
Spearman correlation	0.545	0.113

Table 2: Accuracy and ranking correlation for Twelve Fold Cross-Validation. It can be seen that the simple cosine similarity between the mean vectors of the two sentences, which we use as baseline, returns a low correlation with human judgments.

On the other hand, it is clear that in the choice between *While living in California I had a dream* and *My life in California was nice, I enjoyed it*, the latter is a more reasonable interpretation of the metaphor.

The annotators relative mean ranking has been sustained by our model, even if its absolute scoring involves an error in binary classification.

The correlation between AMT annotation ordering and our model's predictions is a by-product of supervised binary learning. Since we are reusing the predictions of a binary classification task, we consider it a form of transfer learning from a supervised binary context to an unsupervised ordering task. In this case, our corpus allows us to perform double transfer learning. First, we used pretrained word embeddings trained to maximize single words' contextual similarity, in order to train on a supervised binary paraphrase dataset. Then, we use the representations acquired in this way to perform an ordering task for which the DNN had not been trained.

The fact that ranked correlations are sustained through binary paraphrase classification is not an obvious result. In principle, a model trained on {0,1} labels could "polarize" its scores to the point where no meaningful ordering would be available. Had this happened, a good performance in a binary task would actually conceal the loss of important semantic information. The fact that there is no necessary connection between binary classification and prediction of gradient labels, and that an increase in one can even produce a loss in the other, is pointed out in Xu et al. (2015), who discuss the relation of paraphrase identification to the recognition of semantic similarity.

6 The Nature of the Metaphor Interpretation Task

Although this task resembles a particular case of paraphrase detection, in many respects it is something different. While paraphrase detection concerns learning content identity or strong cases of semantic similarity, our task involves the interpretation of figurative language.

In a traditional paraphrase task, we should maintain that "The candidate is a fox" and "The candidate is cunning" are invalid paraphrases. First, the superficial informational content of the two sentences is different. Second, without further context we might assume that the candidate is an actual fox. We ignore the context of the phrase.

In this task the frame is different. We assume that the first sentence contains a metaphor. We summarize this task by the following question.

Given that X is a metaphor, which one of the given candidates would be its best literal interpretation?

We trained our model to move along a similar learning pattern. This training frame can produce the apparent, but false paradox that two acceptable paraphrases such as *The Council is on fire* and *The Council is burning* are assigned a low score by our model. If the first element is a metaphor, the second element is, in fact, a bad literal interpretation. A higher score is correctly assigned to the candidate *People in the Council are very excited.*

7 Conclusions

We present a new kind of corpus to evaluate metaphor paraphrase detection, following the approach presented in Bizzoni and Lappin (2017) for paraphrase grading, and we construct a novel type of DNN architecture for a set of metaphor interpretation tasks. We show that our model learns an effective representation of sentences, starting from the distributional representations of their words. Using word embeddings trained on very large corpora proved to be a fruitful strategy. Our model is able to retrieve from the original semantic spaces not only the primary meaning or denotation of words, but also some of the more subtle semantic aspects involved in the metaphorical use of terms.

We based our corpus' design on the view that paraphrase ranking is a useful way to approach the metaphor interpretation problem.

We show how this kind of corpus can be used for both supervised learning of binary classification, and for gradient judgment prediction.

The neural network architecture that we propose encodes each sentence in a 10 dimensional vector representation, combining a CNN, an LSTM RNN, and two densely connected neural layers. The two input representations are merged through concatenation and fed to a series of densely connected layers.

We show that such an architecture is able, to an extent, to learn metaphor-to-literal paraphrase.

While binary classification is learned in the training phase, it yields a robust correlation in the ordering task through the softmax sigmoid distributions generated for binary classification. The model learns to classify a sentence as a valid or invalid literal interpretation of a given metaphor, and it retains enough information to assign a gradient value to sets of sentences in a way that correlates with our crowd source annotation.

Our model doesn't use any "alignment" of the data. The encoders' representations are simply concatenated. This gives our DNN considerable flexibility in modeling interpretation patterns. It can also create complications where a simple alignment of two sentences might suffice to identify a similarity. We have considered several possible alternative versions of this model to tackle this issue.

In future we will expand the size and variety of our corpus. We will perform a detailed error analysis of our model's predictions, and we will further explore different kinds of neural network designs for paraphrase detection and ordering. Finally, we intend to study this task "the other way around" by detecting the most appropriate metaphor to paraphrase a literal reference sentence or phrase.

Acknowledgments

We are grateful to our colleagues in the Centre for Linguistic Theory and Studies in Probability (CLASP), FLoV, at the University of Gothenburg for useful discussion of some of the ideas presented in this paper, and to three anonymous reviewers for helpful comments on an earlier draft. The research reported here was done at CLASP, which is supported by a 10 year research grant (grant 2014-39) from the Swedish Research Council.

References

Rodrigo Agerri. 2008. Metaphor in textual entailment. In *COLING 2008, 22nd International Conference on Computational Linguistics, Posters Proceedings, 18-22 August 2008, Manchester, UK.* pages 3–6. http://www.aclweb.org/anthology/C08-2001.

Eneko Agirre, Carmen Banea, Daniel M. Cer, Mona T. Diab, Aitor Gonzalez-Agirre, Rada Mihalcea, German Rigau, and Janyce Wiebe. 2016. Semeval-2016 task 1: Semantic textual similarity, monolingual and cross-lingual evaluation. In *Proceedings of the 10th International Workshop on Semantic Evaluation, SemEval@NAACL-HLT 2016, San Diego, CA, USA, June 16-17, 2016.* pages 497–511. http://aclweb.org/anthology/S/S16/S16-1081.pdf.

Yuri Bizzoni and Shalom Lappin. 2017. Deep learning of binary and gradient judgments for semantic paraphrase. *Proceedings of IWCS 2017* .

Danushka Bollegala and Ekaterina Shutova. 2013. Metaphor interpretation using paraphrases extracted from the web. *PloS one* 8(9):e74304.

Liang-Chieh Chen, George Papandreou, Iasonas Kokkinos, Kevin Murphy, and Alan L. Yuille. 2016. Deeplab: Semantic image segmentation with deep convolutional nets, atrous convolution, and fully connected crfs. *CoRR* abs/1606.00915. http://arxiv.org/abs/1606.00915.

Jonathan Dunn, Jon Beitran De Heredia, Maura Burke, Lisa Gandy, Sergey Kanareykin, Oren Kapah, Matthew Taylor, Dell Hines, Ophir Frieder, David Grossman, et al. 2014. Language-independent ensemble approaches to metaphor identification. In *28th AAAI Conference on Artificial Intelligence, AAAI 2014.* AI Access Foundation.

Zornitsa Kozareva. 2015. Multilingual affect polarity and valence prediction in metaphors. In *Proceedings of the 6th Workshop on Computational Approaches to Subjectivity,Sentiment and Social Media Analysis, WASSA@EMNLP 2015, 17 September2015, Lisbon, Portugal.* page 1. http://aclweb.org/anthology/W/W15/W15-2901.pdf.

Tina Krennmayr. 2015. What corpus linguistics can tell us about metaphor use in newspaper texts. *Journalism Studies* 16(4):530–546.

Siwei Lai, Liheng Xu, Kang Liu, and Jun Zhao. 2015. Recurrent convolutional neural networks for text classification. In *Proceedings of the Twenty-Ninth AAAI Conference on Artificial Intelligence.* AAAI Press, AAAI'15, pages 2267–2273. http://dl.acm.org/citation.cfm?id=2886521.2886636.

Tomas Mikolov, Ilya Sutskever, Kai Chen, Greg S Corrado, and Jeff Dean. 2013. Distributed representations of words and phrases and their compositionality. In C. J. C. Burges, L. Bottou, M. Welling, Z. Ghahramani, and K. Q. Weinberger, editors, *Advances in Neural Information Processing Systems 26*, Curran Associates, Inc., pages 3111–3119.

Saif Mohammad, Ekaterina Shutova, and Peter D. Turney. 2016. Metaphor as a medium for emotion: An empirical study. In *Proceedings of the Fifth Joint Conference on Lexical and Computational Semantics, *SEM@ACL 2016, Berlin, Germany, 11-12 August 2016.* http://aclweb.org/anthology/S/S16/S16-2003.pdf.

Razvan Pascanu, Caglar Gulcehre, Kyunghyun Cho, and Yoshua Bengio. 2014. How to construct deep recurrent neural networks. *Proceedings of the Second International Conference on Learning Representations (ICLR 2014)* .

Tara N. Sainath, Oriol Vinyals, Andrew W. Senior, and Hasim Sak. 2015. Convolutional, long short-term memory, fully connected deep neural networks. In *2015 IEEE International Conference on Acoustics, Speech and Signal Processing, ICASSP 2015, South Brisbane, Queensland, Australia, April 19-24, 2015.* pages 4580–4584. https://doi.org/10.1109/ICASSP.2015.7178838.

Ekaterina Shutova. 2010. Automatic metaphor interpretation as a paraphrasing task. In *Human Language Technologies: The 2010 Annual Conference of the North American Chapter of the Association for Computational Linguistics.* Association for Computational Linguistics, Stroudsburg, PA, USA, HLT '10, pages 1029–1037. http://dl.acm.org/citation.cfm?id=1857999.1858145.

Ekaterina Shutova and Simone Teufel. 2010. Metaphor corpus annotated for source-target domain mappings. In *LREC.* volume 2, pages 2–2.

Richard Socher, Eric H. Huang, Jeffrey Pennington, Andrew Y. Ng, and Christopher D. Manning+. 2011. Dynamic Pooling and Unfolding Recursive Autoencoders for Paraphrase Detection. In *Advances in Neural Information Processing Systems 24.*

Peter D. Turney. 2013. Distributional semantics beyond words: Supervised learning of analogy and paraphrase. *CoRR* abs/1310.5042. http://arxiv.org/abs/1310.5042.

Tony Veale, Ekaterina Shutova, and Beata Beigman Klebanov. 2016. *Metaphor: A Computational Perspective.* Synthesis Lectures on Human Language Technologies. Morgan & Claypool Publishers. https://doi.org/10.2200/S00694ED1V01Y201601HLT031.

Soroush Vosoughi, Prashanth Vijayaraghavan, and Deb Roy. 2016. Tweet2vec: Learning tweet embeddings using character-level cnn-lstm encoder-decoder. In *Proceedings of the 39th International ACM SIGIR Conference on Research and Development in Information Retrieval*. ACM, New York, NY, USA, SIGIR '16, pages 1041–1044. https://doi.org/10.1145/2911451.2914762.

Jin Wang, Liang-Chih Yu, K. Robert Lai, and Xuejie Zhang. 2016. Dimensional sentiment analysis using a regional CNN-LSTM model. In *Proceedings of the 54th Annual Meeting of the Association for Computational Linguistics, ACL 2016, August 7-12, 2016, Berlin, Germany, Volume 2: Short Papers*. http://aclweb.org/anthology/P/P16/P16-2037.pdf.

Wei Xu, Chris Callison-Burch, and Bill Dolan. 2015. Semeval-2015 task 1: Paraphrase and semantic similarity in twitter (pit). In *Proceedings of the 9th International Workshop on Semantic Evaluation (SemEval 2015)*. Association for Computational Linguistics, Denver, Colorado, pages 1–11. http://www.aclweb.org/anthology/S15-2001.

A Report on the 2018 VUA Metaphor Detection Shared Task

Chee Wee Leong, Beata Beigman Klebanov
Educational Testing Service
{cleong,bbeigmanklebanov}@ets.org

Ekaterina Shutova
University of Amsterdam
e.shutova@uva.nl

Abstract

As the community working on computational approaches to figurative language is growing and as methods and data become increasingly diverse, it is important to create widely shared empirical knowledge of the level of system performance in a range of contexts, thus facilitating progress in this area. One way of creating such shared knowledge is through benchmarking multiple systems on a common dataset. We report on the shared task on metaphor identification on the VU Amsterdam Metaphor Corpus conducted at the NAACL 2018 Workshop on Figurative Language Processing.

1 Introduction

Metaphor use in everyday language is a way to relate our physical and familiar social experiences to a multitude of other subjects and contexts (Lakoff and Johnson, 2008); it is a fundamental way to structure our understanding of the world even without our conscious realization of its presence as we speak and write. It highlights the unknown using the known, explains the complex using the simple, and helps us to emphasize the relevant aspects of meaning resulting in effective communication. Consider the following examples of metaphor use in Table 1.

Metaphor has been studied in the context of political communication, marketing, mental health, teaching, assessment of English proficiency, among others (Beigman Klebanov et al., 2018; Gutierrez et al., 2017; Littlemore et al., 2013; Thibodeau and Boroditsky, 2011; Kaviani and Hamedi, 2011; Kathpalia and Carmel, 2011; Landau et al., 2009; Beigman Klebanov et al., 2008; Zaltman and Zaltman, 2008; Littlemore and Low, 2006; Cameron, 2003; Lakoff, 2010; Billow et al., 1997; Bosman, 1987); see chapter 7 in Veale et al. (2016) for a recent review.

M: *The alligator's teeth are like white **daggers***
I: The alligator have white and pointed teeth.

M: *He **swam** in a **sea** of diamonds.*
I: He is a rich person.

M: *Authority is a **chair**, it needs **legs** to **stand**.*
I: Authority is useless when it lacks support.

M: *In Washington, people change **dance partners** frequently, but not the **dance**.*
I: In Washington, people work with one another opportunistically.

M: *Robert Muller is like a **bulldog** — he will get what he wants.*
I: Robert Muller will work in a determined and aggressive manner to get what he wants.

Table 1: Metaphorical sentences (**M**) characterized by metaphors in bold and their literal interpretations (**I**)

In this paper, we report on the first shared task on automatic metaphor detection. By making available an easily accessible common dataset and framework for evaluation, we hope to contribute to the consolidation and strengthening of the growing community of researchers working on computational approaches to figurative language. By engaging a variety of teams to test their systems within a common evaluation framework and share their findings about more or less effective architectures, features, and data sources, we hope to create a shared understanding of the current state of the art, laying a foundation for further work.

This report provides a description of the shared task, dataset and metrics, a brief description of each of the participating systems, a comparative evaluation of the systems, and our observations about trends in designs and performance of the

Proceedings of the Workshop on Figurative Language Processing, pages 56–66
New Orleans, Louisiana, June 6, 2018. ©2018 Association for Computational Linguistics

systems that participated in the shared task.

2 Related Work

Over the last decade, automated detection of metaphor has become an increasingly popular topic, which manifests itself in both a variety of approaches and in an increasing variety of data to which the methods are applied. In terms of methods, approaches based on feature-engineering in a supervised machine learning paradigm explored features based on concreteness and imageability, semantic classification using WordNet, FrameNet, VerbNet, SUMO ontology, property norms, and distributional semantic models, syntactic dependency patterns, sensorial and vision-based features (Bulat et al., 2017; Köper and im Walde, 2017; Gutierrez et al., 2016; Shutova et al., 2016; Beigman Klebanov et al., 2016; Tekiroglu et al., 2015; Tsvetkov et al., 2014; Beigman Klebanov et al., 2014; Dunn, 2013; Neuman et al., 2013; Mohler et al., 2013; Hovy et al., 2013; Tsvetkov et al., 2013; Turney et al., 2011; Shutova et al., 2010; Gedigian et al., 2006); see Shutova et al. (2017) and Veale et al. (2016) for reviews of supervised as well as semi-supervised and unsupervised approaches.

Recently, deep learning methods have been explored for token-level metaphor detection (Rei et al., 2017; Gutierrez et al., 2017; Do Dinh and Gurevych, 2016). As discussed later in the paper later, the fact that all but one of the participating teams for the shared task experimented with neural network architectures testifies to the increasing popularity of this modeling approach.

In terms of data used for evaluating metaphor detection systems, researchers used specially constructed or selected sets, such as adjective noun pairs (Gutierrez et al., 2016; Tsvetkov et al., 2014), WordNet synsets and glosses (Mohammad et al., 2016), annotated lexical items (from a range of word classes) in sentences sampled from corpora (Özbal et al., 2016; Jang et al., 2015; Hovy et al., 2013; Birke and Sarkar, 2006), all the way to annotation of all words in running text for metaphoricity (Beigman Klebanov et al., 2018; Steen et al., 2010); Veale et al. (2016) review additional annotated datasets. By far the largest annotated dataset is the VU Amsterdam Metaphor Corpus; it has also been used for evaluating many of the cited supervised learning-based systems. Due to its size, availability, reliability of annotation,

and popularity in current research, we decided to use it to benchmark the current field of supervised metaphor detection approaches.

3 Task Description

The goal of this shared task is to detect, at the word level, all metaphors in a given text. Specifically, there are two tracks, namely, **All Part-Of-Speech (POS)** and **Verbs**. The former track is concerned with the detection of all content words, i.e., nouns, verbs, adverbs and adjectives that are labeled as metaphorical while the latter track is concerned only with verbs that are metaphorical. We excluded all forms or *be*, *do*, and *have* for both tracks. Each participating individual or team can elect to compete in the All POS track, Verbs track, or both. The competition is organized into two phases: training and testing.

3.1 Dataset

We use the VU Amsterdam Metaphor Corpus (VUA) (Steen et al., 2010) as the dataset for our shared task. The dataset consists of 117 fragments sampled across four genres from the British National Corpus: **Academic**, **News**, **Conversation**, and **Fiction**. Each genre is represented by approximately the same number of tokens, although the number of texts differs greatly, where the news archive has the largest number of texts. We randomly sampled 23% of the texts from each genre to set aside for testing, while retaining the rest for training. The data is annotated using the MIP-VU procedure with a strong inter-annotator reliability of $\kappa > 0.8$. It is based on the MIP procedure (Group, 2007), extending it to handle metaphoricity through reference (such as marking *did* as a metaphor in *As the weather broke up, so did their friendship*) and allow for explicit coding of difficult cases where a group of annotators could not arrive at a consensus. The tagset is rich and is organized hierarchically, detecting various types of metaphors, words that flag the presense of metaphors, etc. In this paper, we consider only the top-level partition, labeling all content words with the tag "function=mrw" (metaphor-related word) as metaphors, while all other content words are labeled as non-metaphors. Table 2 shows the overall statistics of our training and testing sets.

To facilitate the use of the datasets and evaluation scripts beyond this shared task in future re-

Data	Training			Testing		
	#texts	#tokens	%M	#texts	#tokens	%M
Verbs						
Academic	12	4,903	31%	4	1,259	51%
Conversation	18	4,181	15%	6	2,001	15%
Fiction	11	4,647	25%	3	1,385	20%
News	49	3,509	42%	14	1,228	46%
All POS						
Academic	12	27,669	14%	4	6,076	24%
Conversation	18	11,994	10%	6	5,302	10%
Fiction	11	15,892	16%	3	4,810	14%
News	49	17,056	20%	14	6,008	22%

Table 2: Verbs and All POS datasets. The table reports the number of text fragments from BNC, number of tokens and percentage of tokens marked as metaphor group by genres.

search, the complete set of task instructions and scripts are published on Github[1]. Specifically, we provide a script to parse the original VUAMC.xml, which was not provided in our download bundle due to licensing restriction, to extract the verbs and other content words required for the shared task. We also provide a set of features used to construct the baseline classification model for prediction of metaphor/non-metaphor classes at the word level, and instructions on how to replicate the baselines.

3.2 Training phase

In this first phase, data is released for training and/or development of metaphor detection models. Participants can elect to perform cross-validation on the training data, or partition the training data further to have a held-out set for preliminary evaluations, and/or set apart a subset of the data for development/tuning of hyper-parameters. However the training data is used, the goal is to have N final systems (or versions of a system) ready for evaluation when the test data is released.

3.3 Testing phase

In this phase, instances for evaluation are released.[2] Each participating system generated predictions for the test instances, for up to N models.[3] Predictions are submitted to CodaLab[4]

and evaluated automatically against the true labels. We selected CodaLab as a platform for organizing the task due to its ease of use, availability of communication tools such as mass-emailing, online forum for clarification of task issues, and tracking of submissions in real time. Submissions were anonymized. Hence, the only statistics displayed were the highest score of all systems per day, and the total number of system submissions per day. The metrics used for evaluation is the F1 score (least frequent class/label, which is "metaphor") with Precision and Recall also available via the detailed results link in CodaLab.

4 Systems

The shared task started on January 12, 2018 when the training data was made available to registered participants. On February 12, 2018, the testing data was released. Submissions were accepted until March 8, 2018. Overall, there were a total of 32 submissions by 8 unique individuals/teams for the Verbs track, and 100 submissions by 11 individuals/teams for the All POS track. All participants in the Verbs track also participated in the All POS track. In total, 8 system papers were submitted describing the algorithms and methodology for generating their metaphor predictions. In the following sections, we first describe the baseline classification models and their feature sets. Next, we report performance results and ranking of the best systems for each of the 8 teams. We also briefly describe the best-performing system for every team. The interested readers can refer to the

---

[1]https://github.com/EducationalTestingService/metaphor/tree/master/NAACL-FLP-shared-task

[2]In principle, participants could have access to the test data by independently obtaining the VUA corpus. The shared task was based on a presumption of fair play by participants.

[3]We set N=12.

[4]https://competitions.codalab.org/competitions/17805

teams' papers for more details.

Baseline Classifiers

We make available to shared task participants a number of features from prior published work on metaphor detection, including unigram features, features based on WordNet, VerbNet, and those derived from a distributional semantic model, POS-based, concreteness and difference in concreteness, as well as topic models.

As baselines, we train two logistic regression classifiers for each track (Verbs and All-POS), with instance weights inversely proportional to class frequencies. Lemmatized unigrams (UL) is a simple yet fairly strong baseline (**Baseline 1**). This feature is produced using NLTK (Bird and Loper, 2004) to generate the lemma of each word according to its tagged POS. As **Baseline 2**, we use the best system from Beigman Klebanov et al. (2016). The features are: lemmatized unigrams, generalized WordNet semantic classes, and difference in concreteness ratings between verbs/adjectives and nouns (UL + WordNet + CCDB).[5]

4.1 System Descriptions

The best-performing system from each participant is described below, in alphabetic order.

bot.zen (Stemle and Onysko, 2018) used word embeddings from different standard corpora representing different levels of language mastery, encoding each word in a sentence into multiple vector-based embeddings which are then fed into an LSTM RNN network architecture. Specifically, the backpropagation step was performed using weightings computed based on the logarithmic function of the inverse of the count of the metaphors and non-metaphors. Their implementation is hosted on Github[6] under the Apache License Version 2.0.

DeepReader (Swarnkar and Singh, 2018) The authors present a neural network architecture that concatenates hidden states of forward and backward LSTMs, with feature selection and classification. The authors also show that re-weighting examples and adding linguistic features (WordNet, POS, concreteness) helps improve performance further.

MAP (Pramanick et al., 2018) used a hybrid architecture of Bi-directional LSTM and Conditional Random Fields (CRF) for metaphor detection, relying on features such as token, lemma and POS, and using word2vec embeddings trained on English Wikipedia. Specifically, the authors considered contextual information within a sentence for generating predictions.

nsu_ai (Mosolova et al., 2018) used linguistic features based on unigrams, lemmas, POS tags, topical LDAs, concreteness, WordNet, VerbNet and verb clusters and trained a Conditional Random Field (CRF) model with gradient descent using the L-BFGS method to generate predictions.

OCOTA (Bizzoni and Ghanimifard, 2018) experimented with a deep neural network composed of a Bi-LSTM preceded and followed by fully connected layers, as well as a simpler model that has a sequence of fully connected neural networks. The authors also experiment with word embeddings trained on various data, with explicit features based on concreteness, and with preprocessing that addresses variability in sentence length. The authors observe that a model that combines Bi-LSTM with the explicit features and sentence-length manipulation shows the best performance. The authors also show that an ensemble of the two types of neural models works even better, due to a substantial increase in recall over single models.

Samsung_RD_PL (Skurniak et al., 2018) explored the use of several orthogonal resources in a cascading manner to predict metaphoricity. For a given word in a sentence, they extracted three feature sets: concreteness score from the Brysbaert database, intermediate hidden vector representing the word in a neural translation framework, and generated logits of a CRF sequence tagging model trained using word embeddings and contextual information. Trained on the VUA data, the CRF model alone outperforms that of a GRU taking all three features.

THU NGN (Wu et al., 2018) created word embeddings using a pre-trained word2vec model and added features such as embedding clusterings and POS tags before using CNN and

---

Bi-LSTM to capture local and long-range dependencies for generating metaphorical labels. Specifically, they used an ensemble strategy in which iterative modeling is performed by training on randomly selected training data and averaging the model predictions for finalized outputs. At the inferencing layer, the authors showed that the best-performing system is one achieved by using a weighted-softmax classifier rather than the Conditional Random Field predictor, since it can significantly improve the recall.

ZIL IPIPAN (Mykowiecka et al., 2018) used word2vec embeddings over ortographical word forms (no lemmatization) as an input for LSTM network for generating predictions. They explored augmenting word embeddings by binarized vectors that reflect the General Inquirer dictionary category of a word and its POS. Experiments were also carried out with different parametrization of LSTM based on type of unit network, number of layers, size of dropout, number of epochs, etc., though vectors enriched with POS information did not result in any improvement.

5 Results

Tables 3 and 4 show the performance and the ranking of all the systems, including the baseline systems. For overall results on All-POS track, three out of the seven systems outperformed the stronger of the two baselines, with the best submitted system gaining 6 F1-score points over the best baseline (0.65 vs 0.59). We note that the best system outperformed the baseline through improved precision (by 10 points), while the recall remained the same, around 0.7.

For the Verbs track, four out of the five systems outperformed both baselines. The best system posted an improvement of 7 F1-score points over best baseline (0.67 vs 0.60), achieved by improvements of about the same magnitude in both recall and precision.

In the following section, we inspect the performance of the different systems more closely.

6 Discussion

6.1 Trends in system design

All the submitted systems but one are based on a neural network architecture. Out of the top three systems that outperform the baseline on All-POS, two introduce explicit linguistic features into the architecture along with the more standard word-embedding-based representations, while the third experiments with using a variety of corpora – including English-language-learner-produced corpora – to compute word embeddings.

6.2 Performance across genres

Tables 3 and 4 show the overall performance for the best submission per team, as well as the performance of these systems by genre. It is clear that the overall F1 scores of 0.62-0.65 for the top three systems do not make explicit the substantial variation in performance across genres. Thus, Academic is the easiest genre, with the best performance of 0.74, followed by News (0.66), with comparable scores for Fiction (0.57) and Conversation (0.55). In fact, this trend holds not only for the top systems but for all systems, including baselines, apart from the lowest-performing system that showed somewhat better results on News than on Academic. The same observations hold for the Verb data. The large discrepancies in performance across different genres underscore the need for wide genre coverage when evaluating metaphor detection systems, as the patterns of metaphor use are quite different across genres and present tasks of varying difficulty to machine learning systems across the board.

Furthermore, we note that the best overall system, which is the only system that improves upon the baseline for every single genre in All-POS evaluation, improved over the baseline much more substantially in the lower-performance genres. Thus, for Academic and News, the increase is 1.4 and 5.2 F1 points, respectively, while the improvements for Conversation and Fiction are 8.1 and 11.1 points, respectively. The best-performing system thus exhibits more stable performance across genres than the baseline, though genre discrepancies are still substantial, as described above.

6.3 Part of Speech

6.3.1 AllPOS vs Verbs

We observe that for the four teams who improved upon the baseline on the Verbs-only track, their best performance on the Verbs was better than on the All-POS track, by 2.1-5 F1 score points.

Rank	Team	P	R	F1	Approach
	All POS (Overall)				
1	THU NGN	0.608	0.700	0.651	word embeddings + CNN + Bi-LSTM
2	OCOTA	0.595	0.680	0.635	word embeddings + Bi-LSTM + linguistic
3	bot.zen	0.553	0.698	0.617	word embeddings + LSTM RNN
4	Baseline 2	0.510	0.696	0.589	UL + WordNet + CCDB + Logistic Regression
5	ZIL IPIPAN	0.555	0.615	0.583	dictionary-based vectors + LSTM
6	Baseline 1	0.521	0.657	0.581	UL + Logistic Regression
7	DeepReader	0.511	0.644	0.570	word embeddings + Di-LSTM + linguistic
8	Samsung_RD_PL	0.547	0.575	0.561	word embeddings + CRF + context
9	MAP	0.645	0.459	0.536	word embeddings + Bi-LSTM + CRF
10	nsu_ai	0.183	0.111	0.138	linguistic + CRF
	All POS (Academic)				
1	THU NGN	0.725	0.746	0.735	word embedding + CNN + Bi-LSTM
2	Baseline 2	0.711	0.731	0.721	UL + WordNet + CCDB + Logistic Regression
3	Baseline 1	0.728	0.701	0.715	UL + Logistic Regression
4	bot.zen	0.743	0.681	0.711	word embeddings + LSTM RNN
5	OCOTA	0.724	0.695	0.709	word embeddings + Bi-LSTM + linguistic
6	ZIL IPIPAN	0.722	0.674	0.697	dictionary-based vectors + LSTM
7	DeepReader	0.641	0.682	0.661	word embeddings + Di-LSTM + linguistic
8	Samsung_RD_PL	0.649	0.631	0.640	word embeddings + CRF + context
9	MAP	0.743	0.526	0.616	word embeddings + Bi-LSTM + CRF
10	nsu_ai	0.283	0.100	0.148	linguistic + CRF
	All POS (Conversation)				
1	THU NGN	0.453	0.711	0.553	word embeddings + CNN + Bi-LSTM
2	OCOTA	0.478	0.607	0.534	word embeddings + Bi-LSTM + linguistic
3	bot.zen	0.469	0.563	0.511	word embeddings + LSTM RNN
4	DeepReader	0.403	0.608	0.485	word embeddings + Di-LSTM + linguistic
5	MAP	0.503	0.456	0.478	word embeddings + Bi-LSTM + CRF
6	Baseline 2	0.334	0.809	0.472	UL + WordNet + CCDB + Logistic Regression
7	Samsung_RD_PL	0.505	0.439	0.470	word embeddings + CRF + context
8	Baseline 1	0.335	0.767	0.466	UL + Logistic Regression
9	ZIL IPIPAN	0.336	0.625	0.437	dictionary-based vectors + LSTM
10	nsu_ai	0.099	0.107	0.102	linguistic + CRF
	All POS (Fiction)				
1	THU NGN	0.483	0.692	0.569	word embeddings + CNN + Bi-LSTM
2	OCOTA	0.460	0.631	0.532	word embeddings + Bi LSTM + linguistic
3	bot.zen	0.474	0.569	0.517	word embeddings + LSTM RNN
4	DeepReader	0.414	0.597	0.489	word embeddings + Di-LSTM + linguistic
5	MAP	0.526	0.445	0.482	word embeddings + Bi-LSTM + CRF
6	ZIL IPIPAN	0.415	0.545	0.471	dictionary-based vectors + LSTM
7	Samsung_RD_PL	0.413	0.531	0.464	word embeddings + CRF + context
8	Baseline 2	0.366	0.614	0.458	UL + WordNet + CCDB + Logistic Regression
9	Baseline 1	0.372	0.594	0.457	UL + Logistic Regression
10	nsu_ai	0.121	0.120	0.120	linguistic + CRF
	All POS (News)				
1	OCOTA	0.606	0.718	0.658	word embeddings + Bi-LSTM + linguistic
2	THU NGN	0.664	0.647	0.655	word embedding + CNN + Bi-LSTM
3	bot.zen	0.608	0.694	0.648	word embeddings + LSTM RNN
4	ZIL IPIPAN	0.649	0.578	0.612	dictionary-based vectors + LSTM
5	Baseline 2	0.567	0.650	0.606	UL + WordNet + CCDB + Logistic Regression
6	Baseline 1	0.591	0.593	0.592	UL + Logistic Regression
7	DeepReader	0.566	0.592	0.579	word embeddings + Di-LSTM + linguistic
8	Samsung_RD_PL	0.571	0.587	0.579	word embeddings + CRF + context
9	MAP	0.681	0.400	0.504	word embeddings + Bi-LSTM + CRF
10	nsu_ai	0.255	0.126	0.169	linguistic + CRF

Table 3: Performance and ranking of the best system per team and baselines for the All-POS track, including split by genre.

Rank	Team	P	R	F1	Approach
				Verbs (Overall)	
1	THU NGN	0.600	0.763	0.672	word embeddings + CNN + Bi-LSTM
2	bot.zen	0.547	0.779	0.642	word embeddings + LSTM RNN
3	ZIL IPIPAN	0.571	0.676	0.619	dictionary-based vectors + LSTM
4	DeepReader	0.529	0.708	0.605	word embeddings + Di-LSTM + linguistic
5	Baseline 2	0.527	0.698	0.600	UL + WordNet + CCDB + Logistic Regression
6	MAP	0.675	0.517	0.586	word embeddings + Bi-LSTM + CRF
7	Baseline 1	0.510	0.654	0.573	UL + Logistic Regression
8	nsu_ai	0.301	0.207	0.246	linguistic + CRF
				Verbs (Academic)	
1	Baseline 2	0.707	0.836	0.766	UL + WordNet + CCDB + Logistic Regression
2	DeepReader	0.684	0.865	0.764	word embeddings + Di-LSTM + linguistic
3	ZIL IPIPAN	0.752	0.768	0.760	dictionary-based vectors + LSTM
4	THU NGN	0.746	0.763	0.755	word embedding + CNN + Bi-LSTM
5	MAP	0.672	0.842	0.748	word embeddings + Bi-LSTM + CRF
6	Baseline 1	0.686	0.808	0.742	UL + Logistic Regression
7	bot.zen	0.769	0.617	0.685	word embeddings + LSTM RNN
8	nsu_ai	0.499	0.908	0.644	linguistic + CRF
				Verbs (Conversation)	
1	THU NGN	0.408	0.656	0.503	word embeddings + CNN + Bi-LSTM
2	bot.zen	0.355	0.729	0.477	word embeddings + LSTM RNN
3	DeepReader	0.366	0.605	0.456	word embeddings + Di-LSTM + linguistic
4	Baseline 2	0.301	0.821	0.441	UL + WordNet + CCDB + Logistic Regression
5	MAP	0.482	0.405	0.440	word embeddings + Bi-LSTM + CRF
6	ZIL IPIPAN	0.333	0.636	0.437	dictionary-based vectors + LSTM
7	Baseline 1	0.294	0.794	0.429	UL + Logistic Regression
8	nsu_ai	0.163	0.271	0.203	linguistic + CRF
				Verbs (Fiction)	
1	THU NGN	0.455	0.784	0.576	word embeddings + CNN + Bi-LSTM
2	bot.zen	0.411	0.766	0.535	word embeddings + LSTM RNN
3	MAP	0.538	0.513	0.525	word embeddings + Bi-LSTM + CRF
4	DeepReader	0.419	0.670	0.515	word embeddings + Di-LSTM + linguistic
5	Baseline 2	0.407	0.667	0.506	UL + WordNet + CCDB + Logistic Regression
6	ZIL IPIPAN	0.414	0.604	0.491	dictionary-based vectors + LSTM
7	Baseline 1	0.390	0.608	0.475	UL + Logistic Regression
8	nsu_ai	0.218	0.190	0.204	linguistic + CRF
				Verbs (News)	
1	THU NGN	0.694	0.744	0.718	word embedding + CNN + Bi-LSTM
2	bot.zen	0.667	0.764	0.712	word embeddings + LSTM RNN
3	Baseline 2	0.677	0.689	0.683	UL + WordNet + CCDB + Logistic Regression
4	ZIL IPIPAN	0.709	0.644	0.675	dictionary-based vectors + LSTM
5	DeepReader	0.644	0.665	0.654	word embeddings + Di-LSTM + linguistic
6	Baseline 1	0.668	0.619	0.643	UL + Logistic Regression
7	MAP	0.746	0.488	0.590	word embeddings + Bi-LSTM + CRF
8	nsu_ai	0.477	0.256	0.333	linguistic + CRF

Table 4: Performance and ranking of the best system per team and baselines for the Verbs track, including split by genre.

Team	All-POS	Verbs	Adjectives	Nouns	Adverbs	Best to Worst
THU NGN	.651	.674 (1)	.651 (2)	.629 (3)	.588 (4)	.09
OCOTA	.635	.669 (1)	.625 (2)	.609 (3)	.569 (4)	.10
bot.zen	.617	.655 (1)	.582 (3)	.594 (2)	.539 (4)	.12
Baseline 2	.589	.616 (1)	.557 (3)	.564 (2)	.542 (4)	.07
ZIL IPIPAN	.583	.619 (1)	.571 (2)	.552 (3)	.484 (4)	.14
Baseline 1	.581	.594 (1)	.578 (2)	.564 (3)	.563 (4)	.03
DeepReader	.570	.605 (1)	.568 (2)	.537 (3)	.521 (4)	.08
SamSung_RD_PL	.561	.615 (1)	.540 (2)	.516 (3)	.498 (4)	.12
MAP	.536	.586 (1)	.527 (2)	.481 (4)	.496 (3)	.10
nsu_ai	.138	.155 (1)	.131 (3)	.136 (2)	.102 (4)	.05
Av. rank among POS	–	1	2.3	2.8	3.9	.09
Rank order correlation with AllPOS performance	1	.94	.92	.98	.81	–

Table 5: Performance (F-score) of the best systems submitted to All-POS track by POS subsets of the test data. In parentheses, we show the rank of the given POS within all POS for the system. The last column shows the overall drop in performance from best POS (ranked 1) to worst (ranked 4).

This could be related to the larger preponderance of metaphors among verbs, which, in turn, leads to a more balanced class distribution in the Verbs data.

6.3.2 AllPOS by POS

To better understand performance patterns across various parts of speech, we break down the All-POS test set by POS, and report performance of each of the best systems submitted to the All-POS track on each POS-based subset of the test data; Table 5 shows the results. First, we observe that the average difference in performance between best and worst POS is 9 points (see column Best to Worst in the Table), with different systems ranging from 3 to 14. We note that the baseline systems are relatively more robust in this respect (3-7 points), while the the top 3 systems exhibit a 9-12 point range of variation in performance by POS. While this gap is substantial, it is much smaller than the 20-point gap observed in by-genre breakdown.

Second, we note that without exception all systems performed best on verbs, and for all but one system performance was worst on adverbs (see "Av. rank among POS" row in Table 5). Performance on adjectives and nouns was comparable for most systems, with slightly better results for adjectives for 7 out of 10 systems. These trends closely follow the proportions of metaphors within each POS:

While 30% of verbs are marked as metaphorical, only 8% of adverbs are thus marked, with nouns and adjectives occupying the middle ground with 13% and 18% metaphors, respectively.

Third, we observe that the relative performance of the systems is quite consistent across POS. Thus, the rank order correlation between systems' overall performance (AllPOS) and their performance on Verbs is 0.94; it is 0.98 for nouns and 0.92 for Adjectives (see the last row of Table 5). In fact, the top three ranks are occupied by the same systems in AllPOS, Verbs, Adjectives, and Nouns categories. The somewhat lower rank order correlation for Adverbs (0.81) reflects Baseline 1 (which ranks 6th overall) posting a relatively strong performance for Adverbs (ranks 3rd), while the ZIL IPIPAN system (ranks 5th overall) shows relatively weak performance on Adverbs (ranks 9th). Overall, the systems' relative standings are not much affected when parceled out by POS-based subsets.

7 Conclusion

This paper summarized the results of the 2018 shared task on metaphor identification in the VUA corpus, held as part of the 2018 NAACL Workshop on Figurative Language Processing. We provided brief descriptions of the participating systems for which detailed papers were submitted; systems' performance in terms of precision, recall, and F-score; and breakdowns of systems' performance by POS and genre.

We observed that the task of metaphor detection seems to be somewhat easier for verbs than for other parts of speech, consistently across participating systems. For genres, we observed a large discrepancy in best and worst performance, with results in the .7s for Academic and in .5s for Conversation data. Clearly, understanding and bridging the genre-based gap in performance is an important avenue for future work.

While most systems employed a deep learning architecture effectively, the baselines that use a traditional feature-engineering design were not far behind, in terms of performance; the stronger baseline came 4th overall. Indeed, some of the contributions explored a combination of a DNN architecture and explicit linguistic features; this seems like a promising direction for future work. Some of the teams made their implementations publicly available, which should facilitate further work on improving performance on this task.

8 Acknowledgements

As organizers of the shared task, we would like to thank all the teams for their interest and participation. Specifically, we would also like to thank Yuri Bizzoni for his help with pre-testing the shared task setup.

References

Beata Beigman Klebanov, Daniel Diermeier, and Eyal Beigman. 2008. Lexical cohesion analysis of political speech. *Political Analysis*, 16(4):447–463.

Beata Beigman Klebanov, Chee Wee Leong, and Michael Flor. 2018. A corpus of non-native written english annotated for metaphor. In *Proceedings of the Annual Meeting of the North American Chapter of the Association for Computational Linguistics*, New Orleans,LA.

Beata Beigman Klebanov, Chee Wee Leong, E Dario Gutierrez, Ekaterina Shutova, and Michael Flor. 2016. Semantic classifications for detection of verb metaphors. In *Proceedings of the 54th Annual Meeting of the Association for Computational Linguistics (Volume 2: Short Papers)*, volume 2, pages 101–106.

Beata Beigman Klebanov, Chee Wee Leong, Michael Heilman, and Michael Flor. 2014. Different texts, same metaphors: Unigrams and beyond. In *Proceedings of the Second Workshop on Metaphor in NLP*, pages 11–17.

Richard M Billow, Jeffrey Rossman, Nona Lewis, Deberah Goldman, and Charles Raps. 1997. Observing expressive and deviant language in schizophrenia. *Metaphor and Symbol*, 12(3):205–216.

Steven Bird and Edward Loper. 2004. Nltk: the natural language toolkit. In *Proceedings of the ACL 2004 on Interactive poster and demonstration sessions*, page 31. Association for Computational Linguistics.

Julia Birke and Anoop Sarkar. 2006. A clustering approach for nearly unsupervised recognition of nonliteral language. In *11th Conference of the European Chapter of the Association for Computational Linguistics*.

Yuri Bizzoni and Mehdi Ghanimifard. 2018. Bigrams and bilstms: Two neural networks for sequential metaphor detection. In *Proceedings of the Workshop on Figurative Language Processing*, New Orleans,LA.

Jan Bosman. 1987. Persuasive effects of political metaphors. *Metaphor and Symbol*, 2(2):97–113.

Luana Bulat, Stephen Clark, and Ekaterina Shutova. 2017. Modelling metaphor with attribute-based semantics. In *Proceedings of the 15th Conference of the European Chapter of the Association for Computational Linguistics: Volume 2, Short Papers*, volume 2, pages 523–528.

Lynne Cameron. 2003. *Metaphor in educational discourse*. A&C Black.

Erik-Lân Do Dinh and Iryna Gurevych. 2016. Token-level metaphor detection using neural networks. In *Proceedings of the Fourth Workshop on Metaphor in NLP*, pages 28–33.

Jonathan Dunn. 2013. What metaphor identification systems can tell us about metaphor-in-language. In *Proceedings of the First Workshop on Metaphor in NLP*, pages 1–10.

Matt Gedigian, John Bryant, Srini Narayanan, and Branimir Ciric. 2006. Catching metaphors. In *Proceedings of the Third Workshop on Scalable Natural Language Understanding*, pages 41–48. Association for Computational Linguistics.

Pragglejaz Group. 2007. Mip: A method for identifying metaphorically used words in discourse. *Metaphor and symbol*, 22(1):1–39.

E Dario Gutierrez, Guillermo Cecchi, Cheryl Corcoran, and Philip Corlett. 2017. Using automated metaphor identification to aid in detection and prediction of first-episode schizophrenia. In *Proceedings of the 2017 Conference on Empirical Methods in Natural Language Processing*, pages 2923–2930.

E Dario Gutierrez, Ekaterina Shutova, Tyler Marghetis, and Benjamin Bergen. 2016. Literal and metaphorical senses in compositional distributional semantic models. In *Proceedings of the 54th Annual Meeting of the Association for Computational Linguistics (Volume 1: Long Papers)*, volume 1, pages 183–193.

Dirk Hovy, Shashank Shrivastava, Sujay Kumar Jauhar, Mrinmaya Sachan, Kartik Goyal, Huying Li, Whitney Sanders, and Eduard Hovy. 2013. Identifying metaphorical word use with tree kernels. In *Proceedings of the First Workshop on Metaphor in NLP*, pages 52–57.

Hyeju Jang, Seungwhan Moon, Yohan Jo, and Carolyn Rose. 2015. Metaphor detection in discourse. In *Proceedings of the 16th Annual Meeting of the Special Interest Group on Discourse and Dialogue*, pages 384–392.

Sujata S Kathpalia and Heah Lee Hah Carmel. 2011. Metaphorical competence in esl student writing. *RELC Journal*, 42(3):273–290.

Hossein Kaviani and Robabeh Hamedi. 2011. A quantitative/qualitative study on metaphors used by persian depressed patients. *Archives of Psychiatry and Psychotherapy*, 4(5-13):110.

Maximilian Köper and Sabine Schulte im Walde. 2017. Improving verb metaphor detection by propagating abstractness to words, phrases and individual senses. In *Proceedings of the 1st Workshop on Sense, Concept and Entity Representations and their Applications, pages 24–30*.

George Lakoff. 2010. *Moral politics: How liberals and conservatives think*. University of Chicago Press.

George Lakoff and Mark Johnson. 2008. *Metaphors we live by*. University of Chicago press.

Mark J Landau, Daniel Sullivan, and Jeff Greenberg. 2009. Evidence that self-relevant motives and metaphoric framing interact to influence political and social attitudes. *Psychological Science*, 20(11):1421–1427.

Jeannette Littlemore, Tina Krennmayr, James Turner, and Sarah Turner. 2013. An investigation into metaphor use at different levels of second language writing. *Applied linguistics*, 35(2):117–144.

Jeannette Littlemore and Graham Low. 2006. Metaphoric competence, second language learning, and communicative language ability. *Applied linguistics*, 27(2):268–294.

Saif Mohammad, Ekaterina Shutova, and Peter Turney. 2016. Metaphor as a medium for emotion: An empirical study. In *Proceedings of the Fifth Joint Conference on Lexical and Computational Semantics*, pages 23–33.

Michael Mohler, David Bracewell, Marc Tomlinson, and David Hinote. 2013. Semantic signatures for example-based linguistic metaphor detection. In *Proceedings of the First Workshop on Metaphor in NLP*, pages 27–35.

Anna Mosolova, Ivan Bondarenko, and Vadim Fomin. 2018. Conditional random fields for metaphor detection. In *Proceedings of the Workshop on Figurative Language Processing*, New Orleans,LA.

Agnieszka Mykowiecka, Aleksander Wawer, and Malgorzata Marciniak. 2018. Detecting figurative word occurrences using word embeddings. In *Proceedings of the Workshop on Figurative Language Processing*, New Orleans,LA.

Yair Neuman, Dan Assaf, Yohai Cohen, Mark Last, Shlomo Argamon, Newton Howard, and Ophir Frieder. 2013. Metaphor identification in large texts corpora. *PloS one*, 8(4):e62343.

Gözde Özbal, Carlo Strapparava, and Serra Sinem Tekiroglu. 2016. Prometheus: A corpus of proverbs annotated with metaphors. In *LREC*.

Malay Pramanick, Ashim Gupta, and Pabitra Mitra. 2018. An lstm-crf based approach to token-level metaphor detection. In *Proceedings of the Workshop on Figurative Language Processing*, New Orleans,LA.

Marek Rei, Luana Bulat, Douwe Kiela, and Ekaterina Shutova. 2017. Grasping the finer point: A supervised similarity network for metaphor detection. In *Proceedings of the 2017 Conference on Empirical Methods in Natural Language Processing*, pages 1537–1546.

Ekaterina Shutova, Douwe Kiela, and Jean Maillard. 2016. Black holes and white rabbits: Metaphor identification with visual features. In *Proceedings of the 2016 Conference of the North American Chapter of the Association for Computational Linguistics: Human Language Technologies*, pages 160–170.

Ekaterina Shutova, Lin Sun, Elkin Darío Gutiérrez, Patricia Lichtenstein, and Srini Narayanan. 2017. Multilingual metaphor processing: Experiments with semi-supervised and unsupervised learning. *Computational Linguistics*, 43(1):71–123.

Ekaterina Shutova, Lin Sun, and Anna Korhonen. 2010. Metaphor identification using verb and noun clustering. In *Proceedings of the 23rd International Conference on Computational Linguistics*, pages 1002–1010. Association for Computational Linguistics.

Filip Skurniak, Maria Janicka, and Aleksander Wawer. 2018. Multim-module recurrent neural networks with transfer learning. a submission for the metaphor detection shared task. In *Proceedings of the Workshop on Figurative Language Processing*, New Orleans,LA.

Gerard J Steen, Aletta G Dorst, J Berenike Herrmann, Anna Kaal, Tina Krennmayr, and Trijntje Pasma. 2010. *A method for linguistic metaphor identification: From MIP to MIPVU*, volume 14. John Benjamins Publishing.

Egon Stemle and Alexander Onysko. 2018. Using language learner data for metaphor detection. In *Proceedings of the Workshop on Figurative Language Processing*, New Orleans,LA.

Krishnkant Swarnkar and Anil Kumar Singh. 2018. Di-lstm contrast : A deep neural network for metaphor detection. In *Proceedings of the Workshop on Figurative Language Processing*, New Orleans,LA.

Serra Sinem Tekiroglu, Gözde Özbal, and Carlo Strapparava. 2015. Exploring sensorial features for metaphor identification. In *Proceedings of the Third Workshop on Metaphor in NLP*, pages 31–39.

Paul H Thibodeau and Lera Boroditsky. 2011. Metaphors we think with: The role of metaphor in reasoning. *PloS one*, 6(2):e16782.

Yulia Tsvetkov, Leonid Boytsov, Anatole Gershman, Eric Nyberg, and Chris Dyer. 2014. Metaphor detection with cross-lingual model transfer. In *Proceedings of the 52nd Annual Meeting of the Association for Computational Linguistics (Volume 1: Long Papers)*, volume 1, pages 248–258.

Yulia Tsvetkov, Elena Mukomel, and Anatole Gershman. 2013. Cross-lingual metaphor detection using common semantic features. In *Proceedings of the First Workshop on Metaphor in NLP*, pages 45–51.

Peter D Turney, Yair Neuman, Dan Assaf, and Yohai Cohen. 2011. Literal and metaphorical sense identification through concrete and abstract context. In *Proceedings of the Conference on Empirical Methods in Natural Language Processing*, pages 680–690. Association for Computational Linguistics.

Tony Veale, Ekaterina Shutova, and Beata Beigman Klebanov. 2016. Metaphor: A computational perspective. *Synthesis Lectures on Human Language Technologies*, 9(1):1–160.

Chuhan Wu, Fangzhao Wu, Yubo Chen, Sixing Wu, Zhigang Yuan, and Yongfeng Huang. 2018. Thu ngn at naacl-2018 metaphor shared task: Neural metaphor detecting with cnn-lstm model. In *Proceedings of the Workshop on Figurative Language Processing*, New Orleans,LA.

Gerald Zaltman and Lindsay H Zaltman. 2008. *Marketing metaphoria: What deep metaphors reveal about the minds of consumers.* Harvard Business Press.

An LSTM-CRF Based Approach to Token-Level Metaphor Detection

Malay Pramanick
Dept. of Computer Science
and Engineering
IIT Kharagpur
West Bengal, India - 721302
malay.pramanick@
iitkgp.ac.in

Ashim Gupta
Dept. of Computer Science
and Engineering
IIT Kharagpur
West Bengal, India - 721302
ashimgupta95@
gmail.com

Pabitra Mitra
Dept. of Computer Science
and Engineering
IIT Kharagpur
West Bengal, India - 721302
pabitra@
cse.iitkgp.ernet.in

Abstract

Automatic processing of figurative languages is gaining popularity in NLP community for their ubiquitous nature and increasing volume. In this era of web 2.0, automatic analysis of metaphors is important for their extensive usage. Metaphors are a part of figurative language that compares different concepts, often on a cognitive level. Many approaches have been proposed for automatic detection of metaphors, even using sequential models or neural networks. In this paper, we propose a method for detection of metaphors at the token level using a hybrid model of Bidirectional-LSTM and CRF. We used fewer features, as compared to the previous state-of-the-art sequential model. On experimentation with VUAMC, our method obtained an F-score of 0.674.

1 Introduction

A *metaphor* is a figure of speech that brings together different concepts, which are often distinct and seemingly unrelated. A metaphor comprises a word or a phrase representing something else, where applying it in its literal sense is often not possible. Metaphors bring in vivid imagery to our communications by drawing an analogy between one thing and another or between actions.

Metaphors also provide a fundamental cognitive and structural role. Lakoff and Johnson (1980) introduced metaphor as a central cognitive device that gives structure to abstract conceptual domains, referred to as the 'target domains', which are described in terms of concrete domains, referred to as the 'source domains'. In our work,

we do not try to ascertain the source or target domains, rather we focus on determining the presence of metaphorically used tokens in any given sentence.

To estimate the frequency of occurrence of metaphors, Shutova and Teufel (2010) conducted a study on a subset of the British National Corpus (Consortium and others, 2007) and manually annotated the metaphorical expressions in that data. They found out that 241 sentences contained at least one metaphor among the 761 sentences considered.

Figurative uses of language are abundant in literature, but they are not restricted to the literary works. Figurative elements of language, especially sarcasm and metaphor, are common in online product reviews, blogs, articles and posts in social networking sites. With the increasing amount of textual data, the number of metaphorical instances is also increasing. As the application of metaphors is pervasive, their interpretation in non-literal ways is required. To process metaphors automatically, their detection is of foremost importance. Their abundance in any language suggests that their detection would benefit the entire Natural Language Processing (NLP) community, for it would benefit methods like paraphrasing, summarization, machine translation, etc. As of now, most of the state of the art machine translations treat text literally and hence errors creep into the automated translations.

There has been an increasing interest in automated processing of metaphors in the NLP community for their pervasiveness in our communications. To analyze and interpret a metaphor, it has to be identified first. Some of the existing computational models for detection of metaphors use a hierarchical organization of conventional

Proceedings of the Workshop on Figurative Language Processing, pages 67–75
New Orleans, Louisiana, June 6, 2018. ©2018 Association for Computational Linguistics

metaphors, or selectional restrictions as provided in lexical resources available or by using word embeddings, or conventional mappings of subject-verb, verb-object, subject-object (Shutova, 2015).

In this paper, we treat the problem of token-level metaphor detection as a sequence tagging problem; and sequence tagging problems, like Parts Of Speech (POS) tagging and Named Entity Recognition (NER), have been long dealt in NLP. We approach token-level metaphor detection, with the help of Long Short-Term Memory (LSTM) and Conditional Random Fields (CRF). We try to identify the metaphors in a running text, irrespective of the type of the metaphor. To observe the effectiveness of our proposed method, we have experimented on VUAMC (Steen et al., 2010b), an open domain text corpus, that has been hand-annotated for metaphors at the token level. Our method obtained the state-of-the-art results as compared to previously reported works on token level metaphor detection.

The rest of the paper is organized as follows. We start in Section 2 by discussing existing literature on metaphor detection which compares to our work in at least one facet and compare these with our methodology. Section 3 discusses the preliminaries. Section 4 presents the motivation behind proposing our method. Section 5 provides information about the dataset used in the experiments and discusses the feature set considered. Section 6 provides the experimental details. Section 7 presents the results of our experiments along with some discussions. Section 8 concludes the paper suggesting possible future works.

2   Related Works

Numerous works have been reported on automated processing of metaphors. Shutova (2015) has made a comprehensive review of computational metaphor identification systems as well as metaphor interpretation systems. Initially, computational approaches to metaphor identification heavily relied on hand-coded knowledge, followed by metaphor identification relying on lexical resources. Recently the NLP community has witnessed a growing interest in statistical and machine learning approaches to metaphor identification. In the following paragraphs, we discuss works done in the past that are related to our approach.

Hovy et al. (2013) presented one of the first approaches to metaphor identification with word vectors. They revisited the idea of selectional preference violation as an indication of metaphorical expression but captured the difference in syntactic relations using dependency trees over words. They used tree kernels, a similarity matrix over tree instances, computed using the number of shared subtrees, to train a Support Vector Machine (Cortes and Vapnik, 1995) (SVM) classifier. To construct the different tree representations, they considered word vector, lemma, POS tag, dependency label, and WordNet (Fellbaum, 1998) supersense representations. They downloaded a list of 329 examples of metaphorical expressions from the web and used 80% as training data, 10% as developmental set and remaining 10% as test set. The authors reported an F-score of 0.75, which indicates the importance of syntactic information and compositionality in metaphor identification.

Haagsma and Bjerva (2016) worked on detecting novel metaphors using selectional preference information. They claim that "metaphor is defined by basicness of meaning and not frequency of meaning". Though the basicness and frequency are correlated, there are instances where the figurative sense of a word has become more frequent than its original literal sense. They proposed different ways for generalizing over selectional preferences obtained from a corpus. One among them was to use the word embeddings for the generalizations directly. They used a neural network with one hidden layer containing 600 hidden units with a sigmoid activation function and the resulting predictions were used as the Predicted Log Probability (P-LP) feature. They evaluated the approaches on the VU Amsterdam Metaphor Corpus (VUAMC).

Tsvetkov et al. (2014) used logistics regression with word vectors and MRC Psycholinguistic Database to get the abstractness and imageability scores. With the abstractness and imageability scores, they used supersenses and vector representation of words as features for Random Forest Classifier to detect metaphor.

Klebanov et al. (2014) considered each of the 'content-word' token in any given text to be classified as metaphorical or not. They used the logistic regression classifier to detect metaphor using unigrams, part of speech, concreteness and topic models as features. Klebanov et al. (2015) tuned the weight parameter to represent concreteness of information and include the difference of concreteness between an adjective and its head noun and between a verb and its direct object, to improve on their previous work.

Do Dinh and Gurevych (2016) presented a neural network based method to detect metaphors at the token level. Their method relied on word embeddings. They experimented with "multilayer perceptrons (MLP), fully connected feedforward neural networks with an input layer, one or more hidden layers, and an output layer". In their experiments, they incorporated labels for tokens with noun, verb, adjective, adverb POS tags as supplied with the VUAMC, as their interest lied in the detection of metaphoricity of content tokens. They also filtered out auxiliary verbs, having lemmas *have*, *be*, or *do*.

Rai et al. (2016) used Conditional Random Fields (CRF) to detect metaphors in an open domain text. For their experiments, they used Syntactic features, Conceptual features, Affective Features and Contextual features. *Lemma, Part of Speech (PoS), Named Entity (NE) type, dependency, and stop word* as a set of syntactic features extracted by using Stanford CoreNLP formed the Syntactic features. *Concreteness, familiarity, imageability, frequency and meaningfulness* extracted from MRC Psycholinguistic Database formed the Conceptual features. *Cognitive state, physical state, trait, attitude, and emotion* extracted from WordNet Affect (Strapparava et al., 2004) formed the Affective features. As Contextual features, they used word embeddings. Using CRF++ (Kudo, 2005) on VUAMC, they reported an F-score of 0.6093.

Do Dinh and Gurevych (2016) filtered out tokens if they did not have noun, verb, adjective or adverb as part of speech. On the other hand, we considered all tokens of the dataset. The reason being that if one word cannot be used metaphorically, it can indicate metaphoricity of another. We used LSTM, which they had suggested in their conclusion. Our approach uses less number of features as compared to that of Rai et al. (2016). We used a hybrid architecture of Bidirectional-LSTM and CRF for metaphor detection.

3 Preliminaries

3.1 Word Embeddings

There is a long history of word embeddings (Hinton et al., 1985; Hinton et al., 1986; Elman, 1990).

Collobert and Weston (2008) tried to define a unified architecture for Natural Language Processing. The architecture deals with raw words and transforms them into real-valued vectors. The architecture learns feature representations that have relevance to many well known NLP tasks like part-of-speech (POS) tagging, chunking, named-entity recognition (NER), learning a language model, recognizing synonyms and semantic role-labeling (SRL), by training a deep neural network.

The word embeddings produced by the method of Turian et al. (2010), are real numbers that are not necessarily in a bounded range, however, generally, the embeddings have a zero mean, though they can be scaled by a hyper-parameter to control their standard deviation.

Mnih and Hinton (2009) used a log-bilinear model as the foundation to their hierarchical model. They were focussed on a learning approach where no expert knowledge was available. The 'word feature vectors' were obtained by generating a random tree of words, training a hierarchical log-bilinear model on it and using the distributed representations the model learns while building the tree of words.

Mikolov et al. (2013b) showed that subsampling of frequent words during the training speeds-up the process, and also improves the accuracy of the vector representations of less frequent words. The most common words are usually less informative as they can easily occur millions of times. To counter the rare and common words imbalance, they used a sub-sampling approach. The work provides a simple but powerful way to represent large pieces of text, keeping the computational complexity to a minimal.

Pennington et al. (2014) explicitly made the model properties that were needed for semantic and syntactic regularities and presented a global log-bilinear model having the advantages of global matrix factorization as well as local context window methods.

3.2 LSTM

Long Short-Term Memory (LSTM) was introduced by Hochreiter and Schmidhuber (1997) to overcome the issue of vanishing gradients in the vanilla recurrent neural networks. They introduced the gating mechanism through LSTM, which made it possible to learn long-term dependencies.

LSTM equations are as follows:

$$i_t = \sigma(\mathcal{W}_{xi} \cdot \mathcal{X}_t + \mathcal{W}_{hi} \cdot \mathcal{H}_{t-1}$$
$$+ \mathcal{W}_{ci} \cdot \mathcal{C}_{t-1} + b_i)$$
$$f_t = \sigma(\mathcal{W}_{xf} \cdot \mathcal{X}_t + \mathcal{W}_{hf} \cdot \mathcal{H}_{t-1}$$
$$+ \mathcal{W}_{cf} \cdot \mathcal{C}_{t-1} + b_f)$$
$$C_t = f_t \odot C_{t-1} + i_t \odot tanh(W_{xc} \cdot \mathcal{X}_t \qquad (1)$$
$$+ \mathcal{W}_{hc} \cdot \mathcal{H}_{t-1} + b_c)$$
$$o_t = \sigma(\mathcal{W}_{xo} \cdot \mathcal{X}_t + \mathcal{W}_{ho} \cdot \mathcal{H}_{t-1}$$
$$+ \mathcal{W}_{co} \cdot \mathcal{C}_t + b_o)$$
$$\mathcal{H}_t = o_t \odot tanh(C_t)$$

In Eq. 1 for the LSTM, σ is the sigmoid function, $\odot$ is the Hadamard product, C_t is the cell state, H_t is the hidden state. i_t, f_t, o_t refer to the input gate, forget gate and output gate respectively.

A Bidirectional-LSTM (Graves and Schmidhuber, 2005) has two LSTM networks. One of the networks is provided the input in the forward direction, whereas the other network is provided the input backward, but both of the networks are connected to the same output layer. In this paper, *Bidirectional-LSTM* is henceforth referred to as Bi-LSTM.

3.3 CRF

While predicting the output tags for a sequence, a system can also make use of the tags predicted in the previous time steps. This can be facilitated by using a Maximum Entropy Markov Model (MEMM) (McCallum et al., 2000) or a Conditional Random Fields based tagging scheme. Conditional Random Fields or CRF was introduced by Lafferty et al. (2001) for building probabilistic models for labeling sequential data. CRF overcomes the problem of label bias. In most problems, CRF provides a better tagging performance as compared to MEMMs (Lafferty et al., 2001; Rozenfeld et al., 2006).

4 Motivation

A standalone word, or token for that matter, cannot be marked for metaphoricity as many words can be used both literally or figuratively, which is determined by the context of the word. Many computational methods have been proposed for metaphor detection in datasets consisting of word tuples like Adjective-Noun (Tsvetkov et al., 2014; Shutova et al., 2016), Noun-Noun (or Type I metaphor as categorised by Krishnakumaran and Zhu (2007)) (Su

et al., 2017; Kesarwani et al., 2017) and Subject-Verb-Object (Tsvetkov et al., 2014; Shutova et al., 2016).

Open domain texts may have more than one type of metaphor and though dependency parsing is pretty accurate these days, metaphorically related words and their indication might not be directly related. So inherently detection of metaphors, at a token level, is a context-sensitive job and a sequential one.

Hybrid models of Bidirectional-LSTM and CRF have been successful in tagging problems like POS tagging, chunking and NER tagging (Huang et al., 2015; Lample et al., 2016). We apply a hybrid model of Bidirectional-LSTM and CRF (henceforth referred to as **Bi-LSTM-CRF**), to look for metaphors at the token level.

5 Data and Feature Set

5.1 Dataset

VU Amsterdam Metaphor Corpus (VUAMC) (Steen et al., 2010b) is a subset of BNC Baby. The Reference Guide to BNC Baby (2003) describes its design and provides information about the way in which it is encoded. VUAMC is one of the "largest available corpus hand-annotated for all metaphorical language use, regardless of lexical field or source domain". It was reported that the corpus was annotated with an inter-annotator reliability in terms of Fleiss' Kappa, $\kappa > 0.8$.

VUAMC consists of randomly selected texts from four registers of the BNC-Baby, namely, **academic texts**, **conversations**, **fiction** and **news texts**. The texts are coded for metaphor. The annotation manual for VUAMC and a detailed documentation of the project have been published in Steen et al. (2010a).

In VUAMC, each lexical unit is annotated as being used literally or metaphorically. Annotation for metaphoricity is done using fine grained tags. XML tags with attribute **function** having value **mrw** indicates that the unit is related to metaphors (mwr expands to metaphor-related words), but they are further divided with the help of attribute **type** which has values between **bridge**, **lit** and **met**. We considered tags with the value of **met** for attribute **type** when attribute **function** has value of **mrw** as metaphorical and label everything else as literal.

5.2 Generating Word Representations

We obtained word embeddings for our experiments by using the open source Google word2vec[1] (Mikolov et al., 2013a; Mikolov et al., 2013b; Mikolov et al., 2013c). We have used the Continuous Bag-Of-Words (CBOW) model of Mikolov et al. (2013a) with a window size of eight (8) words. CBOW uses a continuous distributed representation of the context but the order of words in the history does not influence the projection.

For training the model, we used the text corpus from recent English Wikipedia dump[2] preprocessed with the Perl script of Matt Mahoney[3] and obtained vectors with a dimension of 200.

By training the model with Wikipedia text corpus, we obtained word embeddings for most of the lemmas and words contained in the VUAMC. For some of the words and some of the lemmas, embeddings were not available. There were some words which were compositions of more than one word, for them we took the component-wise average of the vectors of the composing words. Averaging retains the property of both of the components. Phrase embedding could have been an alternative, but averaging sufficed our purpose. Numerical tokens of VUAMC had to be dealt separately as the Perl script removes non-alphabetical characters from the corpus during the preprocessing. So years were represented by the embedding of the word 'year', amount was represented by that of 'dollars', component-wise averaged with embedding for 'million' or 'billion' if mentioned in the token, and so on. For the words whose representations were still not available, a constant vector was used.

In XML file of the VUAMC, the Part-Of-Speech (POS) for the tokens are provided by the "type" attribute. For our experiments, we needed the vector representations of the POS. For their representations instead of using one-hot encoding or some randomly initialized vectors, we trained Google word2vec only on the sequence of POS tags as present in the VUAMC and used the CBOW model to generate vectors of dimension 20 for the POS. While training word2vec on the sequence of POS tags, we did not include the labels for metaphoricity, keeping the embedding genera-

tion for the POS unsupervised.

5.3 Features

The features that we considered for our experiments are as follows :

1. Token

2. Lemma of the token

3. Part-Of-Speech (POS)

4. Whether the lemma and the word are same

5. Whether the lemma is present in the token

Token or word (converted to lower case, if not originally in the XML file of VUAMC) was the most essential component for the feature vector as we were addressing the problem of token-level metaphor detection. So for every experiment performed for this paper, the token was common. The word embedding of the token as generated in subsection 5.2 was considered as a part of the feature vector, and referred to as 'Token'.

Similarly, for the lemma of the token as provided by the "lemma" attribute in XML file of VUAMC, word embeddings as generated in subsection 5.2 was considered and referred to as 'Lemma' in later sections. The generated POS embeddings were used to represent the Part-Of-Speech as provided by the "type" attribute in XML file of VUAMC and referred to as 'POS'.

For the features 4 and 5, we have used one hot encoding. For each of them, there were only two possible scenarios, yes and no, so vectors of dimension 2 did the work. Features 4 and 5 represent the relation between the lemma and the token, so collectively they are referred to as 'Word-Lemma Relations'.

The feature vector of a token, as input to the model, was a concatenation of the representation of the features described above in the order they have been mentioned. When we experimented for the contribution of each of the features over the token, we omitted some features while retaining the others, but we maintained the order for our ease.

6 Experiments

6.1 Baselines

As one of our baselines, we used the results from Do Dinh and Gurevych (2016). Using neural network, they experimented on each of the contained

---

[1]https://code.google.com/archive/p/word2vec/
[2]https://dumps.wikimedia.org/enwiki/latest/
[3]http://mattmahoney.net/dc/textdata.html

genres in VUAMC (news, conversation, fiction, academic) separately; for each subcorpora, they used a random subset of 76% of the data as a training set, 12% as development set and 12% as test set. They also reported the performance of their system on the complete corpus, with a 76%, 12%, 12% split. We compared with their precision, recall and F1-measure regarding metaphorically used tokens for their tuned neural network on a feature set of **Token+POS+Conc** i.e. with a feature set consisting of **Token**, **POS** and **Concreteness rating**.

As for our other baseline, we considered the results from Rai et al. (2016), as reported by them. They used conditional random fields (CRF) for detection of metaphors and experimented on each of the genres contained in VUAMC, as well as on the complete dataset. For the genres, they have reported precision and recall (for metaphor class), from which we can calculate the F-measure for the metaphor class. On the complete dataset, they have reported precision, recall and F-measure, with which we compared the performance of our method.

6.2 Experimental Setup

We considered all tokens, irrespective of their POS tag supplied with the VUAMC. We ignored the punctuations like comma (,), exclamation mark (!), period (.), and quotation mark (') , as punctuation marks cannot be used metaphorically, to the best of our knowledge.

For each of the tokens considered, the feature vector was computed as described in section 5. As the punctuation marks were not considered, the tokens belonging to a particular sentence were clubbed together, in the order they appear in the sentence in VUAMC. As the label for metaphoricity, each token is marked as negative or positive representing **literal** and **metaphorical** tokens, respectively.

As sentences of the dataset are not of equal length, we padded them with constant vectors, labeled negative for metaphoricity. In a running text, if the end of sentences are not marked, an automatic processor for sentences can be used to mark them.

We used a Bi-LSTM-CRF architecture similar to the ones presented by Collobert et al. (2011), Huang et al. (2015) and Lample et al. (2016). Our architecture used a Bidirectional-LSTM with a layer of CRF above it.

Our model with back-propagation updated parameters with every batch. We used a batch size of 128 while training. We used a learning rate of 0.0005 and had set the gradient clipping to 5. We used Adam (Kingma and Ba, 2014) as our learning method with a dropout of 0.5. Our model used a single LSTM layer for forward and a single LSTM layer for backward propagations. Each of the layers had a dimension of 100. It was observed that changing the dimensions did not significantly improve the results.

The system is trained and tested on the complete corpus, leaving out the metadata of the genre they belong to in the British National Corpus (BNC). We did a 10-fold cross validation on the entire dataset, with the order of the sentences changed randomly. We rearranged the sentences so that the sentences belonging to the same genre did not necessarily get clubbed together as originally in the dataset. The performance of the system with the suggested features is evaluated on the basis of Precision, Recall and F1-score.

To check whether a feature contributes to the results, we also experimented on an incremental basis, i.e. adding features on top of the others. We also checked separately for the features along with the word embeddings for the words (tokens). We did this with a 10-fold cross-validation.

6.3 Fig-Lang18 Shared Task

The shared task on metaphor detection in the First Workshop on Figurative Language Processing[4], co-located with NAACL 2018 targets detecting "all content-word metaphors in a given text". The shared task also uses the VUAMC dataset (referred to as VUA in the shared task). It has a separate evaluation only for the verb metaphors.

The training as well as the test data consists of text ids and sentence ids along with the respective sentences from the VUAMC. The test phase has test instances (one set of instances for all-POS and another only for the verb metaphors), over which the submitted predictions are evaluated.

For our training and testing purpose, we had the text ids and sentence ids as provided for the shared task, from which we could get the respective sentences from the VUAMC and thus generate the feature vectors for each of their tokens (leaving aside the punctuation marks), as described in

---

[4]https://competitions.codalab.org/competitions/17805

Method	Precision	Recall	F_1-score
Do Dinh and Gurevych (2016)	0.5899	0.5355	0.5614
Rai et al. (2016)	0.6333	0.5871	0.6093
Bi-LSTM-CRF (Embeddings only for tokens)	0.7036	0.5755	0.6327
Bi-LSTM-CRF (All of the considered features)	0.7283	0.6253	0.6740

Table 1: Results for complete VU Amsterdam Metaphor Corpus.

Method	Precision	Recall	F_1-score
Only Token	0.7036	0.5755	0.6327
Token + Word-Lemma Relations	0.7040	0.5876	0.6330
Token + POS	0.7252	0.5784	0.6399
Token + Lemma	0.7495	0.6213	0.6657
Token + Lemma + POS	0.7239	0.6297	0.6729
Token + Lemma + POS + Word-Lemma Relations	0.7283	0.6253	0.6740

Table 2: Results for Feature Selection on the complete VU Amsterdam Metaphor Corpus with Bi-LSTM-CRF.

section 5. If any punctuation mark was to be evaluated, it was to be given a negative level for metaphoricity.

We trained on the training set as decided for the task, using the same system of Bi-LSTM-CRF as used in the previous subsection, with all of the features considered. We did not train separately for verb metaphors but used the same system to evaluate the verb metaphors also.

7   Results and Discussions

Using Bi-LSTM-CRF only with the word embeddings of the tokens of the sentences, gives better results as compared to the baselines, as shown in Table 1.

We have also reported the results of experiments for feature selection in Table 2. As it can be seen in Table 2, using word embeddings of the lemmas along with the tokens, improved the results by a huge scale. Adding embeddings for the POS also improved the results. POS tags are provided with VUAMC, but for a dataset, if the POS are not available, they can be generated by using the available POS taggers.

Do Dinh and Gurevych (2016) and Rai et al. (2016) used concreteness ratings but for our method, the results hardly change if we consider concreteness ratings. As Do Dinh and Gurevych (2016) have pointed out, this could be due to *one-dimensionality* of the abstractness (or concreteness) feature.

The results of the experiments on the shared task data have been reported in Table 3. Our method obtained an F-measure of 0.6541 over the entire test set of the shared task but an F-measure of 0.5362 for the all-POS instances and 0.5859 for the verb instances.

8   Conclusion and Future Work

We presented a method for token level metaphor detection using Bi-LSTM-CRF. Our method uses word-embeddings of the token as well as its lemmatized form. Our method compares well with the state-of-the-art system that considers a huge set of features, which we beat with fewer features without filtering out any particular type of word.

The context that we had considered for our experiments was one sentence at a time, but an indication of metaphorically related words can also be across sentences and for those scenarios, the global context is expected to help. So in our future work, we intend to take wider context into consideration.

Acknowledgments

We would like to thank Sonam Singh, Priyanka Sinha and António Anastásio Bruto da Costa for their valuable feedback on the initial draft of this paper. We would also like to thank the anonymous reviewers for their valuable comments and feedback.

Data	Accuracy	Precision	Recall	F-measure
All POS Instances	0.8575	0.6446	0.4591	0.5362
Verb Instances	0.7807	0.6753	0.5173	0.5859
Overall Test Set	0.9172	0.7331	0.5904	0.6541

Table 3: Results on Shared Task.

References

Lou Burnard. 2003. Reference guide for bnc-baby.

Ronan Collobert and Jason Weston. 2008. A unified architecture for natural language processing: Deep neural networks with multitask learning. In *Proceedings of the 25th international conference on Machine learning*, pages 160–167. ACM.

Ronan Collobert, Jason Weston, Léon Bottou, Michael Karlen, Koray Kavukcuoglu, and Pavel Kuksa. 2011. Natural language processing (almost) from scratch. *Journal of Machine Learning Research*, 12(Aug):2493–2537.

British National Corpus Consortium et al. 2007. British national corpus version 3 (bnc xml edition). *Distributed by Oxford University Computing Services on behalf of the BNC Consortium. Retrieved February*, 13:2012.

Corinna Cortes and Vladimir Vapnik. 1995. Support-vector networks. *Machine learning*, 20(3):273–297.

Erik-Lân Do Dinh and Iryna Gurevych. 2016. Token-level metaphor detection using neural networks. In *Proceedings of the fourth workshop on metaphor in NLP*, pages 28–33.

Jeffrey L Elman. 1990. Finding structure in time. *Cognitive science*, 14(2):179–211.

Christiane Fellbaum. 1998. *WordNet*. Wiley Online Library.

Yulia Tsvetkov Leonid Boytsov Anatole Gershman and Eric Nyberg Chris Dyer. 2014. Metaphor detection with cross-lingual model transfer. In *Proceedings of the Annual Meeting of the Association for Computational Linguistics*.

Alex Graves and Jürgen Schmidhuber. 2005. Framewise phoneme classification with bidirectional lstm networks. In *Neural Networks, 2005. IJCNN'05. Proceedings. 2005 IEEE International Joint Conference on*, volume 4, pages 2047–2052. IEEE.

Hessel Haagsma and Johannes Bjerva. 2016. Detecting novel metaphor using selectional preference information. In *Proceedings of the fourth workshop on metaphor in NLP*, pages 10–17.

GE Hinton, DE Rumelhart, and RJ Williams. 1985. Learning internal representations by back-propagating errors. *Parallel Distributed Processing: Explorations in the Microstructure of Cognition*, 1.

Geoffrey E Hinton, James L Mcclelland, and David E Rumelhart. 1986. Distributed representations, parallel distributed processing: explorations in the microstructure of cognition, vol. 1: foundations.

Sepp Hochreiter and Jürgen Schmidhuber. 1997. Long short-term memory. *Neural computation*, 9(8):1735–1780.

Dirk Hovy, Shashank Shrivastava, Sujay Kumar Jauhar, Mrinmaya Sachan, Kartik Goyal, Huying Li, Whitney Sanders, and Eduard Hovy. 2013. Identifying metaphorical word use with tree kernels. In *Proceedings of the First Workshop on Metaphor in NLP*, pages 52–57.

Zhiheng Huang, Wei Xu, and Kai Yu. 2015. Bidirectional lstm-crf models for sequence tagging. *arXiv preprint arXiv:1508.01991*.

Vaibhav Kesarwani, Diana Inkpen, Stan Szpakowicz, and Chris Tanasescu. 2017. Metaphor detection in a poetry corpus. In *Proceedings of the Joint SIGHUM Workshop on Computational Linguistics for Cultural Heritage, Social Sciences, Humanities and Literature*, pages 1–9.

Diederik P Kingma and Jimmy Ba. 2014. Adam: A method for stochastic optimization. *arXiv preprint arXiv:1412.6980*.

Beata Beigman Klebanov, Chee Wee Leong, Michael Heilman, and Michael Flor. 2014. Different texts, same metaphors: Unigrams and beyond. In *Proceedings of the Second Workshop on Metaphor in NLP*, pages 11–17.

Beata Beigman Klebanov, Chee Wee Leong, and Michael Flor. 2015. Supervised word-level metaphor detection: Experiments with concreteness and reweighting of examples. In *Proceedings of the Third Workshop on Metaphor in NLP*, pages 11–20.

Saisuresh Krishnakumaran and Xiaojin Zhu. 2007. Hunting elusive metaphors using lexical resources. In *Proceedings of the Workshop on Computational approaches to Figurative Language*, pages 13–20. Association for Computational Linguistics.

Taku Kudo. 2005. Crf++: Yet another crf toolkit. *Software available at http://crfpp. sourceforge. net*.

John Lafferty, Andrew McCallum, and Fernando CN Pereira. 2001. Conditional random fields: Probabilistic models for segmenting and labeling sequence data.

George Lakoff and Mark Johnson. 1980. *Metaphors we live by*. University of Chicago press.

Guillaume Lample, Miguel Ballesteros, Sandeep Subramanian, Kazuya Kawakami, and Chris Dyer. 2016. Neural architectures for named entity recognition. *arXiv preprint arXiv:1603.01360*.

Andrew McCallum, Dayne Freitag, and Fernando CN Pereira. 2000. Maximum entropy markov models for information extraction and segmentation. In *Icml*, volume 17, pages 591–598.

Tomas Mikolov, Kai Chen, Greg Corrado, and Jeffrey Dean. 2013a. Efficient estimation of word representations in vector space. *arXiv preprint arXiv:1301.3781*.

Tomas Mikolov, Ilya Sutskever, Kai Chen, Greg S Corrado, and Jeff Dean. 2013b. Distributed representations of words and phrases and their compositionality. In *Advances in neural information processing systems*, pages 3111–3119.

Tomas Mikolov, Wen-tau Yih, and Geoffrey Zweig. 2013c. Linguistic regularities in continuous space word representations. In *hlt-Naacl*, volume 13, pages 746–751.

Andriy Mnih and Geoffrey E Hinton. 2009. A scalable hierarchical distributed language model. In *Advances in neural information processing systems*, pages 1081–1088.

Jeffrey Pennington, Richard Socher, and Christopher Manning. 2014. Glove: Global vectors for word representation. In *Proceedings of the 2014 conference on empirical methods in natural language processing (EMNLP)*, pages 1532–1543.

Sunny Rai, Shampa Chakraverty, and Devendra K Tayal. 2016. Supervised metaphor detection using conditional random fields. In *Proceedings of the Fourth Workshop on Metaphor in NLP*, pages 18–27.

Binyamin Rozenfeld, Ronen Feldman, and Moshe Fresko. 2006. A systematic cross-comparison of sequence classifiers. In *Proceedings of the 2006 SIAM International Conference on Data Mining*, pages 564–568. SIAM.

Ekaterina Shutova and Simone Teufel. 2010. Metaphor corpus annotated for source-target domain mappings. In *LREC*, volume 2, pages 2–2.

Ekaterina Shutova, Douwe Kiela, and Jean Maillard. 2016. Black holes and white rabbits: Metaphor identification with visual features. In *Proceedings of the 2016 Conference of the North American Chapter of the Association for Computational Linguistics: Human Language Technologies*, pages 160–170.

Ekaterina Shutova. 2015. Design and evaluation of metaphor processing systems. *Computational Linguistics*, 41(4):579–623.

Gerard J Steen, Aletta G Dorst, J Berenike Herrmann, Anna Kaal, Tina Krennmayr, and Trijntje Pasma. 2010a. *A method for linguistic metaphor identification: From MIP to MIPVU*, volume 14. John Benjamins Publishing.

Gerard J Steen, Aletta G Dorst, J Berenike Herrmann, Anna A Kaal, and Tina Krennmayr. 2010b. Vu amsterdam metaphor corpus.

Carlo Strapparava, Alessandro Valitutti, et al. 2004. Wordnet affect: an affective extension of wordnet. In *LREC*, volume 4, pages 1083–1086.

Chang Su, Shuman Huang, and Yijiang Chen. 2017. Automatic detection and interpretation of nominal metaphor based on the theory of meaning. *Neurocomputing*, 219:300–311.

Yulia Tsvetkov, Leonid Boytsov, Anatole Gershman, Eric Nyberg, and Chris Dyer. 2014. Metaphor detection with cross-lingual model transfer. In *Proceedings of the 52nd Annual Meeting of the Association for Computational Linguistics (Volume 1: Long Papers)*, volume 1, pages 248–258.

Joseph Turian, Lev Ratinov, and Yoshua Bengio. 2010. Word representations: a simple and general method for semi-supervised learning. In *Proceedings of the 48th annual meeting of the association for computational linguistics*, pages 384–394. Association for Computational Linguistics.

Unsupervised Detection of Metaphorical Adjective-Noun Pairs

Malay Pramanick
Department of Computer Science
and Engineering
IIT Kharagpur
West Bengal, India - 721302
`malay.pramanick@`
`iitkgp.ac.in`

Pabitra Mitra
Department of Computer Science
and Engineering
IIT Kharagpur
West Bengal, India - 721302
`pabitra@`
`cse.iitkgp.ernet.in`

Abstract

Metaphor is a popular figure of speech. Popularity of metaphors calls for their automatic identification and interpretation. Most of the unsupervised methods directed at detection of metaphors use some hand-coded knowledge. We propose an unsupervised framework for metaphor detection that does not require any hand-coded knowledge. We applied clustering on features derived from Adjective-Noun pairs for classifying them into two disjoint classes. We experimented with adjective-noun pairs of a popular dataset annotated for metaphors and obtained an accuracy of 72.87% with k-means clustering algorithm.

1 Introduction

Figurative or non-literal elements are ubiquitous in human languages. Usage of non-literal language is popular in day-to-day communications. In this era of Web 2.0, generation of textual data is enormous and thus intractable to be labeled by humans to figure out something from them.

Metaphor is one of the most popular figures of speech. Metaphors are common in online product reviews, blogs, articles and posts in social networking sites. So it has become important for computers to detect metaphors. Interpretation of metaphors comes after their detection in any given text. Also, detection and interpretation of metaphors would definitely help other Natural Language Processing (NLP) tasks like machine translation and summarization.

In 1980, Lakoff and Johnson (1980) proposed Conceptual Metaphor Theory (CMT), in which they claimed that metaphor is not only a property of the language but also a cognitive mechanism that describes our conceptual system. Thus metaphors are devices that transfer the property from one domain to another unrelated or different domain.

Many supervised as well as unsupervised works have been reported on metaphor detection (Shutova, 2015). Supervised methods require annotated dataset and thus resources are required. Most of the existing unsupervised methods use some hand-coded knowledge, making them hard to scale. Many words can be used metaphorically as well as literally, and words are added to the dictionary on a regular basis. So hand-crafted knowledge about domains cannot be relied upon for a long time, as language is an ever-changing phenomenon necessitating updates of the knowledge base from time to time.

In this paper, we categorically propose an unsupervised framework for metaphor detection without using any hand-coded knowledge, making it robust to scale and adaptive to language change. Using the Adjective-Noun (AN) pairs from the dataset created by Tsvetkov et al. (2014), validations were performed using accuracy as measure and the proposed method demonstrated significant results.

2 Related Works

In the recent years, there has been a growing interest in statistical metaphor processing. Many methods, supervised as well as unsupervised, have been proposed for metaphor detection (Shutova, 2015).

Fass (1991) proposed one of the first approaches for metaphor identification and interpretation. The system looked for violated semantic constraints, which are also known as selectional preferences, for identification of metaphors.

TroFi (Trope Finder) (Birke and Sarkar, 2006), is a system that classifies whether a verb is used literally or non-literally, through 'nearly unsupervised' techniques. The system is based on statistical word-sense disambiguation techniques (Karov and Edelman, 1998; Stevenson and Wilks, 2003)

Proceedings of the Workshop on Figurative Language Processing, pages 76–80
New Orleans, Louisiana, June 6, 2018. ©2018 Association for Computational Linguistics

and clustering techniques. "TroFi uses sentential context instead of selectional constraint violations or paths in semantic hierarchies" (Birke and Sarkar, 2006).

Wilks et al. (2013) revisited the idea of violation of selectional preferences. To determine whether a sentence contains a metaphor they extracted the subject and direct object for each verb, using the Stanford Parser. After extraction of verbs from the sentence, they checked for preference violations with the help of WordNet (Miller, 1995; Fellbaum, 1998) and VerbNet (Schuler, 2005) and coming across a violation, they marked it as 'Preference Violation metaphor'. They also considered the 'conventional metaphors' and determined them by using the senses in WordNet.

Based on the theory of meaning, Su et al. (2017) presented a metaphor detection technique, considering the difference between the source and target domains in the semantic level rather than the categories of the domains. They extracted subject-object pair by a dependency parser, which they referred to as 'concept-pair'. They compared the cosine similarity of the concept-pair and from the WordNet, they verified whether the subject was a hypernym or hyponym of the object. When the cosine similarity was below a particular threshold and the 'concept-pair' did not have a hypernym-hyponym relation, it was categorized as metaphorical, otherwise literal.

3 Motivation and Feature Selection

3.1 Cosine Similarity

Pramanick and Mitra (2017) used cosine similarity to detect metaphors in a supervised way. They showed that cosine similarity of contextually dissimilar words can be used for metaphor detection, which they base on the claim that words have "multiple degrees of similarity". Their method aims at detecting metaphors in general, so cosine similarity should be helpful in detecting metaphorical Adjective-Noun pairs.

3.2 Abstractness Ratings

According to Köper and im Walde (2017), "abstract words refer to things that can not be seen, heard, felt, smelled, or tasted as opposed to concrete words." Abstractness of any word is studied by placing the word on a scale ranging between abstract and concrete, known as abstractness ratings. Thus abstractness ratings represent the de-

gree of the abstractness of the thing the word refers to. Abstractness ratings have been shown as a determining factor for metaphor detection (Turney et al., 2011; Dunn, 2013; Tsvetkov et al., 2014; Klebanov et al., 2015; Köper and im Walde, 2016).

3.3 Edit Distance

Alliteration, *assonance* and *consonance* are figures of speech, in which there is a repetition of letters or sounds. Literary devices are rarely used in isolation, so a way to project the repetitions of letters might help in detection of metaphors, especially if the source of the AN pairs is verse.

To project the repetition of letters, we used edit distance. Given two strings **a** and **b**, the edit distance is the minimum number of edit operations that transforms **a** into **b**. The problem with this representation is that the length of the words varies. So we used the ratio of the edit distance to the length of the word. We considered edit distance from *adjective* to *noun* divided by the length of the *adjective*.

The edit distance is not symmetric. It is not necessarily that EditDistance(**a**, **b**) = EditDistance(**b**, **a**). So we also used the edit distance from *noun* to *adjective*, divided by the length of the *noun*.

3.4 Summary of the Features

The features thus considered are :

1. Abstractness rating of the Adjective

2. Abstractness rating of the Noun

3. Modulus of ((Abstractness rating of the adjective) - (Abstractness rating of the noun))

4. Cosine similarity of the Adjective and the Noun

5. Edit distance from the Adjective to the Noun, divided by the length of the Adjective

6. Edit distance from the Noun to the Adjective, divided by the length of the Noun

4 Experiments and Results

4.1 Dataset

Tsvetkov et al. (2014) created a large annotated dataset of Adjective-Noun (AN) pairs (henceforth referred to as **TSV** in this paper). The training set *TSV-Train* consists of 884 metaphorical AN pairs and 884 literal AN pairs, and the test set *TSV-Test* contains 100 metaphorical AN pairs and 100 literal AN pairs. The data was collected by two annotators by using public resources, which was then reduced by at least one additional person "by removing duplicates, weak metaphors and metaphorical phrases (such as *drowning students*) whose interpretation depends on the context".

Literal	Metaphorical
acute bronchitis	acute ignorance
beaten boxer	beaten path
clouded sky	clouded face
deflated tire	deflated meaning
enormous ship	enormous ego
fragile glass	fragile health
growing plant	growing imbalance
heated oven	heated discussion
shattered glass	shattered dreams
terminal station	terminal poverty
unforgiving soldier	unforgiving heights
velvet jeans	velvet voice
whispering kids	whispering breeze
young girl	young money

Table 1: Annotated AN Pairs from TSV-Train

Literal	Metaphorical
angry protester	angry welt
bald eagle	bald assertion
clear sky	clear explanation
empty can	empty promise
dry skin	dry wit
raw meat	raw emotion
sour cherry	sour mood
white sand	white anger

Table 2: Annotated AN Pairs from TSV-Test

4.2 Feature Extraction

We have discussed the features that were used for our experiments and the motivation behind them. Now we discuss how we obtained those features for our experiments. The dataset had some words with accents, which we removed with Unicode (NFKD) normalization during preprocessing, as required for feature extraction.

4.2.1 Cosine Similarity

To obtain the vector representation of words, we used the Google word2Vec[1] (Mikolov et al., 2013), an open source tool. We used text corpus from the latest English Wikipedia dump[2] to train the model and obtained word embeddings of dimension 200.

Word vectors were unavailable for some words and most of them contained a hyphen (-). For each of such words, we tried to find its vector by removing the hyphen, still, if the vector was not obtained, we considered the component-wise average of the vector representation of the parts separated by hyphen.

After getting the word vectors for the adjective and the noun, we calculated their cosine similarity, for our experiments.

4.2.2 Abstractness Ratings

For our experiments, we used the abstractness ratings proposed by Köper and im Walde (2017). They used "a fully connected feed forward neural network with up to two hidden layers" with word vectors of dimension 300 to obtain the ratings, which have been made public.

We took the abstractness ratings of the adjective and noun and divided each of them by ten (10). The division was performed so as to make the ratings comparable to the cosine similarity, as the abstractness ratings range from 0.0 to 10.0. If the abstractness ratings were not scaled, they could have overshadowed the other features considered.

For the words whose ratings were not available, we tried to obtain the rating by removing the hyphen if present. If the abstractness rating was still not obtained, we tried to obtain the abstractness rating by the taking the average of the abstractness ratings of the parts separated by the hyphen.

4.2.3 Edit Distance

With the set of ASCII characters as the alphabet under consideration, the edit operations considered were :

- **Substitution** of a single symbol by another symbol from the alphabet

- **Insertion** of a single symbol from the alphabet

- **Deletion** of a single symbol

Features	Accuracy
Abstractness Ratings	72.31%
Abstractness Ratings + Cosine Similarity	72.56%
Abstractness Ratings + Cosine Similarity + Edit Distance	72.87%

Table 3: Accuracy of K-Means for Entire Dataset

Features	Training Set	Test Set
Abstractness Ratings	71.21%	82.5%
Abstractness Ratings + Cosine Similarity	71.44%	82.5%
Abstractness Ratings + Cosine Similarity + Edit Distance	71.55%	84%

Table 4: Accuracy of K-Means for Training Data and Test Data

4.3 Clustering

K-means was adopted as the clustering algorithm for our experiments. Given a set of d data points, k-means aims to partition the set into k $(k < d)$ sets. For our experiments, we needed two clusters representing metaphors and literals and we can fix the number of clusters in the k-means clustering algorithm.

First, we ran the k-means algorithm to cluster the entire data provided in the dataset. The algorithm was run with the features described above and without the labels of AN pairs being metaphorical or literal as provided in the dataset. K-means was used to partition the data into two disjoint clusters. Randomly we labeled one of the clusters as metaphorical and the other as literal, and calculated the accuracy. If the calculated accuracy was below 50%, we interchanged the cluster labels and calculated the accuracy. This was done as we had two clusters and we did not know which one was supposed to be metaphorical. The accuracy of the algorithm on the entire data of the dataset is summarized in Table 3.

The dataset comes with divisions of training set and test set. So we ran the k-means clustering algorithm with the training set and obtained the clusters. Similar as above, we measured the accuracy for the training set. With the clusters received after running the clustering algorithm on the training data, we used them to predict the labels (metaphorical or literal) of the test data. As the labels were decided for the clusters of the training data, we used the same labels and report the accuracy in Table 4.

5 Discussions

Dependency parsers can be used to extract the nouns along with their adjectival modifiers from running texts to look for Adjective-Noun metaphors or Type-III metaphors as categorized by Krishnakumaran and Zhu (2007). For our experiments, we used TSV, a popular annotated dataset for type-III metaphors.

Turney et al. (2011) used hand-annotated abstractness scores for words to develop their system and reported an accuracy of 0.79 for adjective–noun metaphors but it was rather evaluated on a limited dataset of only 10 adjectives and they had used logistic regression, a supervised method.

Tsvetkov et al. (2014) reported an F-score of 0.85 on the Adjective-Noun classification which is better than the F-score as reported by Shutova et al. (2016). But our method being unsupervised, we cannot compare with their results as they have reported in terms of Precision, Recall and F-score.

6 Conclusion

The paper proposes an unsupervised framework for identification of metaphorical adjective-noun word pairs which was evaluated on the large TSV dataset. Cosine similarity and derivatives of abstractness ratings and edit distance were used for clustering.

The proposed framework does not rely on hand-coded knowledge and learns from patterns using machine learning, providing a statistical approach with significant results, which would help as the language changes. The features used in the experiments can also be used for other languages as they are language independent.

Acknowledgements

We would like to thank Priyanka Sinha and Biswajoy Ghosh for their valuable feedback on the initial draft of this paper. We would also like to thank the anonymous reviewers for their valuable comments and feedback.

References

Julia Birke and Anoop Sarkar. 2006. A clustering approach for nearly unsupervised recognition of nonliteral language. In *EACL*.

Jonathan Dunn. 2013. What metaphor identification systems can tell us about metaphor-in-language. In *Proceedings of the First Workshop on Metaphor in NLP*, pages 1–10.

Dan Fass. 1991. met*: A method for discriminating metonymy and metaphor by computer. *Computational Linguistics*, 17(1):49–90.

Christiane Fellbaum. 1998. *WordNet*. Wiley Online Library.

Yael Karov and Shimon Edelman. 1998. Similarity-based word sense disambiguation. *Computational linguistics*, 24(1):41–59.

Beata Beigman Klebanov, Chee Wee Leong, and Michael Flor. 2015. Supervised word-level metaphor detection: Experiments with concreteness and re-weighting of examples. In *Proceedings of the Third Workshop on Metaphor in NLP*, pages 11–20.

Maximilian Köper and Sabine Schulte im Walde. 2016. Distinguishing literal and non-literal usage of german particle verbs. In *HLT-NAACL*, pages 353–362.

Maximilian Köper and Sabine Schulte im Walde. 2017. Improving verb metaphor detection by propagating abstractness to words, phrases and individual senses. *SENSE 2017*, page 24.

Saisuresh Krishnakumaran and Xiaojin Zhu. 2007. Hunting elusive metaphors using lexical resources. In *Proceedings of the Workshop on Computational approaches to Figurative Language*, pages 13–20. Association for Computational Linguistics.

George Lakoff and Mark Johnson. 1980. *Metaphors we live by*. University of Chicago press.

Tomas Mikolov, Ilya Sutskever, Kai Chen, Greg S Corrado, and Jeff Dean. 2013. Distributed representations of words and phrases and their compositionality. In *Advances in neural information processing systems*, pages 3111–3119.

George A Miller. 1995. Wordnet: a lexical database for english. *Communications of the ACM*, 38(11):39–41.

Malay Pramanick and Pabitra Mitra. 2017. A metaphor detection approach using cosine similarity. In *International Conference on Pattern Recognition and Machine Intelligence*, pages 358–364. Springer.

Karin Kipper Schuler. 2005. Verbnet: A broad-coverage, comprehensive verb lexicon.

Ekaterina Shutova, Douwe Kiela, and Jean Maillard. 2016. Black holes and white rabbits: Metaphor identification with visual features. In *HLT-NAACL*, pages 160–170.

Ekaterina Shutova. 2015. Design and evaluation of metaphor processing systems. *Computational Linguistics*, 41(4):579–623.

Mark Stevenson and Yorick Wilks. 2003. Word sense disambiguation. *The Oxford Handbook of Comp. Linguistics*, pages 249–265.

Chang Su, Shuman Huang, and Yijiang Chen. 2017. Automatic detection and interpretation of nominal metaphor based on the theory of meaning. *Neurocomputing*, 219:300–311.

Yulia Tsvetkov, Leonid Boytsov, Anatole Gershman, Eric Nyberg, and Chris Dyer. 2014. Metaphor detection with cross-lingual model transfer.

Peter D Turney, Yair Neuman, Dan Assaf, and Yohai Cohen. 2011. Literal and metaphorical sense identification through concrete and abstract context. In *Proceedings of the Conference on Empirical Methods in Natural Language Processing*, pages 680–690. Association for Computational Linguistics.

Yorick Wilks, Adam Dalton, James Allen, and Lucian Galescu. 2013. Automatic metaphor detection using large-scale lexical resources and conventional metaphor extraction. In *Proceedings of the First Workshop on Metaphor in NLP*, pages 36–44.

Phrase-Level Metaphor Identification using Distributed Representations of Word Meaning

Omnia Zayed, John P. McCrae, Paul Buitelaar
Insight Centre for Data Analytics
Data Science Institute
National University of Ireland Galway
IDA Business Park, Lower Dangan, Galway, Ireland
`firstname.lastname@insight-centre.org`

Abstract

Metaphor is an essential element of human cognition which is often used to express ideas and emotions that might be difficult to express using literal language. Processing metaphoric language is a challenging task for a wide range of applications ranging from text simplification to psychotherapy. Despite the variety of approaches that are trying to process metaphor, there is still a need for better models that mimic the human cognition while exploiting fewer resources. In this paper, we present an approach based on distributional semantics to identify metaphors on the phrase-level. We investigated the use of different word embeddings models to identify verb-noun pairs where the verb is used metaphorically. Several experiments are conducted to show the performance of the proposed approach on benchmark datasets.

1 Introduction

Metaphor is a stylistic device used to enrich the language and represent abstract concepts using the properties of other concepts. It is considered as an analogy between a tenor (target concept) and a vehicle (source concept) by exploiting common similarities. The sense of a concept such as *"harmful plant"* can be transferred to another concept's sense such as *"poverty"* by exploiting the properties of the first concept. This then can be expressed in our everyday language in terms of linguistic metaphoric expressions such as *"...eradicate poverty"*, *"...root out the causes of poverty"*, or *"...the roots of poverty are..."*[1] (Lakoff and Johnson, 1980; Veale et al., 2016). In this work, a word or an expression is a metaphor if it has at least one basic/literal sense (more concrete, physical) and a secondary metaphoric sense (abstract,

non-physical) which resonates semantically with the basic sense (Steen et al., 2010; Hanks, 2016).

Metaphor processing is one of the most challenging problems for many natural language processing tasks such as machine translation, text summarization and text simplification. Moreover, metaphor processing could be helpful for wider applications such as political discourse analysis (Charteris-Black, 2011) and psychotherapy (Witztum et al., 1988; Gutiérrez et al., 2017).

Understanding metaphors requires deeper levels of language processing that go beyond the sentence surface level. Among the main challenges of the computational modelling of metaphors is their pervasiveness in language which makes them occur frequently in everyday language. Moreover, metaphors are often conventionalised to such an extent that they exhibit no defined lexical patterns or signals. Previous approaches relies on extensive lexical resources to identify metaphors and to capture their semantic features. Feature extraction from an annotated corpus is a challenge as well, not only due to the complexity of the task itself but also due to the lack of high quality annotated corpora. The process of creating such a corpus depends on the task definition as well as the targeted application and often requires significant effort and time.

In this paper, we introduce a semi-supervised approach that makes use of distributed representations of word meaning to capture metaphoricity. We focus on identifying verb-noun pairs where the verb is used metaphorically. We extract verb-noun grammar relations using the Stanford parser (Chen and Manning, 2014). We then employ pre-trained word embeddings models to measure the semantic similarity between the candidate and a predefined seed set of metaphors. A similarity threshold, which was optimised on a sample dataset, is used to classify the given candidate. Evaluation

---

[1]These examples could be found in the United Nations Parallel Corpus (Ziemski et al., 2016).

Proceedings of the Workshop on Figurative Language Processing, pages 81–90
New Orleans, Louisiana, June 6, 2018. ©2018 Association for Computational Linguistics

of the presented approach was carried out on various test sets using different word embeddings algorithms. Additionally, a performance comparison is carried out against the results of the state-of-the-art approach on benchmark datasets.

2 Related Work

One of the most common tasks of the computational processing of metaphors is "metaphor identification" which is concerned with recognising (detecting) the metaphoric expressions in the input text. Metaphor detection could be done on the word-level (token-level) or on the phrase-level by extracting grammatical relations.

In this paper, we are interested in phrase-level linguistic metaphor detection, focusing on verb-noun phrases (grammatical relations) by employing semantic representation of word meaning. Therefore, due to space limitation, we will discuss the most relevant research in this regard in this section. An extensive literature review is presented in (Zhou et al., 2007; Shutova, 2015). Some recent work on metaphor detection has been looking into the utilization of semantic representations through word embeddings representations to design supervised systems for metaphor detection (Rei et al., 2017; Bulat et al., 2017; Shutova et al., 2016). Our approach also utilises such representations but in a semi-supervised manner to avoid the need for large training corpora.

Rei et al. (2017) introduced a neural network architecture to detect adjective-noun and verb-noun metaphoric constructions. Their system comprises three main components which are: word gating, vector representation mapping and a weighted similarity function. The word gating is used to model the association between the properties of the source and target domains which is done via a non-linear transformation of the word embeddings vectors of the given candidate pair. The word embeddings used in this step are obtained from a pre-trained model. Then, a vector representation mapping is carried out to prepare a "new metaphor-specific" vector space using the original word embeddings. Finally, a weighted cosine similarity function is used to automatically select the important vector dimensions for the metaphor detection task. The authors experimented with different pre-trained word representations, namely skip-gram model and an attribute-based model. Two different datasets, which were referred to as the TSV dataset

(Tsvetkov et al., 2013) and the MOH dataset (Mohammad et al., 2016), were used to train the system and optimise its parameters as well as to assess its performance.

Bulat et al. (2017) is a recent approach that investigated whether property-based semantic word representation can provide better concept generalisation for detecting metaphors than dense linguistic representation. The authors proposed property-based vectors through cross-modal mapping between dense linguistic representations and a property-norm semantic space. The authors built a count-based distributional vector and employed a skip-gram model trained on Wikipedia articles as their dense linguistic representations. The property-norm semantic space is obtained from the property-norm dataset (McRae et al., 2005). The TSV dataset is used to train and test a support vector machine (SVM) classifier to classify adjective-noun pairs using the introduced cognitively salient properties as features.

An interesting approach, which employed multi-model embeddings of visual and linguistic features to detect metaphoricity in text, is introduced by Shutova et al. (2016). The proposed approach obtained linguistic word embeddings using a log-linear skip-gram model trained on Wikipedia text and obtained visual embeddings using a deep convolutional neural network trained on image data. This was done for both the words and phrases of adjective-noun and verb-noun pairs individually. Then, the cosine similarity function has been employed to measure the distance between the phrase vector and the corresponding vectors of its constituent words. Metaphor classification is done based on an optimised threshold output of the cosine similarity function. The authors used the TSV and the MOH datasets to train and test their system in addition to optimising the classification thresholds.

Modelling metaphor in a distributional semantic space through linear transformation to improve vector representation has been investigated by Gutiérrez et al. (2016). The authors introduced a compositional distributional semantic framework to identify adjective-noun metaphoric expressions.

A variety of lexical and semantic features including lexical abstractness and concreteness, imageability, named entities, part-of-speech tags, and the word's supersenses[2] using WordNet (Fell-

---

[2]the WordNet lexicographer name of the words first sense

baum, 1998) have been employed to develop supervised systems to detect metaphors (Köper and Schulte im Walde, 2017; Tsvetkov et al., 2013; Hovy et al., 2013; Turney et al., 2011).

Shutova et al. (2010) was among the earliest approaches to computational modelling of metaphor, avoiding task-specific hand-crafted knowledge and huge annotated resources. They introduced a semi-supervised approach to identify verb-noun metaphors using corpus-driven distributional clustering. Their strategy is based on clustering abstract nouns based on their contextual features in order to capture the metaphorical senses associated with the source concept. The system exploits a small set of metaphoric expressions as a seed to detect metaphors in a semi-supervised manner. In a follow-up work, Shutova and Sun (2013) investigated the use of hierarchical graph factorization clustering to derive a network of concepts in order to learn metaphorical associations in an unsupervised way which then was used as features to identify metaphors. We consider the work introduced by Shutova et al. (2010) as a baseline for our proposed approach, thus we are going to explain its reimplementation details in subsection 3.3.

Birke and Sarkar (2006) introduced TroFi, which is considered the first statistical system to identify the metaphorical senses of verbs in a semi-supervised way. The authors adapted a statistical similarity-based word sense disambiguation approach to cluster literal and non-literal senses. A predefined set of seed sentences is utilised to compute the similarity between a given sentence and the seed sentences.

3 Methodology

The idea behind our approach is based on finding synonyms and near-synonyms of metaphors. Our approach employs vector representation and semantic similarity to classify verb-noun pairs extracted from a sentence using a parser as potential candidates for metaphoric classification. A candidate is classified as a metaphor or not by measuring its semantic similarity to a predefined small seed set of metaphors which acts as our existing known metaphors sample. Metaphoric classification is performed based on a previously calculated similarity threshold value on a development dataset. The following subsections explain the hypothesis behind this work and our proposed approach in addition to the reimplementation of

the state-of-the-art semi-supervised system used as our baseline system.

3.1 Hypothesis

Our hypothesis in this work is that a given candidate should have common characteristics and semantic features with some positive examples of metaphors. However, simply calculating the similarity between a given verb-noun candidate and a metaphoric seed is not enough due to the effect of each of the verb and the noun on the overall similarity score. For example, consider a metaphoric seed such as *"break agreement"* and two given candidates such as *"break promise"* and *"break glass"*. The semantic similarities between the word embeddings vectors of the seed and the two candidates measured by the cosine similarity function are 0.5304 and 0.6376, respectively, using a pre-trained Word2Vec (Mikolov et al., 2013) word embedding model on the Google News dataset. This indicates that both candidates are similar to the seed and there is not enough information to tell which one should be classified as a metaphor. Table 1 shows the similarity values of the two candidates and the most similar metaphoric seeds from the predefined seed set. We decided to look into the individual words of the candidate considering the fact that semantically similar or related words will be placed near each other in the embeddings space while unrelated words will be far apart. Therefore, we expect that the noun *"promise"* will be in the neighbourhood of *"agreement"* in the semantic space, while *"glass"* will not. So if both candidates share similar verbs, classification could be done based on the similarity of the nouns; in that case, *"break promise"* can be classified as metaphor due to the vicinity of its noun to the noun of the metaphoric seed while *"break glass"* will not. Since using one positive (metaphoric) example is not enough for precise classification, we used a small set of verb-noun pairs, hereafter referred to as the seed set, where the verb is used metaphorically. The specification of the seed set will be explained in detail in section 4.

3.2 Approach

We start with the seed set of metaphoric verb-noun pairs as $S = \{(V, N)\}$. Given a target verb-noun candidate (v_t, n_t) that needs to be classified, we calculate the distance between every verb v_s in S and the verb of the candidate v_t using the cosine distance measure as follows:

Candidate	Metaphoric Seed	Cosine Similarity	Candidate	Metaphoric Seed	Cosine Similarity
	break agreement	0.6376		break agreement	0.5304
	hold back truth	0.4560		hold back truth	0.3435
	fix term	0.3653		frame question	0.3109
	spell out reason	0.3385		face hour	0.2949
break promise	seize moment	0.3384	break glass	block out thought	0.2701
	glimpse duty	0.3224		seize moment	0.2677
	grasp term	0.3019		throw remark	0.2583
	frame question	0.2959		skim over question	0.2509
	accelerate change	0.2927		mend marriage	0.2375
	throw remark	0.2776		spell out reason	0.2354

Table 1: The cosine similarity between the candidates "break promise" and "break glass" and the top 10 metaphoric seeds in the seed set using a pre-trained Word2Vec word embedding model on Google News dataset.

$$D_{ts} = d(v_t, v_s) \ \ \forall v_s \in S$$

This gives a list of verbs ranked according to the distance to the verb of the candidate; we then select the top n nearest verbs and we get the nouns associated with them in the seed set as follows:

$$Y_{v_t} = top_n\{n_s : (v_s, n_s) \in S\} \text{ by } D_{ts}$$

Finally, the average of the distances between these nouns and the target noun in the candidate phrase is calculated. If this average is less than a threshold δ then the candidate phrase will be classified as a metaphoric expression as follows:

$$\frac{1}{|Y_{v_t}|} \sum_{n_s \in Y_{v_t}} [d(n_t, n_s)] \leq \delta$$

Table 2 shows the cosine distance between the verbs and the nouns of the candidates *"break promise"* and *"break glass"* verses the verbs and the nouns of the top 10 metaphoric seeds from the seed set using a pre-trained Word2Vec word embedding model on the Google News dataset; those 10 seeds have the most similar (nearest in terms of distance) verbs to the candidate verb.

3.3 Baseline

We consider the system introduced by Shutova et al. (2010) as our baseline system. In this subsection, we are going to explain in detail the reimplementation of this approach and the related findings. The system consists of four main components which are: a seed set, a clustering component, a candidate extraction component, and a filtering component. The seed set is obtained from the British National Corpus (BNC) (Burnard,

2009) and consists of 62 metaphoric verb-noun pairs (more details are given in section 4). Spectral clustering (Meila and Shi, 2001) is used to cluster the abstract concepts (nouns) and the concrete concepts (verbs) then an association (mapping) is drawn between the two clusters using the seed set. The candidate extraction component employs the Robust Accurate Statistical Parsing (RASP) parser (Briscoe et al., 2006) to extract verb-subject and verb-direct object grammar relations. After that, the linked clusters (through the seed set) is used to identify potential metaphoric candidates. The filtering component is finally used to filter out these candidates based on a selectional preferences strength (SPS) measure (Resnik, 1993). The verbs exhibiting weak selectional preferences are considered to have lower metaphorical potential. An SPS threshold was set experimentally to be 1.32, thus, the candidates which verbs have an SPS value below this threshold are discarded.

In our reimplementation, we employed the Stanford Parser instead of the RASP Parser to extract the grammar relations and to implement the filtering component to calculate the SPS. SPS is calculated using a simplified Resnik model which models the association of the verb (predicate) with the noun (instead of a class) from the BNC corpus. The verb clusters were originally developed using VerbNet (Schuler, 2006) and the noun clustering were developed using the 2,000 most frequent nouns in the BNC corpus. Since the clusters were obtained from a relatively small dataset we suspected that it might lead to a limited coverage, which will be later shown in the system evaluation.

Cand. V	Seed's V	CosDist	Cand. N	Seed's N	CosDist	Cand. N	Seed's N	CosDist
	break	0		agreement	0.7479		agreement	1.0093
	hold back	0.6591		truth	0.7736		truth	0.8872
	mend	0.6935		marriage	0.9381		marriage	0.9419
	fix	0.6952		term	0.8085		term	1.0252
break	catch	0.6966	promise	contagion	1.0126	glass	contagion	0.9089
	throw	0.7035		remark	0.8513		remark	0.9559
	seize	0.7201		moment	0.8556		moment	0.9510
	impose	0.7350		decision	0.8207		control	0.9506
	impose	0.7350		control	0.9107		decision	0.9987
	frame	0.7371		question	0.8462		question	0.9424

Table 2: The cosine distance between the verbs and nouns of the candidates "break promise" and "break glass" verses the verbs and the nouns of the top 10 metaphoric seeds in the seed set using a pre-trained Word2Vec word embedding model on Google News dataset.

This is one of the limitations of this system; a candidate is either in the clusters or not. And if the candidate's noun appeared in a noun cluster but this cluster was not mapped to the cluster where the verb occurs the candidate will be discarded.

4 System Architecture

As described in Figure 1 below, our system consists of three main components: a parser, a seed set of metaphoric expressions and a pre-trained word embedding model.

Parser: Since our aim is to identify metaphors on the phrase-level, the Stanford parser is used to extract the grammar relations in a given sentence. We used the recurrent neural network (RNN) parser in the Stanford CoreNLP toolkit (Manning et al., 2014) to extract dependencies focusing on verb-subject and verb-direct object grammar relations.

Seed Set: We used the seed set of Shutova et al. (2010) to act as our set of existing known metaphoric expressions (positive examples). The seed set consists of 62 verb-subject and verb-direct object phrases where the verb is used metaphorically[3]. These seeds are extracted originally from a subset of the BNC corpus which contains 761 sentences. These sentences were annotated for grammatical relations to extract the specified grammar relations which are then filtered and manually annotated for metaphoricity. Examples of the

metaphors in the seed set are *"mend marriage, break agreement, cast doubt, and stir excitement"*.

Word Embedding Model: This work utilises distributional vector representation of word meaning to calculate semantic similarity between a candidate and a seed set. Word2Vec and GloVe (Pennington et al., 2014) are two widely used word embeddings algorithms to construct embeddings vectors based on the distributional hypothesis (Firth, 1957) but using different machine learning techniques. In this work, we investigated the effect of using different pre-trained models and similarity measures as shown in detail in the next section.

5 Experimental Settings

In this section, we give an overview of the experimental settings of our proposed approach and the test sets that are used to assess the performance of the methodology described above.

5.1 Models and Parameters

The utilised similarity measures, word embeddings models, and system's parameters are defined as follows:

Similarity Measures: We examined two similarity measures as follows:

- Cosine Distance Metric: The cosine similarity function measures the cosine of the angle between two vectors. Given the vectors u and v, the cosine distance can be defined as:

$$1 - \cos(u, v)$$

---

[3]The seed set provided to us by Shutova et al. (2010) consists of 52 pairs out of which 11 are verb-subjects and 41 are verb-direct object

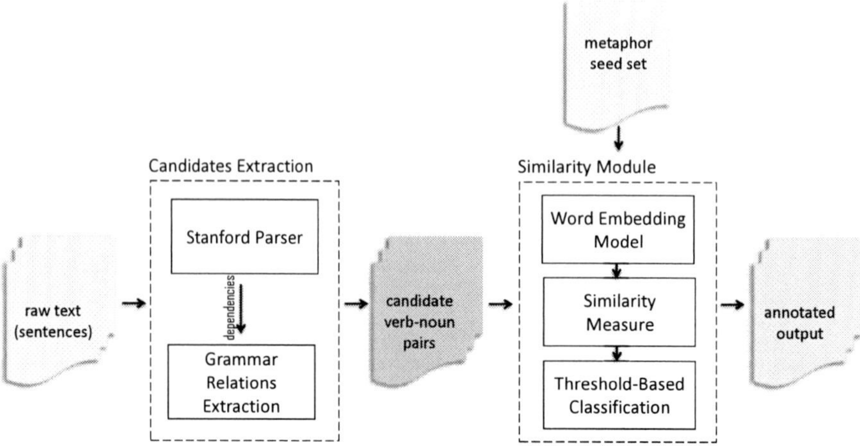

Figure 1: The Overall System Architecture.

– Word Mover's Distance (WMD) (Kusner et al., 2015): could be defined as the minimum travelling distance from one word embeddings vector to the other.

Embeddings Models: We experimented with two different pre-trained vector representations of word embeddings which are:

– Word2Vec Google News[4]: The model is trained on about 100 billion words from the Google News dataset and contains 300-dimensional vectors for 3 million words using the approach described in (Mikolov et al., 2013). The model is based on the skip-gram neural network architecture which employs the negative sampling training algorithm and sub-sampling frequent words using a window-size of 10.

– GloVe Common Crawl[5]: We used a pre-trained model on the Common Crawl dataset containing 840 billion tokens of web data (about 2 million words). The vectors are 300-dimensional using 100 training iteration.

For simplicity, we used a single vector representation for each word ignoring multi-word combina-

tions such as phrasal verbs, examples of which include e.g. *"hold back, flip through"*; we are planning to address this issue in the future.

System's Parameters: We performed experiments on a development set to select the values of the parameters top_n and δ mentioned in subsection 3.2. The best value obtained for n is found to be top 10 nearest verbs. The suitable distance average threshold δ is found to be 0.80 for the GloVe Creative-Commons-840 model and 0.85 for the Word2Vec Google-News model. These values give a good trade-off between false positives and false negatives.

5.2 Test Sets

Two different test sets are used to evaluate our approach as follows:

VUA Test Set: We use a subset of the training verbs dataset from the VU Amsterdam Metaphor Corpus (VUA) (Steen et al., 2010) provided by the NAACL 2018 Metaphor Shared Task [6]. The original VUA corpus is a subset of the BNC Baby corpus consists of 117 texts covering various genres which are academic, conversation, fiction, and news. Although the dataset is annotated on the token-level, its availability and the fact that it is

---

[4] https://code.google.com/archive/p/word2vec/

[5] https://nlp.stanford.edu/projects/glove/

[6] https://github.com/EducationalTestingService/metaphor/tree/master/NAACL-FLP-shared-task

already annotated encouraged us to use it for assessing our approach. The verbs dataset consists of around 17,240 annotated verbs; we retrieved the original sentences of these verbs from the VUA corpus, which yielded around 8,000 sentences. We then parsed these sentences using the Stanford Parser and extracted around 5,000 verb-direct object relations. Arbitrary 300 verb-noun pairs (160 positive and 145 negative examples) are selected to be our test set where the verb is used metaphorically or literally. Table 3 shows some examples from this test set.

MOH dataset: Shutova et al. (2016) introduced a manually annotated dataset of verb-subject and verb-object pairs. The dataset has been referred to as MOH as it was originally obtained from Mohammad et al. (2016) who annotated different senses of verbs in WordNet for metaphoricity. Verbs were selected if they have more than three senses and less than ten senses. Then the example sentences from WordNet for each verb were extracted and annotated by 10 annotators using crowd-sourcing. In a next step, the verb-subject and verb-direct object grammar relations were extracted out of the original dataset. The final dataset consists of 647 pairs out of which 316 instances are metaphorical and 331 instances are literal.

Metaphor	Not Metaphor
reveal approach	collect passport
break corporation	use power
make money	abolish power
see language	perform shuffle
make error	decorate wall
face criticism	put stage
give access	read book
lay foundation	research joke
make time	tell story
abuse status	give key

Table 3: Examples from the VUA test set.

6 Evaluation

In this section, we evaluate our approach using different test sets, pre-trained word embeddings models and similarity measures. Additionally, we compare the performance of our approach against the baseline system explained in subsection 3.3. We used four standard evaluation metrics, namely precision, recall, F-score and accuracy.

6.1 Results

We applied our system to the three test sets introduced above and compared it to the defined baseline system. Table 4 shows the results of the experiment carried out on the VUA test set. It also shows the results obtained from the baseline system. Table 5 shows the performance of our system on the whole MOH dataset.

6.2 Discussion and Analysis

It can be seen from the results above that our approach performs better using GloVe as the pre-trained word embedding model and using cosine distance as the similarity metric. It is also noted that the system suffers from a low recall when using the Word2Vec model with the cosine distance function. This might be due to the limited coverage of the seed set where the top 10 most similar metaphors are not enough to detect new candidates of metaphors. We manually examined our system's output on the MOH dataset. Our system was able to correctly detect metaphoric expressions such as *"absorb knowledge, attack cancer, blur distinction, buy story, capture essence, swallow word, visit illness, wear smile"* as well as literal ones such as *"attack village, build architect, leak container, steam ship, suck poison"*. Some of the false positives, where our system detection was metaphor while the gold label was not, include *"ascend path, blur vision, buy love, communicate anxiety, jam mechanism, lighten room, line book, push crowd"* which could be regarded as metaphors depending on the context.

Our system was able to spot some inconsistency in the annotations of the VUA test set. For example, the verb-noun pair *"win election"* is detected as metaphor by our system while we realised that it has 3 different annotations across the rest of the VUA dataset (the verb *"win"* annotated once as a metaphor and twice as not metaphor while having *"election"* as its direct object). Additionally, in the VUA corpus the verb *"win"* is annotated as metaphor with similar abstract concepts such as in *"win match"* and *"win bid"*. This is one of the differences between preparing a dataset for word-level detection as the VUA corpus or preparing a dataset for phrase-level detection. Moreover, it shows that a verb-noun pair may or may not be metaphoric based on the context. Also, it highlights the minor differences in the views of the

			Precision	Recall	F–score	Accuracy
Shutova et al. (2010) distributional clustering approach			**0.7500**	0.0197	0.0385	0.4915
Our approach	Word2Vec	WMD	0.556	0.8487	0.6719	0.5729
		cosine distance	0.7455	0.2697	0.3961	0.5763
	GloVe	WMD	0.5565	**0.9079**	0.6900	0.5797
		cosine distance	0.6377	0.8684	**0.7354**	**0.6780**

Table 4: Evaluation on the VUA test set of 300 verb-noun pairs and a performance comparison to the baseline system.

			Precision	Recall	F–score	Accuracy
Shutova et al. (2010) distributional clustering approach			**1.0000**	0.0095	0.0189	0.5148
Our approach	Word2Vec	WMD	0.5321	0.8413	0.6519	0.5599
		cosine distance	0.8727	0.1524	0.2595	0.5739
	GloVe	WMD	0.5243	**0.8571**	0.6506	0.5490
		cosine distance	0.6317	0.7460	**0.6841**	**0.6625**

Table 5: Evaluation on the MOH dataset of 647 verb-noun pairs and a performance comparison to the baseline system.

definition of metaphor itself between Lakoff and Johnson (1980) and Steen et al. (2010), which in turn emphasises that the metaphorical sense does not depend solely on the properties of individual words (Gutiérrez et al., 2016).

The results also indicate that the baseline system has a very low recall on the introduced test sets. The reason behind that, as mentioned in subsection 3.3, is that it utilises clusters developed using the BNC corpus, which likely limit the coverage of the system adding into account the limitation of the small seed set (as in our approach). For example, out of the 300 pairs in the VUA test set only 7 candidates were included in the final classification as the rest of the words were not seen before in the clusters. Similarly, out of the 647 pairs in the MOH dataset only 4 were able to be recognised as candidates.

Our system's performance could be improved by increasing the size of the seed set and optimising the system's parameters accordingly (which we are planing to address in the future). In order to investigate this point, we did an additional experiment using 10-fold cross-validation of the MOH dataset in which we included 10 different splits from the dataset as our seed set of metaphors. The best results in terms of precision, recall, F-score, and accuracy are 0.5945, 0.756, 0.6657, and 0.6290, respectively. These results are obtained using the GloVe word embedding model pre-trained on the Common Crawl dataset and the cosine distance as similarity function with the same parameters values. In this experiment, we noticed that the values of n and the threshold δ should be adapted according to the increase in the number of seeds.

We did not to compare our results to Shutova et al. (2016) or Rei et al. (2017) as these systems are not directly comparable to ours. Shutova et al. (2016) is using a different test split from the MOH dataset to evaluate their system. Moreover, both works proposed fully supervised approaches in which they utilise negative (literal) examples as well as positive (metaphoric) examples to train their systems, whereas our approach is semi-supervised (similar to (Shutova et al., 2010)) which uses only the positive (metaphoric) examples. Therefore, carrying out a performance comparison will be imperfect.

7   Conclusion and Future Work

In this work, we presented a semi-supervised approach to detect metaphors using distributional representation of word meaning. Different word embeddings models have been investigated to identify phrase-level metaphors focusing on verb-noun expressions. The system utilises a predefined seed set of metaphoric expressions to detect unseen metaphoric expression(s) in a given sentence. As discussed, in contrast to other state-of-the-art approaches, our proposed approach employs fewer lexical resources and does not require annotated datasets or highly-engineered features. This gives it a flexibility to be easily adapted to new languages or text types. We have performed several experiments to assess the performance of our approach on benchmark datasets. As part of our future work, we are planning to investigate the effect of increasing the number of seeds on the system's coverage and to extend this approach to detect other metaphoric syntactic constructions taking into account multi-word expressions such as phrasal verbs.

Acknowledgments

This work was supported by Science Foundation Ireland under Grant Number SFI/12/RC/2289 (Insight).

References

Julia Birke and Anoop Sarkar. 2006. A clustering approach for nearly unsupervised recognition of non-literal language. In *In Proceedings of the 11th Conference of the European Chapter of the Association for Computational Linguistics*, EACL '06, pages 329–336, Trento, Italy.

Ted Briscoe, John Carroll, and Rebecca Watson. 2006. The second release of the RASP system. In *Proceedings of the Joint Conference of the International Committee on Computational Linguistics and the Association for Computational Linguistics*, COLING-ACL '06, pages 77–80, Stroudsburg, PA, USA. Association for Computational Linguistics.

Luana Bulat, Stephen Clark, and Ekaterina Shutova. 2017. Modelling metaphor with attribute-based semantics. In *Proceedings of the 15th Conference of the European Chapter of the Association for Computational Linguistics*, pages 523–528, Valencia, Spain. Association for Computational Linguistics.

Lou Burnard. 2009. About the British National Corpus. *http://www.natcorp.ox.ac.uk/ corpus/index.xml*.

Jonathan Charteris-Black. 2011. Metaphor in Political Discourse. In *Politicians and Rhetoric: The Persuasive Power of Metaphor*, pages 28–51. Palgrave Macmillan UK, London.

Danqi Chen and Christopher Manning. 2014. A fast and accurate dependency parser using neural networks. In *Proceedings of the 2014 Conference on Empirical Methods in Natural Language Processing*, EMNLP '14, pages 740–750, Doha, Qatar. Association for Computational Linguistics.

Christiane Fellbaum. 1998. *WordNet: An Electronic Lexical Database*. MIT Press.

John R. Firth. 1957. A synopsis of linguistic theory 1930-55. *Studies in Linguistic Analysis (special volume of the Philological Society)*, 1952-59:1–32.

E. Darío Gutiérrez, Guillermo A. Cecchi, Cheryl Corcoran, and Philip Corlett. 2017. Using automated metaphor identification to aid in detection and prediction of first-episode schizophrenia. In *Proceedings of the 2017 Conference on Empirical Methods in Natural Language Processing*, EMNLP '17, pages 2923–2930, Copenhagen, Denmark.

E. Darío Gutiérrez, Ekaterina Shutova, Tyler Marghetis, and Benjamin Bergen. 2016. Literal and metaphorical senses in compositional distributional semantic models. In *Proceedings of the 54th Annual Meeting of the Association for Computational Linguistics*, pages 183–193, Berlin, Germany. Association for Computational Linguistics.

Patrick Hanks. 2016. Three kinds of semantic resonance. In *Proceedings of the 17th EURALEX International Congress*, pages 37–48, Tbilisi, Georgia.

Dirk Hovy, Shashank Srivastava, Sujay Kumar Jauhar, Mrinmaya Sachan, Kartik Goyal, Huiying Li, Whitney Sanders, and Eduard Hovy. 2013. Identifying metaphorical word use with tree kernels. In *Proceedings of the First Workshop on Metaphor in NLP*, pages 52–56, Atlanta, Georgia. Association for Computational Linguistics.

Maximilian Köper and Sabine Schulte im Walde. 2017. Improving verb metaphor detection by propagating abstractness to words, phrases and individual senses. In *Proceedings of the 1st Workshop on Sense, Concept and Entity Representations and their Applications*, SENSE '18, pages 24–30, Valencia, Spain.

Matt J. Kusner, Yu Sun, Nicholas I. Kolkin, and Kilian Q. Weinberger. 2015. From word embeddings to document distances. In *Proceedings of the 32nd International Conference on Machine Learning*, volume 37 of *ICML'15*, pages 957–966, Lille, France.

George Lakoff and Mark Johnson. 1980. *Metaphors we Live by*. University of Chicago Press, Chicago, USA.

Christopher D. Manning, Mihai Surdeanu, John Bauer, Jenny Finkel, Steven J. Bethard, and David McClosky. 2014. The Stanford CoreNLP natural language processing toolkit. In *Proceedings of 52nd Annual Meeting of the Association for Computational Linguistics: System Demonstrations*, pages

55–60, Baltimore, Maryland, USA. Association for Computational Linguistics.

Ken McRae, George S. Cree, Mark S. Seidenberg, and Chris McNorgan. 2005. Semantic feature production norms for a large set of living and nonliving things. *Behavior Research Methods*, 37(4):547–559.

Marina Meila and Jianbo Shi. 2001. A random walks view of spectral segmentation. In *Proceedings of the 8th International Workshop on Artificial Intelligence and Statistics*, AISTATS 2001, Florida, USA.

Tomas Mikolov, Ilya Sutskever, Kai Chen, Greg Corrado, and Jeffrey Dean. 2013. Distributed representations of words and phrases and their compositionality. In *Proceedings of the 26th International Conference on Neural Information Processing Systems - Volume 2*, NIPS'13, pages 3111–3119, Lake Tahoe, Nevada, USA. Curran Associates Inc.

Saif M. Mohammad, Ekaterina Shutova, and Peter D. Turney. 2016. Metaphor as a medium for emotion: An empirical study. In *Proceedings of the 5th Joint Conference on Lexical and Computational Semantics*, *Sem '16, pages 23–33, Berlin, Germany.

Jeffrey Pennington, Richard Socher, and Christopher D. Manning. 2014. GloVe: Global vectors for word representation. In *Proceedings of the 2014 Conference on Empirical Methods in Natural Language Processing*, EMNLP '14, pages 1532–1543, Doha, Qatar. Association for Computational Linguistics.

Marek Rei, Luana Bulat, Douwe Kiela, and Ekaterina Shutova. 2017. Grasping the finer point: A supervised similarity network for metaphor detection. In *Proceedings of the 2017 Conference on Empirical Methods in Natural Language Processing*, EMNLP '17, pages 1537–1546, Copenhagen, Denmark. Association for Computational Linguistics.

Philip Stuart Resnik. 1993. *Selection and Information: A Class-based Approach to Lexical Relationships*. Ph.D. thesis, University of Pennsylvania, Philadelphia, PA, USA.

Karin Kipper Schuler. 2006. *VerbNet: A Broad-Coverage, Comprehensive Verb Lexicon*. Ph.D. thesis, University of Pennsylvania, Philadelphia, PA, USA.

Ekaterina Shutova. 2015. Design and evaluation of metaphor processing systems. *Computational Linguistics*, 41(4):579–623.

Ekaterina Shutova, Douwe Kiela, and Jean Maillard. 2016. Black holes and white rabbits: Metaphor identification with visual features. In *Proceedings of the 15th Annual Conference of the North American Chapter of the Association for Computational Linguistics: Human Language Technologies*, NAACL-HLT '16, pages 160–170, San Diego, California, USA. The Association for Computational Linguistics.

Ekaterina Shutova and Lin Sun. 2013. Unsupervised metaphor identification using hierarchical graph factorization clustering. In *Proceedings of the 2013 Annual Conference of the North American Chapter of the Association for Computational Linguistics: Human Language Technologies*, NAACL-HLT '13, pages 978–988, Atlanta, Georgia. The Association for Computational Linguistics.

Ekaterina Shutova, Lin Sun, and Anna Korhonen. 2010. Metaphor identification using verb and noun clustering. In *Proceedings of the 23rd International Conference on Computational Linguistics*, COLING '10, pages 1002–1010, Beijing, China. Association for Computational Linguistics.

Gerard J. Steen, Aletta G. Dorst, J. Berenike Herrmann, Anna Kaal, Tina Krennmayr, and Trijntje Pasma. 2010. *A Method for Linguistic Metaphor Identification: From MIP to MIPVU*. Converging evidence in language and communication research. John Benjamins Publishing Company.

Yulia Tsvetkov, Elena Mukomel, and Anatole Gershman. 2013. Cross-lingual metaphor detection using common semantic features. In *Proceedings of the First Workshop on Metaphor in NLP*, pages 45–51, Atlanta, Georgia. Association for Computational Linguistics.

Peter D. Turney, Yair Neuman, Dan Assaf, and Yohai Cohen. 2011. Literal and metaphorical sense identification through concrete and abstract context. In *Proceedings of the 2011 Conference on Empirical Methods in Natural Language Processing*, EMNLP '11, pages 680–690, Edinburgh, Scotland, UK. Association for Computational Linguistics.

Tony Veale, Ekaterina Shutova, and Beata Beigman Klebanov. 2016. Metaphor: A Computational Perspective. *Synthesis Lectures on Human Language Technologies*, 9(1):1–160.

Eliezer Witztum, Onno van der Hart, and Barbara Friedman. 1988. The use of metaphors in psychotherapy. *Journal of Contemporary Psychotherapy*, 18(4):270–290.

Chang-Le Zhou, Yun Yang, and Xiao-Xi Huang. 2007. Computational mechanisms for metaphor in languages: A survey. *Journal of Computer Science and Technology*, 22(2):308–319.

Michal Ziemski, Marcin Junczys-Dowmunt, and Bruno Pouliquen. 2016. The United Nations Parallel Corpus v1.0. In *Proceedings of the 10th International Conference on Language Resources and Evaluation*, LREC '16, pages 3530–3534, Portoro, Slovenia.

Bigrams and BiLSTMs
Two neural networks for sequential metaphor detection

Yuri Bizzoni

Centre for Linguistic Theory and
Studies in Probability (CLASP),
Department of Philosophy,
Linguistics and Theory of Science,
University of Gothenburg.
`firstname.lastname@gu.se`

Mehdi Ghanimifard

Centre for Linguistic Theory and
Studies in Probability (CLASP),
Department of Philosophy,
Linguistics and Theory of Science,
University of Gothenburg.
`firstname.lastname@gu.se`

Abstract

We present and compare two alternative deep
neural architectures to perform word-level
metaphor detection on text: a bi-LSTM model
and a new structure based on recursive feedforward concatenation of the input. We discuss different versions of such models and the
effect that input manipulation - specifically, reducing the length of sentences and introducing
concreteness scores for words - have on their
performance. [1]

1 Paper's contribution

This paper describes our contribution to the shared
task on metaphor detection published by NAACL
2018's First Workshop on Figurative Language
Processing.

In this paper, we will:

1. Present and compare two neural network
   models, (1) a bidirectional recurrent neural
   networks for long distance compositions and
   (2) a novel bigram based model for local
   compositions.

2. Show the results of ablation experiments on
   these two models.

3. Present some input manipulations and feature
   enrichment to improve their performance.

The implementation code and additional supple-
mentary material is available here: `https://
github.com/GU-CLASP/ocota`

2 Introduction

Automatic metaphor detection is the task of automatically identifying metaphors in a text or dataset

(Veale et al., 2016). Traditionally, the main approaches to this problem have been of two kinds:
either a set of manually crafted rules was applied
to a text, or a machine learning algorithm was
trained on a source dataset to identify patterns of
features identifying metaphoricity. In the latter
case, typically used features were "psycholinguistics" features such as abstractness or imageability
[2]; hypernym-hyponym coercions as modeled by
resources like WordNet; sequence probabilities as
given by language models; and semantic spaces
or word embeddings. Similar trends can also be
observed in works dealing with other figures of
speech (Zhang and Gelernter, 2015).

The use of word embeddings in metaphor processing - both in detection and interpretation -
is particularly widespread, and distributional semantic spaces may represent the single most consistently used "tool" in this task. Su et al.
(2017) combine word embeddings and WordNet
hypernym/hyponym information to detect nominal
predicative metaphors of the kind "X is Y" and to
select a more literal target - thus producing a paraphrase of the metaphor.

Shutova et al. (2017) use unsupervised and
weakly supervised learning to detect metaphors,
exploiting syntax-aware distributional word vectors.

Gong et al. (2017) use figurative language detection - sarcasm and metaphor - as a way to explore word vector compositionality and try to use
simple cosine distance to tell metaphoric from literal sentences: a word being out of context in a
sentence has a likelihood of being metaphoric.

The reason why semantic spaces are consis-

---

[1] The model product of this paper competed in The Workshop on Figurative Language's Shared Task with team name
OCOTA.

[2] Recent trends tend to see metaphoricity as a nuanced
rather than binary property, and to take into consideration the
correlation between figurativity and affective scoring (Köper
and im Walde, 2016), an umbrella term usually including four
psycolinguistic properties: abstractness, arousal, imageability and valence (Köper and Im Walde, 2016).

Proceedings of the Workshop on Figurative Language Processing, pages 91–101
New Orleans, Louisiana, June 6, 2018. ©2018 Association for Computational Linguistics

tently used in metaphor detection lies in the conception that metaphor, like metonymy and other figures of speech (Nastase and Strube, 2009), is a mainly contextual phenomenon. In this view, a metaphor is fundamentally composed of two different semantic domains, in which one domain acts as source - and is used literally - while the other acts as target - and is used figuratively.

In this frame, semantic spaces appear to be a very flexible and powerful frame to model such semantic domains in terms of words' clustering and distributional similarity (Mohler et al., 2014). Also, semantic spaces are relatively easy to build and handle, giving them an advantage over more time-consuming resources, such as very large knowledge bases and "is A" bases from web corpora, as in Li et al. (2013).

Gutierrez et al. (2016) use the flexibility of word vectors to study the compositional nature of metaphors and the possibility of modeling it in a semantic space.

Tsvetkov et al. (2014) use distributional spaces, together with several other resources such as imageability scores and abstractness to detect metaphors in English and apply a transfer learning system through pivoting on bilingual dictionaries to detect metaphors in multiple language.

A composite approach using both distributional features and psycho-linguistics scores for lexical items is also used by Rai et al. (2016) to perform metaphor detection using conditional random fields.

Metaphor detection with semantic spaces has also been explored in a multimodal frame by Shutova et al. (2016), where systems using only text-based distributional vectors are compared against systems using distributional vectors enriched with visual information.

The link between distributional information and metaphors appears so relevant that some studies presenting new general distributional approaches have elected metaphor detection as a benchmark to test their models (Srivastava and Hovy, 2014), and studies using diversified sets of resources for their classifiers report that distributional vectors are the best performing single device to tackle metaphor detection (Köper and im Walde, 2016).

Finally, Bulat et al. (2017) present a different kind of semantic space, not context-based but attribute-based, to detect and generalize over metaphoric patterns. In such spaces, words are represented by the attributes of the concepts they represent, so that for example *ant* is represented by elements such as *an insect, is black* etc. The authors describe a system to map conventional distributional spaces to pre-existent attribute-based spaces and show that such approach helps detecting metaphoric bigrams.

A recent approach is that of using neural networks for metaphor detection with pretrained word embeddings initialization. Bizzoni et al. (2017) and Rei et al. (2017) proved that this is a valuable strategy to predict metaphoricity in datasets of bigrams without any extra contextual or explicit world knowledge representations. While Bizzoni et al. (2017) show how a simple fully connected neural network is able to learn pre-existing a dataset of metaphoric bigrams with high accuracy and to achieve a better performance than previous approaches, Rei et al. (2017) present an ad-hoc neural design able to compose and detect metaphoric bigrams in two different datasets.

Do Dinh and Gurevych (2016) apply a series of perceptrons to the Amsterdam Corpus combined with word embeddings and part-of-speech tagging, reaching a f-score of .56.

Interestingly, a similar approach - a combination of fully connected networks and pre-trained word embeddings - has also been used as a pre-processing step to metaphor detection, in order to learn word and sense abstractness scores to be used as features in a metaphor identification pipeline (Köper and im Walde, 2017).

3 Corpus

Metaphor processing suffers from a problem of data scarcity: annotated corpora for metaphor detection are relatively rare and of modest proportions.

In this work we will use the VU Amsterdam Metaphor Corpus (Krennmayr and Steen, 2017) train and test our models. To this date, the VU Amsterdam Metaphor Corpus (VUAMC) the largest publicly available annotated corpus for metaphor detection.

Metaphor corpora in other languages do exits, but, to the best of our knowledge, suffer of the same problem of data scarcity.

The VUAMC is divided into four sub-categories representing four different genres: news texts, fiction, academic texts and conversations. Every word in the corpus is manually annotated by several annotators for metaphoricity. In the corpus, metaphor, simile and personification are equated, while also implicit metaphors are taken into consideration. For example, in the sentence *To embark on such a step is not necessarily to succeed immediately in realizing it* the word *it* is considered an implicit metaphor since it refers to the words *step* that was used metaphorically.

The corpus covers about 190,000 lexical units, randomly selected from the BNC Baby corpus.

According to Krennmayr and Steen (2017), the genre with a higher percentage of manually detected metaphors is academic texts (18.5%), followed by news (16.4%), fiction ("only" 11.9%) and conversation (7.7%). Given the very fine-grained nature of metaphor annotation applied to the corpus, the authors also find that the parts of speech that tend to be used metaphorically most often are prepositions and verbs, followed adjectives and nouns.

Due to its dimensions, diversity and accessibility, the VU Amsterdam Metaphor Corpus has been used in a number of studies. Using it can provide a direct comparison to important previous works and proposed models. This makes of the VUAMC a valuable resource for metaphor detection and processing.

Nonetheless, the VU Amsterdam Metaphor Corpus presents some difficulties: the semantic annotation of metaphor can be extremely fine-grained and cross the boundaries with word sense disambiguation.

For example, in the sentence:

> The 63-year-old head of Pembridge Investments, through which the bid is being mounted says, 'rule number one in this business is: the more luxurious the luncheon rooms at headquarters, the more inefficient the business'.[*ale-fragment01-5*]

three words were annotated as metaphoric: *head, through, mounted, rule, in, this* and *headquarters*.

Sometimes the annotation itself can be puzzling or questionable. In the sentence:

> There are other things he has, on his own admission, not fully investigated, like the value of the DRG properties, or which part of the DRG business he would keep after the break up . [*ale-fragment01-7*]

the following words are annotated as metaphoric: *things, on, admission, part, keep* and *after*.

While the very fine-grained metaphoricity of *things, part* and *keep* is to some extent still understandable - these terms are not used in their physical sense to indicate material objects, such as a concrete slice of something, or the act of physically keeping something with oneself - the metaphoric nature of *admission* remains quite opaque. At the same time, it is not clear why the annotators ignored the metaphoric interpretation of *the break up*.

There are also harder to explain examples, at least from our perspective. The sentence

> Going to bed with Jean fucking, fucking shite! [*kbd-fragment07-2586*]

is annotated as completely literal - no metaphoric usage is detected by the annotators.

In the sentence

> Take that fucking urbane look off your face and face reality, Adam [*fpb-fragment01-1343*]

the following words are annotated as metaphoric: *take, that, off, face*.

All the remaining terms have to be considered as literal, which looks slightly incoherent with the previous fine-grained metaphoricity annotations.

4 Models

4.1 Architectures

In this work we present two alternative neural architectures to process sentences as input and predict words' metaphoricity as output.

The first model we discuss is composed of a bi-directional LSTM (Schuster and Paliwal, 1997) and two fully connected or dense layers, having respectively dimensionality of 32, 20 and 1. We will also show results for deeper and more shallow alternative versions of this model.

Sun and Xie (2017) recently tried to tackle verb metaphor detection on the TroFi corpus (Birke and Sarkar, 2006) using Bi-LSTMs with word embeddings. For their study they tried different kinds of input: using the whole sentence; using a sub-sequence composed of the target verb and all its dependents; using a sub-sequence composed of the target verb, its subject and its object. Interestingly, they show that the simplest approach -

taking into consideration the whole sentence - returns the best results, with an F score only slightly lower than that achieved by a composite approach taking into consideration all of the previous different inputs together.

The main difference with our architecture is the presence of the final Perceptrons (fully connected networks). Sun and Xie (2017) don't mention further hidden layers beyond the bi-LSTM.

We also don't have any form of syntactic preprocessing and we only use the sequence of the standard word embeddings to represent the whole sentence. Finally, we are interested in considering the different performances of bi-LSTMs on different part-of-speech elements: metaphor recognition on functional words is supposedly harder, since these words have a more complex semantic signature in distributional spaces.

In this spirit we find worth it approaching the problem with a relatively "standard" neural framework.

The second model we discuss is a simple sequence of fully connected neural networks.

We present the design of this architecture in Figure 1.

This model is a generalization of neural architectures for bigram phrase compositions as tested on Adjective-Noun phrases in Bizzoni et al. (2017). While a similar approach is already attempted in Do Dinh and Gurevych (2016), we introduce a recursive variant which can make the compositions deeper and while allowing wide window sizes. There have been more sophisticated architectures such as Kalchbrenner et al. (2014), which take a similar approach for sentence representation with convolutional neural networks, but we propose a simpler method only using dense compositions.

We built our architecture using the Python library Keras (Chollet et al., 2015).

For both our models we used Adam optimizer.

4.2 Input manipulation

We compare two different features representations: 1. different word embeddings, 2. concreteness scores as word representations. In addition to ablation test for feature representations, we examined the effect of breaking sentences in shorter sequences.

Embeddings We tried two types of pre-trained word embeddings both with 300 dimensions: (1)

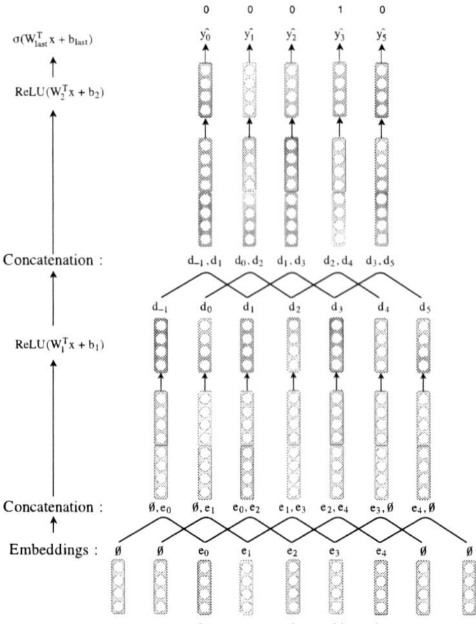

Figure 1: Bigram composition networks with depth $n = 2$.

GloVe (Pennington et al., 2014) (2) Word2Vec (Mikolov et al., 2013). Since these vector spaces are trained on different corpora, there are some out-of-vocabulary words, we represent these words with zero vectors. Additionally, Word2Vec is using a sub-sampling technique for more efficiency which consequently it doesn't cover most frequent words. In order to expand the word-coverage, we also trained GloVe embeddings on British National Corpus (Consortium et al., 2007) from which the VUAMC corpus was sampled, and compared it with both pre-trained Word2Vec embeddings on Google News corpus and standard GloVe embeddings trained on Common Crawl corpus.

Explicit features It has been observed in several works that metaphoricity judgments are partially related to a gap in concreteness between the target word and its context. Köper and im Walde (2017) try detecting all metaphoric verbs in the Amsterdam corpus using this single feature. Bizzoni et al. (2017) show how a network trained for metaphor detection on pairs of word embeddings can "side-learn" noun abstractness.

A metaphor functioning on this axis is composed of an abstract and a concrete element: in such case, usually, the concrete element is the metaphoric one. The expression "In a window of 5 years, between 2011 and 2016" could be considered a metaphor playing on this level, where the more concrete word "window" has a metaphoric sense.

There are kinds of metaphors functioning at different semantic levels: for example a synesthesia, which can be considered a sub-type of metaphor, is an expression where a word linked to a sensorial field is used to refer to a term that pertains to another sensorial field.

In this case, the features used metaphorically are usually on a similar level of abstractness. However, for our purposes the abstract-concrete features may be among the most important to take into consideration.

While the abstract-concrete polarity is represented in distributional embeddings, it is possible that taking such features more explicitly into consideration would help a neural classifier. Brysbaert et al. (2014) released a list of almost forty thousand English words annotated along the concrete-abstract axis, annotated by over four thousand participants.

We try using such scores as an extra dimension for the distributional embeddings: we thus obtain sequences of 301-dimensional embeddings, the last dimension being the human rating of concreteness. For the out-of-vocabulary words we use the average concreteness value of 2.5.

This resource allows us to assign to (almost) every word in the dataset an explicit concreteness score. When a word might have more than one sense, the annotations seem to use the most concrete one: for example the word "node" has a concreteness score of 4 out of 5. For comparison the words "output" and "literally" have a score of 2.48 and the word "being" has a score of 1.93.

It must be noted that the abstract-concrete gap is not necessarily the best way to describe the kind of metaphors represented in this specific corpus. The network should be able to mark as metaphoric words in this dataset that have a low level of concreteness, such as "approach" (2.76), in equally abstract contexts, such as "latest corporate reveals laid-back approach" (here "approach" was marked as metaphoric in VUAMC).

Many of the metaphoric uses outlined here are so ingrained in language that their actual concrete origins may be under-represented not only in modern day corpora, but even in many mod-

Concreteness score window	number of words
1-2	38 262
2-3	36 730
3-4	28 664
4-5	14 473

Table 1: Concrete and abstract tokens in VUAM corpus according to Brysbaert et al. (2014) dataset.

ern day annotators' minds. We discussed various cases of this problem in the section about the corpus: words that have gradually assumed a new and main sense in the English language are often annotated as metaphors in the VUAMC.

Nonetheless, the abstract-concrete polarity remains one of the main semantic dimensions to interpret and understand metaphors and has been explicitly used in several metaphor detection tasks with promising results.

We can thus partly revert to feature engineering and see whether adding this dimension can improve the performance of our models.

Sentence breaking Including long sentences in our training dataset makes it necessary to consistently pad short sentences with zero-vectors. In our experiments we have seen that this seems to slow down and harm training for our models, since they will try to learn both patterns for sequences of pre-trained embeddings and patterns for long sequences of vectors filled with 0s.

To partly avoid this problem, we can break long sentences into two or more shorter elements. We assume that long distance information is not particularly important here to detect metaphoricity, while long padding can affect performance.

4.3 Preprocessing

We chose a maximum sentence length of 50: while the longest sentence in the dataset is 87 words, the vast majority of the elements in the dataset is less than 50 words long. Out of vocabulary words, which are words that did not have a corresponding vector in our embedding space, were replaced by a mock vector of all zeros. After shuffling the dataset, we use the first 1000 sentences of the corpus as test, and the rest of the data for training (11122 sentences). We used the same training and test data for all reported results.

4.4 Loss function

The design of the models is to predict the metaphoricity of each word in a sentence. The predicted value from a final layer with sigmoid activation is compared with the labeled data and usual logarithmic loss is used. However, most words do not have specified metaphoric or literal annotations in the dataset. Instead of assigning a non-metaphor value to unspecified tokens in a string, we modified the loss function in order to generate zero loss for these tokens.

4.5 Training

After shuffling the training data, 1000 samples are taken as holdout to find the overfitting point. With batch size 64 and and early stopping patience 3 based on validation loss we trained each model up to 15 epochs.

5 Results

5.1 Embeddings

Through a comparison of different semantic spaces, we found that the best performing space was GloVe trained on 42B Common Crawl, of dimensionality 300.

For the rest of our experiments we used these embeddings.

5.2 Baseline

In Table 2, we compare the results obtained from previous works on this task, and the performance of the "vanilla" settings of our model including a simple LSTM as our baselines. The comparison with Do Dinh and Gurevych (2016) shows that deploying deeper and more complex architectures on this set does not return particularly large improvements: we achieve an F1-score one point higher than Do Dinh and Gurevych (2016)'s results on a setting enriched with POS tags, and two points higher than the simplest model proposed in the paper.

It can be observed that our bigram composition architecture seems to produce comparable results considering the previous works. The influence of LSTM architectures appears thus further diminished.

Table 3 presents precision, recall and F-score values for several concatenation windows of our composition model. These results can be compared to the ones we obtain with deep Bi-LSTM models. Without external features such as concreteness or POS tagging, composing the input improves the model's performance up to a window of 3. Larger windows reduce the performance of the model.

In Table 4 we report the tests with different settings on depth and width of each layer.

It seems that widening the dimensionality of the Bi-LSTM itself beyond a certain limit does not improve - and rather harms - the model's performance in classification.

Regarding our first model, completely relying on the power of the Bi-LSTM architecture is not enough, and deeper fully connected layers are clearly playing a role.

We can also see that inserting a fully connected layer before the Bi-LSTM returns better results. This layer has a number of nodes as large as the number of dimensions of the input token embeddings. It can be another clue that the most relevant information for this task has to be searched in the word embeddings composing the sentence and their immediate surrounding, rather than in the structure of the whole sequence.

In conclusion, our results show that a quite standard deep neural architecture fed with good word embeddings can return promising results in metaphor detection. The "compositional" architecture also achieves comparable results, with an F score only a couple of points lower than that of the Bi-LSTM, indicating that "forcing" a network to give particular attention to the short or immediate context of each word in the data can improve its performance all the while reducing its depth, complexity and number of parameters. While this approach is not the one returning the absolute best F score, we consider the trade-off between its simplicity and its performance worth noting.

Our results also show a negative aspect: while we consider our models' performances encouraging, there is an ample room for improvement.

5.3 Feature experiments

Interestingly adding explicit semantic information such as concreteness ratings in our input - which means, somehow, reverting to feature engineering - did produce better results for the composition architecture, but not yet for our Bi-LSTM.

Table 5 show the results of our best performing models when the concreteness of the individual token was explicitly added to the embeddings.

Architecture	F1
Haagsma and Bjerva (2016)	.53
Do Dinh and Gurevych (2016)[3]	.56
Dense(1)	.22
LSTM(32)	.43
Bi-LSTM(32)	.46
Bi-LSTM(32)+Dense(20)	.50
Dense(300)+Bi-LSTM(32)+Dense(20)	**.56**
Concat(n=2)+Dense(300)	.55

Table 2: Performance of different models compared to the score reported by two relevant works in the literature. We report the performance of simpler models and their combinations as baselines. We used some abbreviations to describe the models in the table. For example, *Dense(1)* represents a single, fully connected layer of output length of 1, *LSTM(32)* is an LSTM with an output length of 32 and *Concat* represents our compositional model. Thus, *Concat(n=2)+Dense(300)* represents the bigram composition model with a concatenation window of 2 combined with a fully connected layer of 300 output units.

N	Precision	Recall	F1 score
1	.627	.459	.530
2	.588	.504	.543
3	.571	.531	**.550**
4	.649	.402	.497

Table 3: F1 for different windows of concatenation (N) in the composition model. N=1 is equivalent to no concatenation.

The results are higher than those returned by the same models trained and tested on the same sentences only with pre-trained distributional embeddings. It appears that simply adding the concreteness feature returns a better performance on the whole dataset. It is worth noting that in this case, and only in this case, the "compositional" architecture is the best performing, while the bi-LSTM has a harder time detecting metaphors in the textual data.

Finally, we try to break long sentences into shorter sequences, as we discussed in 4.2. The metaphors identified in the VUAM corpus do not generally require long-distance information to be detected. We can observe that this method improves the performance of our models: this is probably because the "noise" due to long padding of short sentences is reduced. Having less contextual information for words tagged as metaphoric or literal does not seem to have a real negative impact on the learning process.

As we show in Table 6, breaking sentences longer than 20 tokens into several short sequences reduces the number of misclassified elements in the set.

Not surprisingly, a combination of these two methods - adding explicit concreteness information and breaking long sentences - returns the best overall results, as can be seen in Table 7.

Finally, since these experiments were originally designed for the shared task in metaphor detection of the First Workshop in Figurative Language (NAACL 2018), in Table 8 we report our best performing models' results on the evaluation set provided in the task.

The last line reports the result from using both models together: as can be seen, the F score we get from taking into consideration the output of both architectures together is higher than the F score of the single models.

We can suppose that the two models are learning to detect slightly different kinds of metaphors - their true positives are not completely overlapping - and they can thus complement each other.

6   Conclusions

In the frame of NAACL 2018's shared task on metaphor detection, we explored two main approaches to detect metaphoricity through deep learning and compared their performances with different kinds of inputs. The overall single best performing system is a deep neural network composed of a bi-LSTM preceded and followed by fully connected layers, having access to concreteness scores for each token and running on relatively short sequences - thus reducing the effects of sentence padding.

We show that adding such features, our model is

Architecture	F1
Bi-LSTM(32)	.46
Bi-LSTM(32)+Dense(20)	.50
Bi-LSTM(400)+Dense(20)	.47
Bi-LSTM(32)+LSTM(32)+Dense(20)	.35
Bi-LSTM(400)+LSTM(32)+Dense(20)	.43
Dense(300)+Bi-LSTM(32)+Dense(20)	**.56**
Dense(300)+Bi-LSTM(300)+Dense(20)	**.56**
Dense(300)+Bi-LSTM(300)+LSTM(20)+Dense(20)	**.57**
Dense(300)+Bi-LSTM(300)+LSTM(100)+Dense(20)	.40

Table 4: Parameter tuning, testing both deeper and wider settings of the model. We write in parenthesis the dimensions each layer: for example *Dense(20)* is a fully connected layer with an output space of dimensionality 20.

N	Precision	Recall	F1
Dense(300)+Bi-LSTM(32)+Dense(20)	.642	.498	.561
Dense(301)+Bi-LSTM(32)+Dense(20)+Conc	.580	.491	.530
Concat(n=2)+Dense(300)+Conc	.554	.570	.562
Concat(n=3)+Dense(300)+Conc	.567	.593	**.580**

Table 5: Results for different models using embeddings enriched with explicit information regarding word concreteness. The first line works as baseline showing a model without input manipulation. *Concat(n=)* represents our compositional model, with *n=* representing the composition window length. *Conc* signifies the usage of concreteness scores. So for example *Concat(n=2)+Dense(300)+Conc* represents our compositional model with concatenation window of 2 combined with a fully connected layer of 300 output units and using the concreteness scores as additional information.

N	Precision	Recall	F1
Dense(300)+Bi-LSTM(32)+Dense(20)	.642	.498	.561
Dense(300)+Bi-LSTM(32)+Dense(20)+Chunk	.671	.570	**.621**
Concat(n=2)+Dense(300)+Chunk	.571	.561	.560
Concat(n=3)+Dense(300)+Chunk	.611	.400	.491

Table 6: Results for different models using sentence breaking to 20 (any sentence longer than 20 tokens is split in two parts treated as complete different sentences). The first line works as baseline showing a model without input manipulation. *Concat(n=)* represents our compositional model, *Chunk* signifies the usage of sentence breaking.

N	Precision	Recall	F1
Dense(300)+Bi-LSTM(32)+Dense(20)	.642	.498	.561
Dense(300)+Bi-LSTM(32)+Dense(20)+Chunk	.670	.571	.620
Dense(301)+Bi-LSTM(32)+Dense(20)+Conc	.581	.490	.531
Dense(301)+Bi-LSTM(32)+Dense(20)+Conc+Chunk	.649	.624	**.636**
Concat(n=3)+Dense(300)+Conc+Chunk	.632	.446	.523

Table 7: Results for different models using embeddings enriched with explicit information regarding word concreteness and sentence breaking to 20 (any sentence longer than 20 tokens is split in two parts treated as complete different sentences). The first lines work as baselines showing the performance of previous models (without any input manipulation, only chunking, only concreteness scores). *Concat(n=)* represents our compositional model, *Chunk* signifies the usage of sentence breaking, *Conc* represents the usage of concreteness scores.

N	Precision	Recall	F1
Dense(300)+Bi-LSTM(32)+Dense(20)	.638	.593	.615
Concat(n=2)+Dense(300)	.642	.498	.561
Combined results	.595	.680	**.635**

Table 8: Results for the evaluation set from the shared dataset competition (NAACL 2018). We used sentence breaking and concreteness information.

able to slightly outperform two baselines recently published.

We also found that combining these two systems gave the best results on the test set provided by the shared task.

Considering the difficult nature of the original annotations, we judge this a promising result. It could be the case that adding more explicit features further helps reduce the number of inconsistent detections on the corpus, but one of the goals of these experiments was that of keeping the feature engineering as contained as possible, reducing the number of external resources used to enrich the input.

We also explored a simpler neural architecture based on the recursive composition of word embeddings. Yielding a slighlty worse performance than the Bi-LSTM architecture, this model still shows that a much simpler architecture can reach interesting results.

7 Future Works

We think that an in depth error analysis of our models' shortcomings might represent an interesting contribution in order to better understand what neural networks are learning when they are learning metaphor detection. In future we would like to perform a systematic analysis of the errors of our networks both when used alone and when used in combination.

We would also like to extend the range of our comparisons to different, and simpler, machine learning algorithms to see to what extent the information provided in input - in terms of distributional information and explicit lexical scores - contributes to the performance of our models. While a consistent body of works on metaphor detection with "traditional" machine learning means already exists, we think that a direct comparison of our networks with other systems might help clarifying the contribution of deep learning to this task.

Acknowledgments

We are grateful to our colleagues in the Centre for Linguistic Theory and Studies in Probability (CLASP), FLoV, at the University of Gothenburg for useful discussion of some of the ideas presented in this paper.

We are also grateful to three anonymous reviewers for their several helpful comments on our earlier draft.

The research reported here was done at CLASP, which is supported by a 10 year research grant (grant 2014-39) from the Swedish Research Council.

References

Julia Birke and Anoop Sarkar. 2006. A clustering approach for nearly unsupervised recognition of non-literal language. In *11th Conference of the European Chapter of the Association for Computational Linguistics*.

Yuri Bizzoni, Stergios Chatzikyriakidis, and Mehdi Ghanimifard. 2017. " deep" learning: Detecting metaphoricity in adjective-noun pairs. In *Proceedings of the Workshop on Stylistic Variation*, pages 43–52.

Marc Brysbaert, Amy Beth Warriner, and Victor Kuperman. 2014. Concreteness ratings for 40 thousand generally known english word lemmas. *Behavior research methods*, 46(3):904–911.

Luana Bulat, Stephen Clark, and Ekaterina Shutova. 2017. Modelling metaphor with attribute-based semantics. In *Proceedings of the 15th Conference of the European Chapter of the Association for Computational Linguistics: Volume 2, Short Papers*, volume 2, pages 523–528.

François Chollet et al. 2015. Keras. `https://github.com/keras-team/keras`.

British National Corpus Consortium et al. 2007. British national corpus version 3 (bnc xml edition). *Distributed by Oxford University Computing Services on behalf of the BNC Consortium. Retrieved February*, 13:2012.

Erik-Lân Do Dinh and Iryna Gurevych. 2016. Token-level metaphor detection using neural networks. In *Proceedings of the Fourth Workshop on Metaphor in NLP*, pages 28–33.

Hongyu Gong, Suma Bhat, and Pramod Viswanath. 2017. Geometry of compositionality. In *AAAI*, pages 3202–3208.

E Dario Gutierrez, Ekaterina Shutova, Tyler Marghetis, and Benjamin Bergen. 2016. Literal and metaphorical senses in compositional distributional semantic models. In *Proceedings of the 54th Annual Meeting of the Association for Computational Linguistics (Volume 1: Long Papers)*, volume 1, pages 183–193.

Hessel Haagsma and Johannes Bjerva. 2016. Detecting novel metaphor using selectional preference information. In *Proceedings of the Fourth Workshop on Metaphor in NLP*, pages 10–17.

Nal Kalchbrenner, Edward Grefenstette, and Phil Blunsom. 2014. A convolutional neural network for modelling sentences. In *Proceedings of the 52nd Annual Meeting of the Association for Computational Linguistics (Volume 1: Long Papers)*, volume 1, pages 655–665.

Maximilian Köper and Sabine Schulte Im Walde. 2016. Automatically generated affective norms of abstractness, arousal, imageability and valence for 350 000 german lemmas. In *LREC*.

Maximilian Köper and Sabine Schulte im Walde. 2016. Distinguishing literal and non-literal usage of german particle verbs. In *HLT-NAACL*, pages 353–362.

Maximilian Köper and Sabine Schulte im Walde. 2017. Improving verb metaphor detection by propagating abstractness to words, phrases and individual senses. In *Proceedings of the 1st Workshop on Sense, Concept and Entity Representations and their Applications*, pages 24–30.

Tina Krennmayr and Gerard Steen. 2017. Vu amsterdam metaphor corpus. In *Handbook of Linguistic Annotation*, pages 1053–1071. Springer.

Hongsong Li, Kenny Q Zhu, and Haixun Wang. 2013. Data-driven metaphor recognition and explanation. *Transactions of the Association for Computational Linguistics*, 1:379–390.

Tomas Mikolov, Ilya Sutskever, Kai Chen, Greg S Corrado, and Jeff Dean. 2013. Distributed representations of words and phrases and their compositionality. In *Advances in neural information processing systems*, pages 3111–3119.

Michael Mohler, Bryan Rink, David B Bracewell, and Marc T Tomlinson. 2014. A novel distributional approach to multilingual conceptual metaphor recognition. In *COLING*, pages 1752–1763.

Vivi Nastase and Michael Strube. 2009. Combining collocations, lexical and encyclopedic knowledge for metonymy resolution. In *Proceedings of the 2009 Conference on Empirical Methods in Natural Language Processing: Volume 2-Volume 2*, pages 910–918. Association for Computational Linguistics.

Jeffrey Pennington, Richard Socher, and Christopher D. Manning. 2014. Glove: Global vectors for word representation. In *Empirical Methods in Natural Language Processing (EMNLP)*, pages 1532–1543.

Sunny Rai, Shampa Chakraverty, and Devendra K Tayal. 2016. Supervised metaphor detection using conditional random fields. In *Proceedings of the Fourth Workshop on Metaphor in NLP*, pages 18–27.

Marek Rei, Luana Bulat, Douwe Kiela, and Ekaterina Shutova. 2017. Grasping the finer point: A supervised similarity network for metaphor detection. *arXiv preprint arXiv:1709.00575*.

Mike Schuster and Kuldip K Paliwal. 1997. Bidirectional recurrent neural networks. *IEEE Transactions on Signal Processing*, 45(11):2673–2681.

Ekaterina Shutova, Douwe Kiela, and Jean Maillard. 2016. Black holes and white rabbits: Metaphor identification with visual features. In *Proceedings of the 2016 Conference of the North American Chapter of the Association for Computational Linguistics: Human Language Technologies*, pages 160–170.

Ekaterina Shutova, Lin Sun, Elkin Dario Gutierrez, Patricia Lichtenstein, and Srini Narayanan. 2017. Multilingual metaphor processing: Experiments with semi-supervised and unsupervised learning. *Computational Linguistics*.

Shashank Srivastava and Eduard Hovy. 2014. Vector space semantics with frequency-driven motifs. In *Proceedings of the 52nd Annual Meeting of the Association for Computational Linguistics (Volume 1: Long Papers)*, volume 1, pages 634–643.

Chang Su, Shuman Huang, and Yijiang Chen. 2017. Automatic detection and interpretation of nominal metaphor based on the theory of meaning. *Neurocomputing*, 219:300–311.

Shichao Sun and Zhipeng Xie. 2017. Bilstm-based models for metaphor detection. In *National CCF Conference on Natural Language Processing and Chinese Computing*, pages 431–442. Springer.

Yulia Tsvetkov, Leonid Boytsov, Anatole Gershman, Eric Nyberg, and Chris Dyer. 2014. Metaphor detection with cross-lingual model transfer. In *Proceedings of the 52nd Annual Meeting of the Association for Computational Linguistics (Volume 1: Long Papers)*, volume 1, pages 248–258.

Tony Veale, Ekaterina Shutova, and Beata Beigman Klebanov. 2016. Metaphor: A computational perspective. *Synthesis Lectures on Human Language Technologies*, 9(1):1–160.

Wei Zhang and Judith Gelernter. 2015. Exploring metaphorical senses and word representations for identifying metonyms. *arXiv preprint arXiv:1508.04515*.

Computationally Constructed Concepts: A Machine Learning Approach to Metaphor Interpretation Using Usage-Based Construction Grammatical Cues

Zachary Rosen
Department of Linguistics
The University of Colorado, Boulder
295 UCB, Boulder, CO 80309
`Zachary.P.Rosen@colorado.EDU`

Abstract

The current study seeks to implement a deep learning classification algorithm using argument-structure level representation of metaphoric constructions, for the identification of source domain mappings in metaphoric utterances. It thus builds on previous work in computational metaphor interpretation (Mohler et al. 2014; Shutova 2010; Bollegala & Shutova 2013; Hong 2016; Su et al. 2017) while implementing a theoretical framework based off of work in the interface of metaphor and construction grammar (Sullivan 2006, 2007, 2013). The results indicate that it is possible to achieve an accuracy of approximately 80.4% using the proposed method, combining construction grammatical features with a simple deep learning NN. I attribute this increase in accuracy to the use of constructional cues, extracted from the raw text of metaphoric instances.

1 Introduction

Lakoff's theory of conceptual metaphor has been highly influential in cognitive linguistic research since its initial publication (Lakoff & Johnson 1980). Conceptual metaphors represent fine-grained mappings of abstract concepts like "love" to more concrete, tangible phenomena, like "journeys" which have material and culturally salient attributes like a PATH, various LANDMARKS, and a THEME which undergoes movement from a SOURCE to a GOAL (Lakoff & Johnson 1980). These tangible phenomena then serve as the basis for models from which speakers can reason about abstract ideas in a culturally transmissible manner. For example, consider the following metaphoric mappings for the metaphor LOVE IS MAGIC, as shown in figure 1.

To date, while automatic metaphor detection has been explored in some length, computational metaphor interpretation is still relatively new, and a growing number of researchers are beginning to explore the topic in greater depth. Recently, work by the team behind Berkeley's MetaNet has shown that a constructional and frame-semantic ontology can be used to accurately identify metaphoric utterances and generate possible source domain mappings, though at the cost of requiring a large database of metaphoric exemplars (Dodge et al. 2015; Hong 2016). Researchers from the Department of Cognitive Science at Xiamen University (Su et al. 2017) report that, using word embeddings, they have created a system that can reliably identify nominal-specific conceptual metaphors as well as interpret them, albeit within a very limited scope–the nominal modifier metaphors that they work with only include metaphors in which the source and target domain share what they refer to as a "direct ancestor", such as in the case of "the surgeon is a butcher", limiting researchers to analyzing noun phrases with modifiers that exist in a single source and target domain. Other approaches have included developing literal paraphrases of metaphoric utterances (Shutova 2010; Bollegala & Shutova 2013), and, as an ancestor to the current study, clustering thematic co-occurents–the AGENT, PATIENT, and ATTRIBUTE of the metaphoric sentence–which allowed researchers to predict a possible source domain label–think: "The bill blocked the way forward", where for the word "bill" the system predicted that it mapped to a "PHYSICAL OBJECT" role in the source domain (Mohler et al. 2014).

2 Construction Grammatical Approaches to Metaphor

The constructional makeup of metaphoric language has been explored at some length by a

Proceedings of the Workshop on Figurative Language Processing, pages 102–109
New Orleans, Louisiana, June 6, 2018. ©2018 Association for Computational Linguistics

LOVER is a MAGICIAN	She cast her spell over me
ATTRACTION is a SPELL	I was spellbound
A RELATIONSHIP is BEWITCHMENT	He has me in a trance

Figure 1: Metaphoric Mapping & Example

handful of researchers to date. Karen Sullivan, for example, has done considerable work on both how syntactic structures (i.e. constructions) restrict the interpretation of metaphoric utterances in predictable ways by both instantiating a semantic frame and mapping the target domain referent to a semantic role *within* the instantiated frame (Sullivan 2006, 2009, 2013). Notable examples of computational implementations of Sullivan's theories include Stickles et al. (2016) and Dodge et al. (2015), who have compiled a database of metaphoric frames–MetaNet–organized into an ontology of source domains for researchers to use in analyzing metaphoric utterances, similar to FrameNet.

One of the advantages of construction grammar with respect to figurative language interpretation lies in the regularity with which constructions establish form-meaning pairings. The various meanings of constructions rely heavily on particular "cues"–cues including the verb, as well as the syntactic template and argument-structure–which point speakers in the direction of a specific interpretation (Goldberg 2006). For the purpose of the current study, I will be focusing on the argument-structure of metaphoric utterances which, though it supplies a rather course-grained view of the meaning of an utterance, provides an excellent and stable constructional cue with respect to its interpretation (Goldberg 2006). As an example of how this might work, consider the difference between "the Holidays are coming up on us" and "we're coming up on the Holidays." In the first sentence, "the Holidays" is established as being mapped to a MOVING OBJECT in the source domain by virtue of its position in the argument-structure of the sentence. Meanwhile, in the second utterance "the Holidays" is mapped to a LOCATION or GOAL in the source domain due to its change in position in the argument-structure of the construction. Implicitly, this means that important information about the interpretation of a construction can be gleaned through extracting the arguments that fill its argument-structure and analyzing these arguments' relationships to one another,

independent of cues beyond the sentence itself.

3 Data Collection

All the examples in this experiment were taken from the EN-Small LCC Metaphor Dataset, compiled and annotated by Mohler et al. (2016). The corpus contains 16,265 instances of conceptual metaphors from government discourse, including immediate context sentences preceding and following them. Each sentence is given a metaphoricity score, ranging from "-1" to "3", where "3" indicates high confidence that the sentence is metaphoric, "0" indicates that the sentence was not metaphoric, and "-1" indicates an invalid syntactic relationship between the target and source domain referents in the sentence (Mohler et al. 2016). Additionally, the corpus is annotated for polarity (negative, neutral, and positive), intensity, and situational protagonists (i.e.: the "government", "individuals", etc.). Though not annotated for every sentence, the most important annotations for this study were the annotations for source-target domain mappings. There was a total of 7,941 sentences annotated for these mappings, with 108 source domain tags, annotated by five annotators (Mohler et al. 2016). Each annotator indicated not only what they thought the source domain was, but also gave the example an additional metaphoricity score based on their opinion.

For the purposes of this study, I only used the metaphoric instances that were annotated for source-target domain mappings. For the source domain labels, I selected the labels made by the annotator who had marked the example for having the highest metaphoricity. I initially attempted to select the metaphoric source domain annotations that had the highest agreement amongst the annotators who had annotated the sentence, but this proved trickier than I had anticipated. After calculating the average Cohen Kappa score (54.4%), I decided that selecting labels based on their associated metaphoricity would be better. This effectively removed two annotators from the pool, who consistently ranked each metaphoric sentence as having a metaphoricity score of 1 or less.

I further restricted the training and test data by excluding multi-word expressions from the dataset for simplicity, though in the future I would very much like to re-test the methods outlined in the rest of this paper including the omitted MWEs. Finally, I removed any source domain annotations that included only a single example and split the data in training and testing data sets, using 85% as training data, and 15% as testing data. Because of my exclusion of MWEs and metaphoric source domain tags that were used only once, this left me with a total of 1985 sentences used in this experiment–1633 of those were used in the training data, and 352 reserved for test data–with 77 source domain labels. The source labels were converted to integers and used as classes in the following Deep Neural Net (DNN) classifier.

4 The Neural Network Approach to Source Domain Interpretation

4.1 Feature Generation

The task in this study is to predict the source domain of a metaphoric utterance using only features extracted from the sentence text. For example, from a sentence like "So, you advocate for the ability to deny people the vote by pushing them into poverty?", and given the target domain referent (in this sentence, "poverty"), can we accurately predict the source domain label "ABYSS" (as annotated in the LCC dataset) using only the text from the sentence? To do so, we wanted to extract from the sentence a representation of its argument structure, and use that to classify the source domain label. The argument structure of a construction is represented by the verb and the arguments it accepts to fulfill the roles defined by both the verb and its semantic frame (Goldberg 2006; Michaelis 2012; Sag 2012; Pustejovsky 2011). Though there are subtle differences between construction grammar and dependency grammar, it is possible to reconstruct the argument-structure of a construction from grammatical dependencies (Osborne & Gross 2012; for a computational implementation of a theoretically similar system to ours, see Hong 2016). For the purposes of this study, I first generated a representation of all the dependency relationships in each sentence from the LCC dataset using the Stanford NLP dependency parser (Chen & Manning 2014). Second, I searched the output list dependencies from the dependency parser for the target domain referent as identified in the

corpus example, and found the verb that it was directly dependent on in the sentence. This ensured that the target domain referent was in its immediate context. Once the verb was found, I then built a representation of the argument structure of the sentence by extracting the following dependencies–(1) the verb for which the target domain referent was a dependency, (2) the subject of the verb in 1, (3) the object of the verb in 1, and if the target domain referent was not included in the subject or direct object, (4) the target domain referent as a nominal modifier and (5) any prepositional arguments that it had as a dependency. Additionally, I extracted (6) the universal dependency tags for each of the arguments in the verb's argument-structure, and converted that into a list of tags that I simply labeled "syntax", or "SYN", based off the assumption that knowing what the dependencies were might help in identifying the exact relationships between the lexemes that had been collected. Finally, these elements along with (7) the target domain referent itself were compiled into a list to be used in the training or test data, and labeled with the pre-identified source domain label assigned to the sentence in the LCC dataset. The output of this process is visually represented in figure 2. The branch of the dependency tree in blue indicates the direct context of the target domain referent–in this case, "poverty".

While these strings provided a representation of the arguments as a set, they did not provide enough information *a priori* to predict the source domain on their own. Sullivan (2013) explains that the backbone of metaphoric utterances is the relationship of the target domain referent to the frame evoked by the construction. Additionally, Goldberg (2006) describes the semantic meaning of constructions as arising from both the nouns contained in their argument-structure, and the meaning implied by the construction's syntactic template. The following features combined Sullivan's relationships of the target domain referent to the construction, with the two observations made by Goldberg about constructional meaning. For the interaction of *the target domain referent with the nouns contained in the argument structure* I used the following interactions as features: (8) the target domain referent and the subject of the local dependency tree (again, in blue in figure 2), (9) the target domain referent and the direct object, and (10) the target domain referent and the nom-

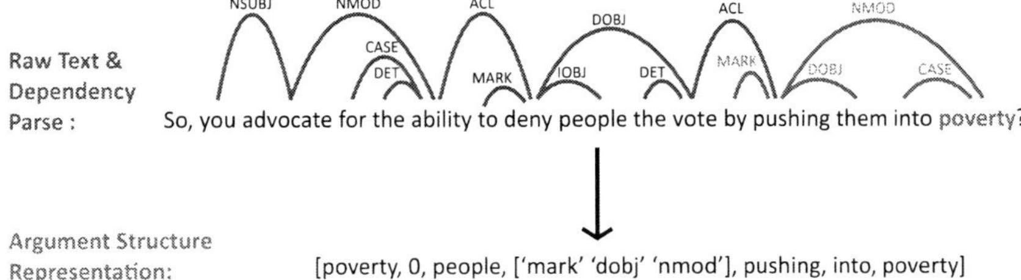

Figure 2: Raw text sentence input to dependency parsed output from Stanford Core NLP's dependency parser. The syntactic roles in order of their index in the dependency parsed sentence are as follows: (0) the target domain referencing noun, (1) the subject, (2) the direct object, (3) the syntactic sisters of the target domain referencing noun, (3) the verb, (4) the preposition/case of a nominal modifier, (5) the head of a nominal modifier. The word in bold was annotated as the target domain referent by annotators.

inal modifier from 4 in the previous paragraph. I then augmented these with the following interactions to represent the interaction of *the target domain referent with the syntactic template*: (11) the target domain referent, the verb, and the subject of the verb, (12) the target domain referent, the verb, and the object of the verb, and (13) the target domain referent, the preposition preceding the nominal modifier, and the nominal modifier. I predicted that these six interactions would approximate the relationship between the target domain referent and its construction-based context, as inspired by previous work in semantic role labeling (Wang et al. 2009; Matsubayashi et al. 2014; and especially Gildea & Jurafsky 2002, where researchers automatically labeled the semantic role of a specific target noun in a given frame). A list of these complex interactions can be seen in figure 3.

These 13 features were then converted into embeddings to be used as inputs in the DNN via the following process. The strings extracted from the dependency parsed, raw text sentence were first lemmatized, then converted from strings into numeric representations in Tensorflow using the tf.contrib.layers sparse column with hash bucket function. The interactions indicated in 8-13 in the prior paragraph were defined using the tf.contrib.layers crossed column function, returning a numeric representation of the interaction. Finally, these numeric representations for all of the features described above were then converted into an embedding layer in order to represent the context of the features as they appeared per each sentence that they extracted from. This was done using the tf.contrib.layers embedding column function, and the number of dimensions for each embedding layer was set uniformly at 13 dimensions.

4.2 Feed Forward DNN Network Architecture

These embedding layers were then used as the inputs into the DNN. In order to quickly prototype the model, I used the tf.contrib.learn library in Tensorflow. The activation function in the network was set to a relu function (tf.nn.relu). The network included a single, fully connected hidden layer, with 77 hidden units which were randomly initialized during training. I implemented a dropout rate of .4 during training to prevent overfitting. Information from the hidden layer was passed to a Softmax layer, and then passed to an output layer for the 77 labels in the train and test data. The reason behind using a single hidden layer was in part because the model training was initially done on a single MacBook Air, and so the model needed to be sufficiently small to train efficiently on that computer. The network was trained for 500 epochs, or until the model reached a training loss less than .006 after the 498th epoch. The early cut-off was decided upon after having run the model 20 times, and having discovered that accuracy was improved by approximately 1.2% if training was cut off immediately after reaching a loss less than .006. The full network architecture can be seen in figure 4.

4.3 Accuracy and Evaluation

The DNN architecture as described accurately predicted the source domain label from the LCC

105

Argument Structure Representation: [poverty, 0, people, ['mark' 'dobj' 'nmod'], pushing, into, poverty]
Target Domain NP x Subject: [poverty, 0]
Target Domain NP x Direct Object: [poverty, people]
Target Domain NP x Head of Nominal Modifier: [poverty, poverty]
Target Domain NP x Verb x Subject: [poverty, pushing, 0]
Target Domain NP x Verb x Direct Object: [poverty, pushing, people]
Target Domain NP x Preposition x Head of Nominal
Modifier: [poverty, into, poverty]

Figure 3: Diagram of the interactions as derived from the previous dependency parsed inputs.

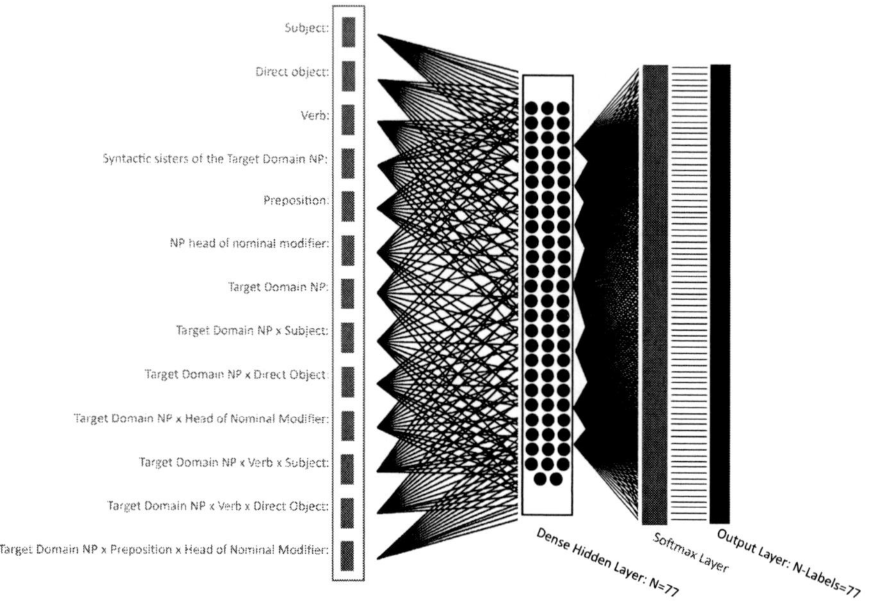

Figure 4: Diagram of the full DNN architecture from input features to output layer.

dataset 80.4% of the time, with a testing loss value of 1.51. I compared the output of the feedforward network to a similar DNN build without the interactions from figure 3 (essentially, only using the extracted argument structure as seen in figure 2). I then also compared the DNN architecture with the interactions in figure 3, to an LSTM neural network without those same constructional features. The results for the highest and lowest accuracy in a set of five test runs for each of these networks are compared in figure 5.

5   Discussion

The results reported indicates that the addition of construction grammatical relations to the feature set used by deep learning algorithms significantly increases the accuracy of metaphoric source domain prediction tasks.

Whilst the inclusion of the lexical units from the dependency parsed sentence are important to build sufficient context for the DNN classifier, the interactions as seen in Figure 3 provide the real predictive power of this system by approximating the relationship between the target domain referent and the interactions of items in the argument-structure of the construction. While we can take for granted from work in both VerbNet and FrameNet (VerbNet: Kipper, Korhonen, Ryant & Palmer 2008; FrameNet: Fillmore et al. 2001; Fillmore, Johnson, & Petruck 2002) proving that the verb is a strong cue for the semantic frame, a stronger predictor for the metaphoric source domain is the interaction of the verb with the arguments in its argument-structure.

In theory, the pipeline from dependencies, to usage-based constructional features, to embeddings for input into the DNN described, would

Network Architecture	Lowest acc	Highest acc
Feed Forward DNN without constructional cues as inputs	77.6%	78.9%
LSTM without constructional cues as inputs	72.1%	73.0%
Feed Forward DNN with constructional cues as inputs	79.2%	80.4%

Figure 5: Highest and lowest accuracy for the three network builds.

appear to assume that the utterance being analyzed has already been identified as metaphoric. In practice, by focusing on the relationship of the target domain referent to a small set of interactions (representing a construction's argument-structure), one could feasibly use a known set of target domain referents in order to identify the source domains that they are mapped to, skipping entirely the need to identify an example as metaphoric. Think of it like this: if a researcher is interested in the kinds of metaphors used to talk about "poverty" in a text, a simple query coupled with the DNN described can find and accurately predict possible source domain labels for all utterances in which "poverty" is used. Coupling the DNN here with a system designed to identify metaphors or even target domain referents in a text, however, would be ideal, and would greatly add to the described DNN's power and utility as a predictive tool.

An additional confound limiting the final accuracy in this experiment was the wide range of conceptual metaphor source domain annotations given by annotators per each utterance in the LCC dataset. Despite it being an excellent resource for researchers interested in metaphor source domain interpretation due to its CMSource annotations, the average inter-annotator agreement for source domain mappings in the corpus was on average approximately 54.4% for the dataset, as calculated by averaging the Cohen-Kappa scores for annotators. While annotators agreed about the relatedness of the source and target domain referents during the annotation process (agreement for "Source Relatedness" and "Target Relatedness" in the LCC dataset were calculated as of 2014 as 95.1% and 94.3% respectively (Mohler et al. 2014)), several of the source domain mappings provided were different from one another in incredibly subtle, but crucial, ways. Take "LMInstance" 22920 from the dataset for example–"This prison is the prison of poverty." Where as one of the annotators labeled the sentence as evoking "CRIME" as the source domain mapping, another indicated that it evoked

the thematically related concept of "CONFINE-MENT" as the source domain. Neither label in this instance appears, at least on first glance, to be intrinsically better than the other.

Adding to this, I actively avoided using examples in which MWEs were identified as the target domain referent–a decision which limited the number of examples used, and thus likely limited the number of times that a specific argument-structure construction in the dataset showed up alongside of an accompanying source-domain label.

In all, the current experiment serves as an example not only of the usefulness of construction grammar to NLP tasks, but of the utility of a cognitive theory of language understanding to computational linguistic inquiry.

6   Acknowledgements

I would like to thank the anonymous reviewers for their excellent feedback, and Michael Mohler of the Language Computer Corporation for the corpus used in this paper. I would also like to thank the wonderful faculty and students at the University of Colorado, Boulder, for their support.

References

Danushka Bollegala and Ekaterina Shutova. 2013. Metaphor interpretation using paraphrases extracted from the web. *PloS ONE* 8(9):e74304.

Danqi Chen and Christopher D Manning. 2014. A fast and accurate dependency parser using neural networks. In *Proceedings of EMNLP 2014*. Association for Computational Linguistics, pages 740–750.

Ellen Dodge, Jisup Hong, and Elise Stickles. 2015. Metanet: Deep semantic automatic metaphor analysis. In *Proceedings of the Third Workshop on Metaphor in NLP*. Association for Computational Linguistics, pages 40–49.

John Feldman and S. Narayanan. 2004. Embodied meaning in a neural theory of language. *Brain and language* 89(2):385–392.

Charles Fillmore, Christopher Johnson, and Miriam Petruck. 2002. Background to framenet. *International Journal of Lexicography* 16(3):235–250.

Charles Fillmore et al. 2001. Building a large lexical databank which provides deep semantics. In Benjamin Tsou and Olivia Kwong, editors, *Proceedings of the 15th Pacific Asia Conference on Language, Information and Computation*. Pacific Asia Conference on Language, Information, and Computation, pages 3–26.

Dedre Gentner et al. 2002. As time goes by: Evidence for two systems in processing spacetime metaphors. *Language and Cognitive Processes* 17(5):537–565.

Daniel Gildea and Daniel Jurafsky. 2002. Automatic labeling of semantic roles. *Linguistics* 28(3):245–288.

Adele Goldberg. 2006. *Constructions at Work: The Nature of Generalization in Language*. Oxford University Press, Inc.

Stefan Gries. 2006. Corpus-based methods and cognitive semantics: The many senses of to run. In Stefan Th. Gries and Anatol Stefanowitsch, editors, *Corpora in Cognitive Linguistics: Corpus-Based Approaches to Syntax and Lexis*, Walter de Gruyter, pages 57–99.

Jisup Hong. 2016. Automatic metaphor detection using constructions and frames. *Constructions and Frames* 8(2):295–322.

Karin Kipper, Anna Korhonen, Neville Ryant, and Martha Palmer. 2008. A large-scale classification of english verbs. *Language Resources and Evaluation Journal* 42(1):21–40.

George Lakoff. 1990. *Women, Fire, and Dangerous Things*. The University of Chicago Press.

George Lakoff and Mark Johnson. 1980. *Metaphors We Live By*. The University of Chicago Press.

R. W. Landacker. 2002. *Concept, image and symbol: cognitive basis of grammar*. Mouton de Gruyter.

R. W. Langacker. 1997. Constituency, dependency, and conceptual grouping. *Cognitive Linguistics* 8(1):1–32.

Dekang Lin. 1998. Automatic retrieval and clustering of similar words. In *Proceedings of the 17th International Conference on Computational Linguistics*. Association for Computational Linguistics, volume 2, pages 768–774.

Z.J. Mason. 2004. Cormet: A computational, corpus-based conventional metaphor extraction system. *Computational Linguistics* 30(1):23–44.

Yuichiroh Matsubayashi et al. 2014. Generalization of semantic roles in automatic semantic role labeling. *Journal of Natural Language Processing* 21(4):841–875.

Matthew McGlone. 1998. Back (or forward?) to the future: The role of perspective in temporal language comprehension. *Journal of Experimental Psychology Learning Memory and Cognition* 24(5):1211–1223.

Laura Michaelis. 2012. Making the case for construction grammar. In Hans Boas and Ivan Sag, editors, *Sign-Based Construction Grammar*, Center for the Study of Language and Information, pages 31–67.

Michael Mohler et al. 2013. Semantic signatures for example-based linguistic metaphor detection. In Ekaterina Shutova, Beata Beigman Klebanov, Joel Tetreault, and Zornitsa Kozareva, editors, *First Workshop on Metaphor in NLP*. Association for Computational Linguistics, pages 27–35.

Michael Mohler et al. 2014. A novel distributional approach to multilingual conceptual metaphor recognition. In *Proceedings of COLING 2014, the 25th International Conference on Computational Linguistics: Technical Papers*. Association for Computational Linguistics, pages 1752–1763.

Michael Mohler et al. 2016. Introducing the LCC metaphor datasets. In *Proceedings of the Language Resources and Evaluation Conference 2016*. European Language Resources Association (ELRA), pages 4221–4227.

James Pustejovsky. 2011. Coercion in a general theory of argument selection. *Linguistics* 49(6):1401–1431.

Ivan Sag. 2012. Sign-based construction grammar: An informal synopsis. In Hans Boas and Ivan Sag, editors, *Sign-Based Construction Grammar*, Center for the Study of Language and Information, pages 61–197.

Ekaterina Shutova. 2010. Automatic metaphor interpretation as a paraphrasing task. In Ben Hachey and Miles Osborne, editors, *Human Language Technologies: The 2010 Annual Conference of the North American Chapter of the Association for Computational Linguistics*. Association for Computational Linguistics, pages 1029–1037.

Elise Stickles et al. 2016. Formalizing contemporary conceptual metaphor theory: A structured repository for metaphor analysis. *Constructions and Frames* 8:166–213.

Chang Su et al. 2017. Automatic detection and interpretation of nominal metaphor based on the theory of meaning. *Neurocomputing* 219:300–311.

Karen Sullivan. 2007. Metaphoric extension and invited inferencing in semantic change. *Culture, Language and Representation, Special Issue: Metaphor and Discourse* pages 257–274.

Karen Sullivan. 2009. Grammatical constructions in metaphoric language. In Barbara Lewandowska-Tomaszcyk and Katerina Dziwirek, editors, *Studies in Corpus Linguistics*, John Benjamins, pages 1–24.

Karen Sullivan. 2013. *Frames and Constructions in Metaphoric Language*. John Benjamins.

Hong-Lin Wang et al. 2009. Semantic role labeling based on dependency relationship. *Computer Engineering* 35(15):82–84.

Neural Metaphor Detecting with CNN-LSTM Model

Chuhan Wu[1], Fangzhao Wu[2], Yubo Chen[1], Sixing Wu[1],
Zhigang Yuan[1] and Yongfeng Huang[1]

[1]Tsinghua National Laboratory for Information Science and Technology,
Department of Electronic Engineering, Tsinghua University, Beijing 100084
[2]Microsoft Research Asia

`{wuch15,ybch14,wu-sx15,yuanzg14,yfhuang}@mails.tsinghua.edu.cn`
`wufangzhao@gmail.com`

Abstract

Metaphors are figurative languages widely used in daily life and literatures. It's an important task to detect the metaphors evoked by texts. Thus, the metaphor shared task is aimed to extract metaphors from plain texts at word level. We propose to use a CNN-LSTM model for this task. Our model combines CNN and LSTM layers to utilize both local and long-range contextual information for identifying metaphorical information. In addition, we compare the performance of the softmax classifier and conditional random field (CRF) for sequential labeling in this task. We also incorporated some additional features such as part of speech (POS) tags and word cluster to improve the performance of model. Our best model achieved 65.06% F-score in the *all POS testing* subtask and 67.15% in the *verbs testing* subtask.

1 Introduction

A metaphor is a type of conceptual mapping to represent one thing as another (Lakofi and Johnson, 1980). They are widely used in verbal and written languages to convey rich linguistic and sentiment information (Steen et al., 2010). Detecting the metaphors in texts are important to mine the semantic and sentiment information better, which is beneficial to many applications such as machine translation, dialog systems and sentiment analysis (Tsvetkov et al., 2014).

However, detecting metaphors is a challenging task. The semantic differences between metaphorical and non-metaphorical texts are often subtle. For example, the sentence *Her hair is a white snowflake* is metaphorical, while the sentence *Her hair is white* doesn't contain metaphors. In addition, detecting metaphors can be influenced by subjective factors, and may need specific domain knowledge (Tsvetkov et al., 2014).

Existing computational approaches to detect metaphors are mainly based on lexicons (Mohler et al., 2013; Dodge et al., 2015) and supervised methods (Turney et al., 2011; Heintz et al., 2013; Klebanov et al., 2014, 2015, 2016). Lexicon-based methods are free from data annotation, but they are unable to detect novel metaphorical usages and capture the contextual information. Supervised methods such as logistic regression classifier (Klebanov et al., 2014) can capture richer metaphor information. However, they need sophisticated hand-crafted features.

To improve the collective techniques on detecting metaphors, the metaphor shared task[1] aims to detect both metaphorical verbs and metaphors with other POS. Given a sentence and their words with specific POS tags, systems are required to determine whether each word is a metaphor. We propose a CNN-LSTM model with CRF or weighted softmax classifier to address this task. Our model can take advantage of both long-range and local information by utilizing both LSTM and CNN layers. We propose to use a weighted softmax classifier to predict the label sequence of sentence, which outperforms the CRF method. We apply a model ensemble strategy to help our model predict more accurately. In addition, we incorporated additional features such as POS tags and word cluster features to further improve our model. Our best model achieved 65.06% F-score on the test data in the *all POS testing* subtask, and 67.15% in the *verbs testing* subtask.

2 CNN-LSTM Model with CRF or Softmax Inference

We model this task as a sequential labeling task and the input is a sentence with a sequence of words. The framework of our CNN-LSTM model

---

[1]https://competitions.codalab.org/competitions/17805

Proceedings of the Workshop on Figurative Language Processing, pages 110–114
New Orleans, Louisiana, June 6, 2018. ©2018 Association for Computational Linguistics

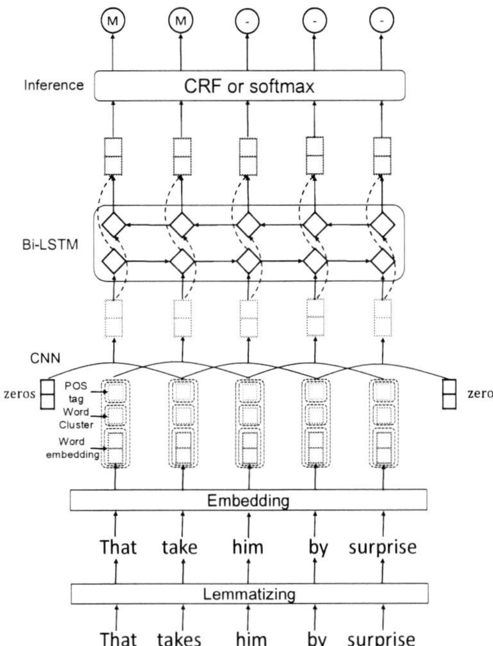

Figure 1: The architecture of our method. The final metaphor labels will be predicted by a CRF or softmax inference layer.

is presented in Figure 1. We will introduce the details of modules in our model from bottom to top.

We follow the approach proposed by Klebanov et al. (2016) to use the lemmatizing strategy. The first module in our model is a lemmatizer. This module is used to lemmatize the verbs in texts via a dictionary. The input is a text with a sequence of word, and output is the text with lemmatized words. Since verbs with different forms can share the same lemmas, using the lemmatized verbs in texts can simplify the semantic information and reduce the number of out-of-vocabulary words. We use the NLTK package (Bird et al., 2009) to transform the verbs into their lemmas.

The second module is an embedding layer. It will convert sequences of words in sentences into sequences of low-dimension dense vectors via a lookup table. The embedding weights of words are obtained by the pre-trained word2vec model and they will be fine-tuned during model training. POS tags are useful in metaphor detecting task (Klebanov et al., 2014). Therefore, we also incorporate the one-hot encoded POS tags as additional features into our neural model, and concate-

nated them with the word embeddings. We use the Stanford parser[2] tool to obtain the POS tag of each word in texts. Since similar words may have similar metaphor information, we also incorporate the word cluster features. They are obtained by clustering the word embedding vectors via k-means method. They are also one-hot encoded and combined with the word embeddings as the final word representations to input the neural network.

The third module in our model is a convolutional neural networks (CNN) to extract local contextual information. Motivated by the multiple kernels CNN used for sequential labeling (Chen et al., 2016), we also apply such CNN with different window sizes to this task.

The fourth module in our model is a bidirectional long short-term memory (Bi-LSTM) layer. This layer is used to extract the long-range information from the CNN feature maps. It will combine the previous and future context information to output the hidden state $\mathbf{h}_i$ at time step i.

The last module is an inference layer. We implement it with two alternatives and compare their performance via experiments.

CRF: We use CRF to predict the metaphor labels of each words. Given the matrix of hidden representations $\mathbf{h} = [\mathbf{h}_1, \mathbf{h}_2, ..., \mathbf{h}_N]$, the conditional probability of the output sequence of label $\mathbf{y}$ is formulated as follows:

$$p(\mathbf{y}|\mathbf{h}; \theta) = \frac{\prod_{i=1}^{N} \psi(\mathbf{h}_i, y_i, y_{i-1})}{\sum_{\mathbf{y}' \in \mathcal{Y}(s)} \prod_{i=1}^{N} \psi(\mathbf{h}_i, y_i', y_{i-1}')}, \quad (1)$$

where $\mathcal{Y}(s)$ is the set of all possible label sequences, θ is the parameters, and $\psi(\mathbf{h}_i, y_i, y_{i-1})$ is the potential function. In our model, we use a simple potential function which is formulated as:

$$\psi(\mathbf{h}_i, y_i, y_{i-1}) = \exp(y_i^T \mathbf{W}^T \mathbf{h}_i + y_{i-1}^T \mathbf{T} y_i), \quad (2)$$

where $\mathbf{W}$ and $\mathbf{T}$ represent the linear transform parameters. The CRF loss function we use is the negative log-likelihood over all training samples, which is formulated as follows:

$$\mathcal{L}_{CRF} = -\sum_{s \in \mathcal{S}} \log(p(\mathbf{y}_s|\mathbf{h}_s; \theta)), \quad (3)$$

where $\mathcal{S}$ is the training set, and $\mathbf{h}_s$ and $\mathbf{y}_s$ are the hidden states and label sequence of sentence s.

---

[2] https://nlp.stanford.edu/software/lex-parser.shtml

Softmax: We use a dense layer with softmax activation function to predict the metaphor label sequences. Motivated by the cost-sensitive cross-entropy (Santos-Rodríguez et al., 2009; Yang et al., 2014; Muller et al., 2014), the loss function of our model is formulated as follows:

$$\mathcal{L}_{Softmax} = -\sum_{s \in \mathcal{S}} \sum_{i=1}^{N} w_{y_i} y_i \log(\hat{y}_i), \quad (4)$$

y_i is the metaphor label of i_{th} word, $\hat{y}_i$ is the predicted score, and w_{y_i} is the loss weight of metaphor label y_i. Since there are much more non-metaphorical words than metaphors, we assign larger loss weight to the positive class. Since the prediction is generated from the lemmatized texts, optimizing the loss in Eq. (4) can tune all parameters in the embedding, CNN and LSTM layers.

Ensemble strategy is usually useful to improve the performance of neural network (Wu et al., 2017). We train our model for 20 times on randomly selected 90% training data. For CRF-based model, the prediction of each token will be obtained by voting. For softmax-based model, the output probability is the averaged logits of all model predictions.

3 Experiment

3.1 Dataset and Experimental Settings

The dataset for this task is the VU Amsterdam Metaphor Corpus (VUA)[3]. There are 12,122 sentences for training, and 4,080 sentences for test. We tune the hyper-parameters of our model via cross validation.

The pre-trained word embeddings are the 300-dim Google embedding[4] released by Mikolov et al. (2013). They were trained by the skip-gram model on about 100-billion words on Google News. These word embedding were fine-tuned during model training.

The hyper-parameters in our model were tuned via cross-validation. The dimension of Bi-LSTM hidden states is 200, the window sizes of CNN filters are 3, 5, 7 and 9 respectively. The number of CNN filters is 100. We set the dropout rate to 0.2 for each layer. The loss weights w_p and w_n of metaphors and non-metaphorical words are set to

2.0 and 1.0 respectively. The class number of word cluster is set 50. The batch size is 50, and the max training epoch is set to 15. The optimizer we use is RMSProp in our experiment. The performance of both *all POS testing* and *verbs testing* subtasks is evaluated by precision, recall and F-score as a standard binary classification task.

3.2 Performance Evaluation

We compare the performance of the variants of our model and several baseline methods. The methods to be compared include: 1) CNN+CRF, using CNN to extract local information and CRF for word-level metaphor detection; 2) *LSTM+CRF*, using Bi-LSTM to obtain the text representation and CRF inference layer; 3) *CNN+LSTM+CRF*, using the combination of LSTM, CNN and CRF inference layer; 4) *CNN+LSTM+CRF+ensemble*, adding ensemble strategy to the CNN+LSTM+CRF model; 5) *CNN+Softmax*, using CNN and weighted softmax classifier for sequential labeling; 6) *LSTM+Softmax*, using Bi-LSTM and softmax inference layer; 7) *CNN+LSTM+Softmax w/o lemma*, using the combination of LSTM, CNN and softmax inference layer, but without the lemmatizing process; 8) *CNN+LSTM+Softmax*, using the combination of LSTM, CNN and softmax inference layer; 9) *CNN+LSTM+Softmax+ensemble*, adding ensemble strategy to the CNN+LSTM+Softmax model. Our official submissions are obtained by model 3), 4), 8), 9) and the different combinations of additional features, which will be discussed in the next subsection.

According to Table 1, we have several observations: (1) The combination of LSTM and CNN outperforms the single CNN and LSTM in both subtasks. It proves that the combination of CNN and LSTM can help to mine both local and long-distance information from texts, which is beneficial for detecting the metaphors in texts. (2) Comparing the modeling using CRF and softmax layer, best precision score can be achieved by using CRF. But the recall and F-score are significantly better when using weighted softmax classifier. This is probably because the numbers of metaphors are usually less than normal non-metaphorical words. The metaphors can be identified better when they are assigned larger loss weights. (3) Improvement can be brought by the lemmatizing process

[3]http://ota.ahds.ac.uk/headers/2541.xml
[4]https://code.google.com/archive/p/word2vec/

Model	Verbs Testing			All POS Testing		
	P	R	F	P	R	F
*CNN+CRF**	.628	.611	.619	.605	.589	.597
*LSTM+CRF**	.633	.609	.621	.604	.586	.595
CNN+LSTM+CRF	.644	.615	.629	**.617**	.597	.607
CNN+LSTM+CRF+ensemble	**.664**	.626	.645	.610	.627	.619
*CNN+Softmax**	.575	.716	.638	.585	.644	.613
*LSTM+Softmax**	.588	.710	.643	.591	.659	.623
*CNN+LSTM+Softmax w/o lemma**	.585	.702	.638	.601	.669	.633
CNN+LSTM+Softmax	.593	.734	.656	.611	.677	.643
CNN+LSTM+Softmax+ensemble	.600	**.763**	**.671**	.608	**.700**	**.651**

Table 1: The performance of different methods. *The results of these baseline methods were not submitted due to the limited submission time. We evaluate their performance using the labels of testing data after the competition.

in both tasks. It may be because the lemmatized verbal metaphors are more simple, and there will be fewer out-of-vocabulary words in the embedding look-up table. (4) the ensenmble strategy can also help our model identify metaphors more accurately. It validates that using a series of models to predict can reduce the data noise and improve the generalization ability of our model.

3.3 Influence of Additional Features

Features	Verbs Testing			All POS Testing		
	P	R	F	P	R	F
None	.584	.717	.644	.583	.665	.621
+POS	.588	.729	.651	.606	.662	.633
+cluster	.589	.723	.649	.606	.665	.634
+POS+cluster	**.593**	**.734**	**.656**	**.611**	**.677**	**.643**

Table 2: The influence of additional features on our best-performance model.

The influence of the POS tags and word clusters is shown in Table 2. Here we use the *CNN+LSTM+Softmax* model to investigate the influence of features. The results show that both POS tags and word cluster features can help improve the performance of detecting metaphors. It proves that POS tags contain useful information to identify the metaphors, since metaphors usually have specific POS tags and they can be easier to be identified by incorporating POS information. Thus, combing the POS tag features is beneficial. Incorporating the word cluster features is also useful to improve the performance. It may be because words with similar semantic information have some inherent relatedness and they share similar metaphor information. Our model can identify such information better if word cluster features are incorporated. In addition, it can also enrich the in-

formation of out-of-vocabulary words, which can improve the generalization ability of our model. Thus, incorporating the word cluster features is also beneficial to detect metaphors.

3.4 Influence of Loss Weight

Since the metaphors are less frequent than normal words, the selection of loss weight is important. We investigate the influence of the loss weight w_p of positive label on the softmax classifier, which is illustrated in Figure 2. The results indicate that using larger w_p can improve the recall score, but the precision will be lower. It proves that controlling the loss weights can improve the F-score performance in this unbalanced classification task. To achieve a better performance, we choose $w_p = 2$ since the F-score performance is best as shown in this figure.

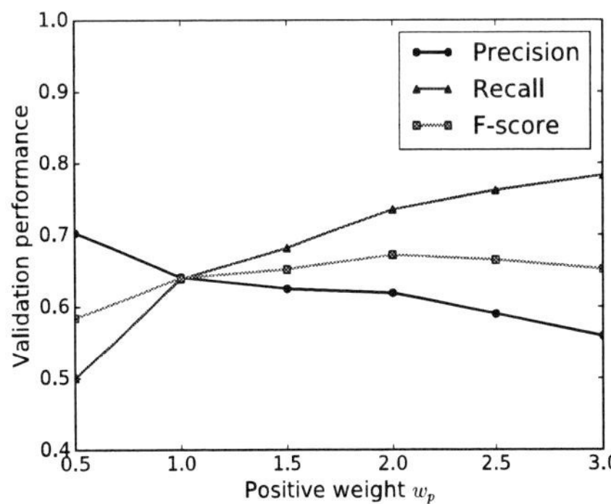

Figure 2: The validation performance of our model using different w_p.

4 Conclusion

In this paper, we introduce our CNN-LSTM model with CRF or softmax layer for the metaphor shared task to detect metaphors in texts. We combine CNN and LSTM to capture both local and long-distance contextual information to represent the input sentences with lemmatizing preprocessing. We compare the performance of using CRF and softmax classifier with weighted loss. In addition, we incorporate additional features including POS tags and word cluster features, and use the ensemble strategy to improve the performance. The experimental results validate the effectiveness of our model on detecting metaphors.

Acknowledgments

The authors thank the reviewers for their insightful comments and constructive suggestions on improving this work. This work was supported in part by the National Key Research and Development Program of China under Grant 2016YFB0800402 and in part by the National Natural Science Foundation of China under Grant U1705261, Grant U1536207, Grant U1536201 and U1636113.

References

Steven Bird, Ewan Klein, and Edward Loper. 2009. *Natural language processing with Python: analyzing text with the natural language toolkit.* " O'Reilly Media, Inc.".

Xinchi Chen, Xipeng Qiu, and Xuanjing Huang. 2016. A feature-enriched neural model for joint chinese word segmentation and part-of-speech tagging. *arXiv preprint arXiv:1611.05384*.

Ellen Dodge, Jisup Hong, and Elise Stickles. 2015. Metanet: Deep semantic automatic metaphor analysis. In *Proceedings of the Third Workshop on Metaphor in NLP*, pages 40–49.

Ilana Heintz, Ryan Gabbard, Mahesh Srivastava, Dave Barner, Donald Black, Majorie Friedman, and Ralph Weischedel. 2013. Automatic extraction of linguistic metaphors with lda topic modeling. In *Proceedings of the First Workshop on Metaphor in NLP*, pages 58–66.

Beata Beigman Klebanov, Ben Leong, Michael Heilman, and Michael Flor. 2014. Different texts, same metaphors: Unigrams and beyond. In *Proceedings of the Second Workshop on Metaphor in NLP*, pages 11–17.

Beata Beigman Klebanov, Chee Wee Leong, and Michael Flor. 2015. Supervised word-level metaphor detection: Experiments with concreteness and reweighting of examples. In *Proceedings of the Third Workshop on Metaphor in NLP*, pages 11–20.

Beata Beigman Klebanov, Chee Wee Leong, E Dario Gutierrez, Ekaterina Shutova, and Michael Flor. 2016. Semantic classifications for detection of verb metaphors. In *Proceedings of the 54th Annual Meeting of the Association for Computational Linguistics (Volume 2: Short Papers)*, volume 2, pages 101–106.

George Lakofi and Mark Johnson. 1980. Metaphors we live by. *Chicago, IL: University of.*

Tomas Mikolov, Kai Chen, Greg Corrado, and Jeffrey Dean. 2013. Efficient estimation of word representations in vector space. *arXiv preprint arXiv:1301.3781.*

Michael Mohler, David Bracewell, Marc Tomlinson, and David Hinote. 2013. Semantic signatures for example-based linguistic metaphor detection. In *Proceedings of the First Workshop on Metaphor in NLP*, pages 27–35.

Philippe Muller, Cécile Fabre, and Clémentine Adam. 2014. Predicting the relevance of distributional semantic similarity with contextual information. In *52nd Annual Meeting of the Association for Computational Linguistics-ACL 2014*, pages 479–488.

Raúl Santos-Rodríguez, Darío García-García, and Jesús Cid-Sueiro. 2009. Cost-sensitive classification based on bregman divergences for medical diagnosis. In *Machine Learning and Applications, 2009. ICMLA'09. International Conference on*, pages 551–556. IEEE.

Gerard J Steen, Aletta G Dorst, J Berenike Herrmann, Anna A Kaal, and Tina Krennmayr. 2010. Metaphor in usage. *Cognitive Linguistics*, 21(4):765–796.

Yulia Tsvetkov, Leonid Boytsov, Anatole Gershman, Eric Nyberg, and Chris Dyer. 2014. Metaphor detection with cross-lingual model transfer. In *Proceedings of the 52nd Annual Meeting of the Association for Computational Linguistics (Volume 1: Long Papers)*, volume 1, pages 248–258.

Peter D Turney, Yair Neuman, Dan Assaf, and Yohai Cohen. 2011. Literal and metaphorical sense identification through concrete and abstract context. In *Proceedings of the Conference on Empirical Methods in Natural Language Processing*, pages 680–690. Association for Computational Linguistics.

Chuhan Wu, Fangzhao Wu, Yongfeng Huang, Sixing Wu, and Zhigang Yuan. 2017. Thu_ngn at ijcnlp-2017 task 2: Dimensional sentiment analysis for chinese phrases with deep lstm. *Proceedings of the IJCNLP 2017, Shared Tasks*, pages 47–52.

Xuesong Yang, Anastassia Loukina, and Keelan Evanini. 2014. Machine learning approaches to improving pronunciation error detection on an imbalanced corpus. In *Spoken Language Technology Workshop (SLT), 2014 IEEE*, pages 300–305. IEEE.

Di-LSTM Contrast : A Deep Neural Network for Metaphor Detection

Krishnkant Swarnkar and **Anil Kumar Singh**
Indian Institute of Technology (BHU), Varanasi, India
{ krishnkant.swarnkar.cse15, aksingh.cse } @iitbhu.ac.in

Abstract

The contrast between the contextual and general meaning of a word serves as an important clue for detecting its metaphoricity. In this paper, we present a deep neural architecture for metaphor detection which exploits this contrast. Additionally, we also use cost-sensitive learning by re-weighting examples, and baseline features like concreteness ratings, POS and WordNet-based features. The best performing system of ours achieves an overall F1 score of 0.570 on All POS category and 0.605 on the Verbs category at the Metaphor Shared Task 2018.

1 Introduction

Lakoff (1993) defines a metaphorical expression as a linguistic expression which is the surface realization of a cross-domain mapping in a conceptual system. On one hand, metaphors play a significant role in making a language more creative. On the other, they also make language understanding difficult for artificial systems.

Metaphor Shared Task 2018 (Leong et al., 2018) aims to explore various approaches for word-level metaphor detection in sentences. The task is to predict whether the target word in the given sentence is metaphoric or not. There are two categories for this shared task. The first one, All POS, tests the models for content words from all types of POS among nouns, adjectives, adverbs and verbs, while the second category, Verbs, tests the models only for verbs.

2 Related Work

Various attempts have been made for metaphor detection in recent years, but only a few of them utilize the power of distributed representation of words (Bengio et al., 2003) combined with deep neural networks. Rei et al. (2017) proposed and evaluated the first deep neural network for metaphor identification on two datasets, Saif M. Mohammad and Turney (2016) and Tsvetkov et al. (2014). Do Dinh and Gurevych (2016) explore MLP classifier with trainable word embeddings on VUAMC corpus and achieve comparable results to other systems which use corpus-based or based on handcrafted features.

Other attempts which employ supervised learning approaches for metaphor detection on VUAMC corpus involve the use of logistic classifier (Beigman Klebanov et al., 2014) on a set of features, which include unigrams, topic models, POS, and concreteness features. Later, Beigman Klebanov et al. (2015) showed a significant improvement by re-weighting examples for cost sensitive learning and experimenting with concreteness information. Gargett and Barnden (2015) focused on utilizing the interactions between concreteness, imageability, and affective meaning for metaphor detection. Rai et al. (2016) explored Conditional Random Fields with syntactic, conceptual, affective, and contextual (word embeddings) features. Beigman Klebanov et al. (2016) experimented with unigrams, WordNet (Miller, 1995) and VerbNet (Schuler, 2006) based features for detection of verb metaphors.

3 Data

The dataset provided for this task is VU Amsterdam Metaphor Corpus (VUAMC). VUAMC is extracted from the British National Corpus (BNC Baby) and is annotated using MIPVU Procedure (Steen, 2010). It contains examples from four genres of text: Academic, News, Fiction and Conversation.

Table 1 and Table 2 summarize the statistics of the data for this shared task.

Proceedings of the Workshop on Figurative Language Processing, pages 115–120
New Orleans, Louisiana, June 6, 2018. ©2018 Association for Computational Linguistics

| | **Content** | **%** |
	Tokens	**Metaphors**
Training Set	72611	15.2%
Test Set	22196	17.9%

Table 1: Summary of data statistics for All POS category (Content Tokens: nouns, adjectives, adverbs and verbs)

| | **Content** | **%** |
	Tokens	**Metaphors**
Training Set	17240	27.8%
Test Set	5873	29.9%

Table 2: Summary of data statistics for Verbs category (Content Tokens: verbs)

4 System Description

This section describes our proposed system for this shared task, which we call Di-LSTM Contrast (illustrated in Figure 1[1]) and is divided into three modules trained in an end to end setting. The input to the model is given as pre-trained word embeddings. An encoder uses these word embeddings to encode the context of the sentence with respect to the target word using forward and backward LSTMs (Hochreiter and Schmidhuber, 1997). The output from the encoder is fed to the feature selection module (section 4.2) for generating contrast-based features for the token word. The classifier module (section 4.3) then predicts the probabilities for the target word being metaphoric.

4.1 Context Encoder

The context encoder is inspired by Bidirectional LSTM (BLSTM, Graves and Schmidhuber (2005)). Given an input sentence $S = \{w_1, w_2, ...w_n\}$, with n as the number of tokens in a sentence and i as the index of target token, we make two sets $A = \{w_1, w_2, ...w_i\}$ and $B = \{w_n, w_{n-1}, ...w_i\}$ and feed them into forward and backward LSTMs respectively. The motivation for this split is to produce the context with respect to the target word (w_i).

$$h_f = LSTM_f(A)$$

$$h_b = LSTM_b(B)$$

The hidden states $h_f \in \mathbb{R}^d$ and $h_b \in \mathbb{R}^d$, so obtained from forward and backward LSTMs are

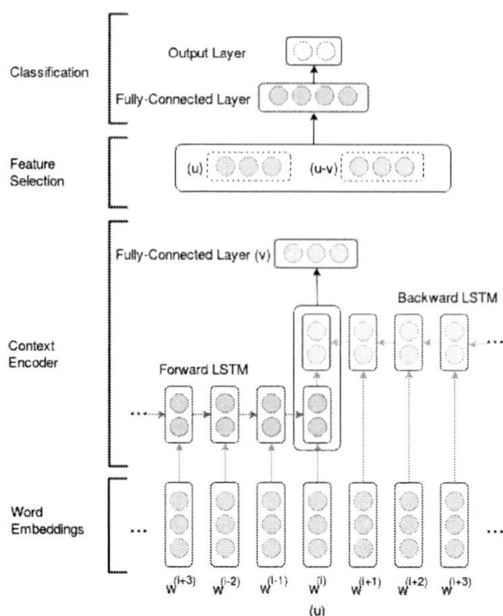

Figure 1: The Architecture of DiLSTM Contrast Model

combined by concatenation or averaging, followed by a fully connected layer to produce $v \in \mathbb{R}^d$, the context encoding.

$$h = [h_f; h_b]$$

$$v = sigmoid(W_{(1)}h + b_{(1)})$$

$W_{(1)} \in \mathbb{R}^{(d \times 2d)}$ is the transformation weight matrix, and $b_{(1)} \in \mathbb{R}^d$ is bias.

4.2 Feature Selection

A combination of the context encoding (v) and the word vector of the target word $u = w_i$ is then fed to the classification module as

$$g = [u; (u - v)]$$

The intuition behind this feature set $g \in \mathbb{R}^{2d}$ is that the properties of the word and the difference between the general and contextual meanings play a major role in determining the metaphoricity of a word (Steen, 2010).

4.3 Classification

The vector g from the previous module is transformed to a hidden layer and then to the output layer to obtain the softmax probabilities ($p \in \mathbb{R}^2$) for metaphoricity.

$$h_1 = sigmoid(W_{(2)}g + b_{(2)})$$

---

[1]Figure generated using https://www.draw.io/

116

Model Variants	Val.	Test All POS	Test Verbs
DC (avg)	0.541	0.538	0.572
DC	0.554	0.542	0.584
DC +R	0.570	0.562	0.590
DC +RL	**0.575**	0.570	**0.605**
Task Baseline	-	**0.589**	0.600

Table 3: Comparision of F1 scores on Validation, All POS (Test) and Verbs (Test) scores between the various approaches. DC = DiLSTM Contrast with concatenation, DC (avg) = DiLSTM Contrast with averaging, R = Reweighting of Examples, L = Additional Linguistic Features (Baseline), Task Baseline = The baseline system used by the task organizers

$$p = softmax(W_{(4)}h_1 + b_{(4)})$$

$W_{(2)} \in \mathbb{R}^{(m \times 2d)}, W_{(4)} \in \mathbb{R}^{(2 \times m)}$ are the weight matrices and $b_{(2)} \in \mathbb{R}^m, b_{(4)} \in \mathbb{R}^2$ are the biases.

To enable the use of some additional binary baseline features (section 6.3), we modify the equations as

$$h_1 = sigmoid(W_{(2)}g + b_{(2)})$$

$$l_2 = W_{(3)}g_{baseline} + b_{(3)}$$

$$l_1 = W_{(4)}h_1 + b_{(4)}$$

$$p = softmax(\alpha\, l_1 + (1 - \alpha)\, l_2)$$

$W_{(2)} \in \mathbb{R}^{(m \times 2d)}, W_{(3)} \in \mathbb{R}^{(2 \times k)}, W_{(4)} \in \mathbb{R}^{(2 \times m)}$ are the corresponding weight matrices, $b_{(2)} \in \mathbb{R}^m, b_{(3)} \in \mathbb{R}^2, b_{(4)} \in \mathbb{R}^2$ are the corresponding biases, $g_{baseline} \in \mathbb{R}^k$ is the baseline feature vector and α is a trainable variable which determines the weights to be given to the baseline features and the contrast features.

5 Implementation Details

We split the provided training data in 90:10 ratio as training set and development set. We use this development set to tune our hyperparameters for the different variations of our model. We use 300-dimensional GloVe vectors (Pennington et al., 2014) trained on 6B Common Crawl corpus as word embeddings, setting the embeddings of out-of-vocabulary words to zero. To prevent overfitting on the training set, we use dropout regularization (Srivastava et al., 2014) and early stopping (Yao et al., 2007). We set the minibatch size to 50 examples and we zero pad the A and B split sets (as defined in section 4.1). More details on the hyperparameter settings can be found in the table 4.

Hyperparameter	Value
GloVe dimension (d$^+$)	300
Hidden dimension (m$^+$)	200
Dropout	0.15
Initial learning rate	0.3
# epochs	30
Early stopping*	2

Table 4: Hyperparameter settings for out best performing model; +: d, m as indicated in section 4; *: stop training after loss divergence for 2 consecutive iterations .

We use TensorFlow (Abadi et al., 2015) library in Python[2] to implement our model. AdaGrad (Duchi et al., 2011) optimizer is used for optimization of the model.

We train our models only on the All POS category training set, and evaluate it on the test sets of both All POS and Verb categories, since the training set for all the verbs is a subset of the ALL POS category .

6 Experiments and Evaluation

In this section, we present evaluation results for our model. Table 3 shows their comparison on the test set using F1 score as the metric for evaluation. Experimental results indicate that our model generalizes well on the tests for both the task categories and the performance trends on tests are consistent with those on validation. Table 3 also shows the performance comparison of the variants of our model with the baseline results for the shares task provided by the organizers. Our best performing model surpasses the baseline results on the Verbs category, while it achieves a lesser but comparable performance with the baseline on

---

[2]https://www.python.org/

Text Genre	All POS			Verbs		
	P	**R**	**F**	**P**	**R**	**F**
Academic	0.641	0.683	0.661	0.736	0.753	0.744
Conversation	0.346	0.724	0.469	0.308	0.729	0.433
Fiction	0.413	0.596	0.488	0.416	0.665	0.512
News	0.566	0.591	0.578	0.643	0.665	0.654
Average	0.491	0.648	0.549	0.525	0.703	0.585
Overall	0.511	0.644	0.570	0.529	0.708	0.605

Table 5: Analysis of our best performing system on the Test Sets (both categories). P = Precision. R = Recall, F = F1 Score

All POS category.

6.1 Experiment with the Encoder

We experiment with the combining function of the hidden states of forward and backward LSTM (in section 4.1) using both averaging and concatenation. The validation results on both the categories show that concatenation performs much better than averaging. This observation is supported by the fact that concatenation followed by a fully connected layer allows more parameterized interactions between the two states than averaging.

6.2 Re-weighting of Training Examples

We employ cost-sensitive learning (Yang et al., 2014) by re-weighting examples for our model. This brings an appreciable improvement in the performance of our model, 1.6% F1 gain on Validation, 2.0% on All POS category (Test) and 0.6% on verb category (Test). This increment in the performance agrees with the previous works on metaphor detection (Beigman Klebanov et al., 2015, 2016) which show the effectiveness of re-weighting training examples on VUAMC corpus.

6.3 Additional Baseline Features

The use of baseline features like WordNet (Miller, 1995) features, part-of-speech tags and Concreteness features (Brysbaert et al., 2014) in our model additionally improves the F1 score by 0.8% on the All POS category (Test) and 1.5% on verb category (Test), though it shows a relatively lesser improvement on the Validation set.

To obtain the POS-tag-based features, we encode the POS tag of the target tokens into a one-hot vector. By Wordnet features, we refer to one-hot encoding of the 26 class classification of the words based on their general meaning. The concreteness features represent the concatenation of the one hot representation of concreteness-mean-binning-BiasDown, and concreteness-mean-binning-BiasUp features (as indicated in Beigman Klebanov et al. (2015, 2016)).

7 Analysis

After the completion of the shared task, we downloaded the publicly available labels of the test data to analyze the results of our best performing model across all the four genres of text (section 3) on both the categories (as shown in the Table 5). Our system performs comparatively better on academic and news texts than on conversation and fiction texts.

8 Conclusion and Future Work

We described a deep neural architecture Di-LSTM Contrast Network for metaphor detection, which we submitted for Metaphor Shared Task 2018 (Leong et al., 2018). We showed that our system achieves appreciable performance solely by using the contrast features, generated by our model using pre-trained word embeddings. Additionally, our model gets a significant performance boost from the use of extra baseline features, and re-weighting of examples.

For our future work, we plan to experiment with CNNs along with LSTM for capturing the context representation of the sentence in light of the target word. Another interesting idea is the use of attention mechanism (Mnih et al., 2014), which has proven to be effective in many NLP tasks.

Acknowledgments

We would like to thank the anonymous reviewers for their helpful reviews and suggestions.

References

Martín Abadi, Ashish Agarwal, Paul Barham, Eugene Brevdo, Zhifeng Chen, Craig Citro, Greg S. Corrado, Andy Davis, Jeffrey Dean, Matthieu Devin, Sanjay Ghemawat, Ian Goodfellow, Andrew Harp, Geoffrey Irving, Michael Isard, Yangqing Jia, Rafal Jozefowicz, Lukasz Kaiser, Manjunath Kudlur, Josh Levenberg, Dandelion Mané, Rajat Monga, Sherry Moore, Derek Murray, Chris Olah, Mike Schuster, Jonathon Shlens, Benoit Steiner, Ilya Sutskever, Kunal Talwar, Paul Tucker, Vincent Vanhoucke, Vijay Vasudevan, Fernanda Viégas, Oriol Vinyals, Pete Warden, Martin Wattenberg, Martin Wicke, Yuan Yu, and Xiaoqiang Zheng. 2015. TensorFlow: Large-scale machine learning on heterogeneous systems. Software available from tensorflow.org.

Beata Beigman Klebanov, Ben Leong, Michael Heilman, and Michael Flor. 2014. Different texts, same metaphors: Unigrams and beyond. In *Proceedings of the Second Workshop on Metaphor in NLP*, pages 11–17. Association for Computational Linguistics.

Beata Beigman Klebanov, Chee Wee Leong, and Michael Flor. 2015. Supervised word-level metaphor detection: Experiments with concreteness and reweighting of examples. In *Proceedings of the Third Workshop on Metaphor in NLP*, pages 11–20. Association for Computational Linguistics.

Beata Beigman Klebanov, Chee Wee Leong, E. Dario Gutierrez, Ekaterina Shutova, and Michael Flor. 2016. Semantic classifications for detection of verb metaphors. In *Proceedings of the 54th Annual Meeting of the Association for Computational Linguistics (Volume 2: Short Papers)*, pages 101–106. Association for Computational Linguistics.

Yoshua Bengio, Réjean Ducharme, Pascal Vincent, and Christian Janvin. 2003. A neural probabilistic language model. *J. Mach. Learn. Res.*, 3:1137–1155.

Marc Brysbaert, AB Warriner, and V Kuperman. 2014. Concreteness ratings for 40 thousand generally known english word lemmas. *BEHAVIOR RESEARCH METHODS*, 46(3):904–911.

Erik-Lân Do Dinh and Iryna Gurevych. 2016. Token-level metaphor detection using neural networks. In *Proceedings of the Fourth Workshop on Metaphor in NLP*, pages 28–33. Association for Computational Linguistics.

John Duchi, Elad Hazan, and Yoram Singer. 2011. Adaptive subgradient methods for online learning and stochastic optimization. *J. Mach. Learn. Res.*, 12:2121–2159.

Andrew Gargett and John Barnden. 2015. Modeling the interaction between sensory and affective meanings for detecting metaphor. In *Proceedings of the Third Workshop on Metaphor in NLP*, pages 21–30. Association for Computational Linguistics.

Alex Graves and Jürgen Schmidhuber. 2005. 2005 special issue: Framewise phoneme classification with bidirectional lstm and other neural network architectures. *Neural Netw.*, 18(5-6):602–610.

Sepp Hochreiter and Jürgen Schmidhuber. 1997. Long short-term memory. *Neural Comput.*, 9(8):1735–1780.

George Lakoff. 1993. *The contemporary theory of metaphor*, 2 edition. Cambridge University Press.

Chee Wee Leong, Beata Beigman Klebanov, and Ekaterina Shutova. 2018. A report on the 2018 vua metaphor detection shared task. In *Proceedings of the Workshop on Figurative Language Processing*, New Orleans, LA.

George A. Miller. 1995. Wordnet: A lexical database for english. *Commun. ACM*, 38(11):39–41.

Volodymyr Mnih, Nicolas Heess, Alex Graves, and Koray Kavukcuoglu. 2014. Recurrent models of visual attention. *CoRR*, abs/1406.6247.

Jeffrey Pennington, Richard Socher, and Christopher D. Manning. 2014. Glove: Global vectors for word representation. In *Empirical Methods in Natural Language Processing (EMNLP)*, pages 1532–1543.

Sunny Rai, Shampa Chakraverty, and Devendra K. Tayal. 2016. Supervised metaphor detection using conditional random fields. In *Proceedings of the Fourth Workshop on Metaphor in NLP*, pages 18–27. Association for Computational Linguistics.

Marek Rei, Luana Bulat, Douwe Kiela, and Ekaterina Shutova. 2017. Grasping the finer point: A supervised similarity network for metaphor detection. *CoRR*, abs/1709.00575.

Ekaterina Shutova Saif M. Mohammad and Peter D. Turney. 2016. Metaphor as a medium for emotion: An empirical study. In *Proceedings of the Fifth Joint Conference on Lexical and Computational Semantics (*Sem)*, Berlin, Germany.

Karin Kipper Schuler. 2006. *VerbNet: A Broad-Coverage, Comprehensive Verb Lexicon*. Ph.D. thesis, University of Pennsylvania.

Nitish Srivastava, Geoffrey Hinton, Alex Krizhevsky, Ilya Sutskever, and Ruslan Salakhutdinov. 2014. Dropout: A simple way to prevent neural networks from overfitting. *J. Mach. Learn. Res.*, 15(1):1929–1958.

G. Steen. 2010. *A Method for Linguistic Metaphor Identification: From MIP to MIPVU*. Converging evidence in language and communication research. John Benjamins Publishing Company.

Yulia Tsvetkov, Leonid Boytsov, Anatole Gershman, Eric Nyberg, and Chris Dyer. 2014. Metaphor detection with cross-lingual model transfer. In *Proceedings of the 52nd Annual Meeting of the Association for Computational Linguistics (Volume 1: Long Papers)*, volume 1, pages 248–258.

X. Yang, A. Loukina, and K. Evanini. 2014. Machine learning approaches to improving pronunciation error detection on an imbalanced corpus. In *2014 IEEE Spoken Language Technology Workshop (SLT)*, pages 300–305.

Yuan Yao, Lorenzo Rosasco, and Andrea Caponnetto. 2007. On early stopping in gradient descent learning. *Constructive Approximation*, 26(2):289–315.

Conditional Random Fields for Metaphor Detection

Anna Mosolova[1], Ivan Bondarenko[2] and Vadim Fomin[3]
[1,2,3]Novosibirsk State University
[1]a.mosolova@g.nsu.ru [2] i.yu.bondarenko@gmail.com [3]wadimiusz@gmail.com

Abstract

We present an algorithm for detecting metaphor in sentences which was used in Shared Task on Metaphor Detection by First Workshop on Figurative Language Processing. The algorithm is based on different features and Conditional Random Fields.

1 Introduction

In this paper, we present a system which predicts metaphoricity of the word depending on its neighbors. We used VU Amsterdam corpus (Steen et al., 2010) given by competition's organizers, 10 features which were also given by competition's organizers and algorithm of Conditional Random Fields for predictions that are depending on previous ones.

2 Related Work

A lot of papers describe methods for metaphor detection, but the closest in performance is the article by Rai et al. (2016). It proposes to use Conditional Random Fields for metaphor detection. The authors also use features based on syntax, concepts, affects, and word embeddings from MRC Psycholinguistic Database and coherence and analogy between words which are taken from word embeddings given by Huang et al. (2012). Moreover, they use synonymy from WordNet.

This work is very similar to our due to some similar features and the main algorithm which is CRF.

3 Data

3.1 Dataset

As a dataset was used VU Amsterdam corpus (Steen et al., 2010). It consists of 117 texts divided into 4 parts (academic, news, fiction, conversation).

It was divided into two parts: train and test. The model was trained on the train set and evaluated on the test set.

3.2 Features

Features were given by competition's organizers. Set of features consists of:

- Unigrams: All words from the training data without any changes;

- Unigram lemmas: All words from the training data in their normal form;

- Part-of-Speech tags: They were generated by Stanford POS tagger 3.3.0 (Toutanova et al. 2003);

- Topical LDA: Latent Dirichlet Allocation (Blei et al., 2003) for deriving a 100-topic model from the NYT corpus years 2003-2007 (Sandhaus, 2008) for representing common topics of public discussions. The NYT data was lemmatized using NLTK (Bird, 2006) and the model was built using the gensim toolkit (R. Řehůřek and P. Sojka, 2010);

- Concreteness: For this feature was used Brysbaert et al. (2013) database of concreteness ratings for about 40,000 English words. The mean ratings, ranging 1-5, are binned in 0.25 increments; each bin is used as a binary feature;

Proceedings of the Workshop on Figurative Language Processing, pages 121–123
New Orleans, Louisiana, June 6, 2018. ©2018 Association for Computational Linguistics

- WordNet: 15 lexical classes of verbs based on their general meanings;

- VerbNet: Classification based on syntactic frames of verbs ;

- Corpus: 150 clusters of verbs using their subcategorization frames and the verb's nominal arguments as features for clustering.

All of these features were described in Beigman Klebanov et al. (2014), Beigman Klebanov et al. (2015) and Beigman Klebanov et al. (2016).

3.3 Algorithm

As an algorithm for classification was used Conditional Random Fields which was described in Lafferty et al. (2001). This algorithm depends on previous predictions making the future ones and it was crucial because metaphoricity of a word in a sentence relies on its neighbors. Also, this classifier can work with a big amount of features, so we used a lot of them in this work and it was helpful for the further results.

4 Experiments

We tried different parameters that were provided in the crfsuite (Okazaki, 2007). There were five training algorithms such as lbfgs (gradient descending using the L-BFGS method), l2sgd (stochastic gradient descend with L2 regularization term), Averaged Perceptron, Passive Aggressive, Adaptive Regularization Of Weight Vector. The best training algorithm was lbfgs.

Moreover, we used a different amount of iterations, and its amount affects the loss because there is no limit to the number of iterations in the lbfgs-algorithm.

Furthermore, some experiments with regularization were conducted. Regularization was used for reducing the generalization error and it is important in CRF. For the selection of the most appropriate parameters for regularization, we used RandomizedSearchCV from scikit-learn (http://scikit-learn.org).

We used sklearn-crfsuite that is the special wrapper of crfsuite written in C for Python (https://github.com/TeamHG-Memex/sklearn-crfsuite) for computing the algorithm.

As a metric for evaluating the score was taken F-score.

The best F-score had the algorithm with 200 iterations, lbfgs-algorithm, c1 regularization and c2 regularization that equal to 0.1.

The result obtained with these parameters was evaluated using a held-out set from the train set. F-score of this model and other experiments are presented in table 1 for All-POS track and for Verb track.

Parameters	F-score for all-POS	F-score for Verbs track
lbfgs, 200 iterations, c1=c2=0.1	0.8621	0.7417
lbfgs, 100 iterations, c1=c2=0.1	0.8593	0.739
lbfgs, 50 iterations, c1=c2=0.1	0.8601	0.7333
lbfgs, 100 iterations, c1=0.2353, c2=0.0329,	0.8586	0.7528
l2sgd, 100 iterations, c2=0.1	0.8455	0.6343
Averaged Perceptron, 100 iterations	0.8303	0.7165
Passive Aggressive, 100 iterations	0.8483	0.7327

Table 1 The results of the experiment for All-POS and Verb tracks.

Adaptive Regularization Of Weight Vector, 100 iterations	0.8459	0.6973

5 Results

As a result, our best-trained model was based on 10 features described below and CRF classifier with lbfgs and 200 iterations and it has F-score equal to 0.8621 for All-POS track. As for the Verb track, the best model was also based on lbfgs, had 100 iterations and c1 equal to 0.2353, c2 equal to 0.0329 with F-score 0.7528.

These results are obtained using validation with a part of the train set, and as for the test set, for All-POS track, the result measured by F-score is 0.138 and for Verb track is 0.246.

The results differ as it is possible that validation on a small part of the train set (33%) is not as accurate as validation on the test set which usually consists of the larger number of sentences.

6 Conclusion

We used Conditional Random Fields for the task of metaphor detection. Due to the large number of features, this classifier worked very well, and it is assumed that increasing the number of features will improve the performance of the algorithm.

References

David M. Blei, Andrew Y. Ng, and Michael I. Jordan. 2003. *Latent Dirichlet Allocation*. Journal of Machine Learning Research, 3:993–1022.

Marc Brysbaert, Amy Beth Warriner, and Victor Kuperman. 2013. *Concreteness ratings for 40 thousand generally known english word lemmas*. Behavior Research Methods, pages 1–8.

Beata Beigman Klebanov, Chee Wee Leong, Michael Heilman, and Michael Flor. 2014. *Different texts, same metaphors: Unigrams and beyond*. In Proceedings of the Second Workshop on Metaphor in NLP, pages 11–17, Baltimore, MD, June. Association for Computational Linguistics.

Beata Beigman Klebanov, Chee Wee Leong, and Michael Flor. 2015. *Supervised word-level metaphor detection: Experiments with concreteness and re-weighting of examples*. In Proceedings of the Third Workshop on Metaphor in NLP, pages 11–20, Denver, Colorado, June. Association for Computational Linguistics.

Huang, Eric H., Richard Socher, Christopher D. Manning, and Andrew Y. Ng. 2012. *Improving word representations via global context and multiple word prototypes*. Proceedings of the 50th Annual Meeting of the Association for Computational Linguistics: Long Papers-Volume 1. Association for Computational Linguistics.

John Lafferty, Andrew McCallum, Fernando Pereira. 2001. *Conditional random fields: Probabilistic models for segmenting and labeling sequence data*. Proc. 18th International Conf. on Machine Learning. Morgan Kaufmann. pp. 282–289.

Naoaki Okazaki. 2007. *CRFsuite: a fast implementation of Conditional Random Fields (CRFs)*. http://www.chokkan.org/software/crfsuite/

Sunny Rai, Shampa Chakraverty, and Devendra K. Tayal. 2016. Supervised metaphor detection using conditional random fields. In Proceedings of the Fourth Workshop on Metaphor in NLP, pages 18–27, San Diego, California. Association for Computational Linguistics.

Radim Řehůřek and Petr Sojka. 2010. *Software Framework for Topic Modelling with Large Corpora*. In Proceedings of the LREC 2010 Workshop on New Challenges for NLP Frameworks, pages 45–50, Valletta, Malta, May. ELRA.

Evan Sandhaus. 2008. *The New York Times Annotated Corpus*. LDC Catalog No: LDC2008T19.

Gerard Steen, Aletta Dorst, Berenike Herrmann, Anna Kaal, Tina Krennmayr, and Trijntje Pasma. 2010. *A Method for Linguistic Metaphor Identification*. Amsterdam: John Benjamins.

Kristina Toutanova, Dan Klein, Christopher Manning, and Yoram Singer. 2003. *Feature-Rich Part-of-Speech Tagging with a Cyclic Dependency Network*. In Proceedings of NAACL, pages 252–259.

Detecting Figurative Word Occurrences Using Recurrent Neural Networks

Agnieszka Mykowiecka
ICS PAS
Jana Kazimierza 5
Warsaw, Poland
agn@ipipan.waw.pl

Aleksander Wawer
ICS PAS
Jana Kazimierza 5
Warsaw, Poland
axw@ipipan.waw.pl

Małgorzata Marciniak
ICS PAS
Jana Kazimierza 5
Warsaw, Poland
mm@ipipan.waw.pl

Abstract

The paper addresses the detection of figurative usage of words in English text. The chosen method was to use neural nets fed by pre-trained word embeddings. The obtained results show that simple solutions, based on word embeddings only, are comparable to complex solutions, using additional information as a result of taggers or a psycholinguistic database. This approach can be easily applied to other languages, even less-studied, for which we only have raw texts available.

1 Introduction

Natural language is a very efficient way of communication. To make the task of learning and remembering language easier, the same linguistic expression can have many different meanings, e.g. *the nearest bank*. What is more, in spite of regular homonymy and polysemy, words or expressions can have a meaning that is different from all literal interpretations. The latter phenomena, called figurative usage, allows for much more creative and rich communication, and makes it more effective, persuasive, and impactful. It is very often used in poetry or literature, but is also quite frequent in everyday language. Although figurative meanings are different from literal ones, there usually exists some linkage between both meanings which make metaphors comprehensive for a hearer/reader. For example, when somebody says *I am a rock* we start to think about being hard and solid. Thus, we can easily understand not just conventional figurative expressions which we already know, but also those that we read or hear for the first time.

The problem which we tried to solve was defined by the organizers of the Figurative Language NAACL Workshop shared task in which we took part as the ZIL-IPIPAN team. In this task, participants were supposed to label, in a given subset of VU Amsterdam Metaphor Corpus (Steen et al., 2010), individual words which were used metaphorically. As people are able to recognize metaphorical usage of a word based on the actual context, we decided to test to what degree it is possible to automatically recognize metaphorical word occurrence using only word embeddings.

2 Related Work

Multiple approaches have been proposed for the problem of detecting metaphors in text. Among many published methods, we only discuss selected ones in this section, especially those based on the Amsterdam metaphor dataset.

In (Beigman Klebanov et al., 2016), the authors apply a logistic regression classifier to test combined lexical and dictionary-based feature spaces.

In (Rai et al., 2016), a conditional random field (CRF) algorithm is proposed. The approach is based on features from the MRC psycholinguistic dictionary (Wilson and Division, 1997) and Word-NetAffect database (a subset of WordNet with emotion annotations).

Perhaps the the method described in (Do Dinh and Gurevych, 2016) is the most relevant to our work, where a neural network is used to recognize word-level metaphoricity. As in our approach, word embeddings are used to represent words. However, the structure of the network is different: it is a dense multi-layer network, while we focus on recurrent networks (such as LSTM), in our opinion more suitable for labelling sequential, word-level data. Interestingly, the authors demonstrate the positive influence of part-of-speech (POS) based features, used to augment word embeddings. The best overall model is based on combining word embeddings, POS and selected MRC dictionary data.

Proceedings of the Workshop on Figurative Language Processing, pages 124–127
New Orleans, Louisiana, June 6, 2018. ©2018 Association for Computational Linguistics

3 Data

The texts in the VU AMC corpus, used in the shared task, originated from the British National Corpus from four genres: News, Fiction, Academic and Conversation. VU AMC was divided into two parts: train and test. The train set was used to prepare classifiers of metaphorical and literal senses of tokens, while a test set was used for evaluation. The numbers of sentences tokens and metaphors of both parts are given in Table 1.

part	sentences	tokens	metaphors	% of met.
train	8,883	106,986	9,022	8.43
test	4,080	58,359	6,822	11.69

Table 1: The test and train datasets in numbers

The solutions were tested on 22,196 tokens from the test set indicated by the organizers.

4 Neural Net Architecture

In our experiments, we adopted the method described in (Wawer and Mykowiecka, 2017) as a starting point. The authors applied neural networks and word embeddings to predict if a noun-adjective phrase has a literal or metaphorical sense or can have both senses depending on its usage. As the current task concerns labelling all words in a sentence, the obvious choice was to use a sequential model. We tested both GRU and LSTM units in a bidirectional architecture, as the important information may be coded both in left and right word context. The implementation is done in Keras with the Tensorflow backend – the model summary is given in Figure 1. The sequential network has to be of a fixed length, thus the maximum length of the sentence was chosen (to be equal to 110). As word representation, we used 300 element GLoVe vectors trained on Wikipedia 2014 and Gigaword 5 (Pennington et al., 2014)

```
Layer (type)                 Output Shape          Param #
=================================================================
input_1 (InputLayer)         (None, 110, 300)      0
_________________________________________________________________
bidirectional_1 (Bidirection (None, 110, 600)      1442400
_________________________________________________________________
dropout_1 (Dropout)          (None, 110, 600)      0
_________________________________________________________________
bidirectional_2 (Bidirection (None, 110, 600)      2162400
_________________________________________________________________
dense_1 (Dense)              (None, 110, 3)        1803
=================================================================
Total params: 3,606,603
Trainable params: 3,606,603
Non-trainable params: 0
```

Figure 1: Basic net architecture

As it might be correct that the information included in word embeddings is not sufficient, we tested the impact of additional information. We extended appropriate word embeddings with more features. Two types of information were considered. First, we added morphological information about part of speech categories. Second, we used information from General Inquirer data.

4.1 Adding part-of-speech data

In our experiments, we tested if enriching data by part-of-speech (POS) had a positive effect on the results. At the beginning, we wanted to extract POS from the xml file of VU AMC available on the shared task page, but it occurred that it contained tokens/parts omitted in the train and test text files, and the tokenization was inconsistent in the text and xml datasets. Because we were not sure of all the changes made to the text data, we tagged the train and test texts with the Stanford tagger (Toutanova et al., 2003) available from `https://nlp.stanford.edu/software/tagger.shtml`, and we applied the bidirectional model. As the tokenization used in the tagger divided strings into finer ones in comparison to VU AMC, we removed redundant tags where it was necessary. For example, in the corpus, there were amounts of money given by one token *£10,000* but the tagger divided them into two tokens: *£* tagged as '#' and *10,000* tagged as 'CD'. As we had to choose one tag we deleted the first one and left the second. There were many similar differences, especially in tokenization of strings containing a digit.

4.2 Adding General Inquirer Data

It has been shown that using information from external dictionaries may be beneficial for training models on the metaphor detection problem. In their baseline paper (Beigman Klebanov et al., 2016) demonstrate the positive influence of features derived from the WordNet dictionary.

For this task, some researchers use not only general purpose dictionaries (such as WordNet) but also more specialized, psychological and psycholinguistic databases of words. For example, the MRC database (Wilson and Division, 1997), a large dictionary listing linguistic and psycholinguistic attributes obtained experimentally, has been applied to metaphor detection in a cross-lingual model transfer scenario (Tsvetkov et al., 2014).

In our experiments, we used another such database: The General Inquirer (Stone et al., 1966). The dictionary (a total of 183 categories assigned to over eleven thousand words that cover a large part of the commonly used English lexicon) contains two sub-parts: the Harvard IV psychosocial dictionary and the Laswell dictionary of values in politics. We conducted our experiments using the Harvard IV part. It contains all three Osgood dimensions (including evaluative dimension, often called sentiment, but also potency and activity), and also many other categories related to pleasure, pain, emotions, various social institutions (sport, politics, religion) and social cognition, cognitive orientation, and emotional states. A more comprehensive description and listing of the categories can be found at http://www.wjh.harvard.edu/ ~inquirer/homecat.htm. The dictionary is only available for English. Its translation would be a complex and challenging task. This might involve validation against many perspectives, both theoretical and empirical, as many groups of researchers contributed their parts of the dictionary over decades. For example, Osgood labels come from factor analysis of a large survey, Laswell dictionary labels are grounded in studies of totalitarian regimes.

We tested for the presence of each input word in the General Inquirer dictionary and created binary input vectors for neural network models, with a '1' indicating that the word belongs to a given category and a '0' otherwise.

5 Results

The main neural net architecture was chosen based on the experience with solving other tasks and data sets (see (Mykowiecka et al., 2018); recognition of figurative/metaphorical senses of Polish phrases in sentences, recognition of temporal relations — work in progress), but still some decisions had to be made as to the number of layers, the number of epoch, and the degree of the dropout. To select the best configuration we planned to perform 10-cross validation on the training data. As our experiments with LSTM networks were time consuming, we eventually decided not to perform them on all 10 folds but on their subset. The exact number of folds are given in Table 2. The results of these preliminary experiments are given in Table 2. The results show that the LSTM units are better

than GRU. The larger number of layers (3 instead of 2) helped slightly for the LSTM network and worsened the results of the GRU network. For the GRU architecture, the 15 epochs are better than 10 or 20; for LSTM, 10 epochs turned out to be the best choice of those three values. Adding information on POS tags helped in the case of the GRU network and had very little influence on the results of the LSTM architecture. The same slight, positive, influence was observed after adding either 20 or 50 features from the General Inquirer to the input of the LSTM network.

type	folds	acc.	P	R	F1
GRU					
2 layers, 15 epochs, dropout 0.4					
	10	-	0.71	0.62	0.66
2 layers, 20 epochs, dropout 0.4					
	2	-	0.71	0.60	0.65
3 layers, 15 epochs, dropout 0.4					
	10	-	0.70	0.61	0.65
3 layers, 10 epochs, dropout 0.4 + POS tags					
	1	0.982	0.68	0.70	0.69
LSTM					
2 layers, 10 epochs, dropout 0.4					
	10	0.985	0.74	0.72	0.73
2 layers, 15 epochs, dropout 0.4					
	10	-	0.71	0.62	0.66
3 layers, 10 epochs, dropout 0.4					
	4	0.984	0.73	0.71	0.72
3 layers, 20 epochs, dropout 0.4					
	2	0.982	0.73	0.62	0.67
2 layers, 10 epochs, dropout 0.4 + POS tags					
	5	0.985	0.75	0.72	0.74
2 layers, 20 epochs, dropout 0.3 + POS tags					
	10	0.985	0.76	0.71	0.74
3 layers, 10 epochs, dropout 0.4 + POS tags					
	4	0.984	0.74	0.71	0.73
2 layers, 10 epochs, dropout 0.4 + GI20					
	5	0.985	0.74	0.72	0.73
2 layers, 5 epochs, dropout 0.4 + GI50					
	10	0.985	0.76	0.71	0.73
2 layers, 10 epochs, dropout 0.4 + GI50					
	10	0.984	0.75	0.72	0.73
2 layers, 10 epochs, dropout 0.3 + POS tags + GI50					
	10	0.985	0.76	0.70	0.73

Table 2: Results of partial 10-fold cross validation on train data set, all-pos task; folds – number of folds processed. GI stands here for the features taken from the General Inquirer. The number indicates how many (beginning) features were taken. POS indicates adding the encoded part of the speech tag.

We applied the models trained on the entire training data on the test data and observed slightly different results (see Table 3). However, the LSTM architecture still turned out to be more effective, generally, and the obtained results were lower that those from the cross-validation schema. The best results (0.58 for all words and 0.62 for

type	lrs	dpt	ep.	add-inf	F1:all	F1:v
LSTM	2	.4	10	-	0.583	0.619
LSTM	2	.4	15	-	0.574	0.602
LSTM	3	.4	10	GI20	0.545	0.563
LSTM	3	.5	7		0.541	0.553
LSTM	3	.4	10	-	0.536	0.544
LSTM	2	.4	7	GI_POS	0.518	0.543
GRU	3	.5	15	-	0.514	0.561
GRU	2	.4	20	-	0.506	0.546
GRU	2	.5	15	-	0.485	0.524
LSTM	3	.4	10	POS	0.475	0.558
LSTM	1	.4	5	-	0.447	0.450
GRU	3	.5	20	-	0.425	0.452
LSTM	1	.4	5	GI50	0.350	0.338

Table 3: Results on the test set ordered by the F1 value (for metaphors only) for the all-pos task. Models differ in type of unit network, number of layers, size of dropout, number of epochs and the type of additional information included apart from embeddings. GI stands here for the features taken from the General Inquirer. The number indicates how many beginning features were taken. POS indicates adding the encoded part of the speech tag.

verbs) were obtained using the model which was not the best one in the cross-validation schema but, nevertheless, it obtained an F-value equal to 0.72 on all the words. In the case of the test data, adding POS names and features from the General Inquirer worsened the results.

6 Conclusions

Recurrent sequential neural networks turned out to be capable of recognizing metaphorical usage of words better than many other already tested approaches. The exact result achieved – F1 equal to 0.73 for the metaphorical words and to 0.58 for the test data in the cross-validation schema – shows that the scores are not very stable and, probably, the optimal net architecture and settings were not already found. An improvement in the results after adding General Inquirer data, at least for some configurations, shows that the enrichment of the vector representation by additional features might be effective and that this idea needs further study.

Acknowledgments

This work was supported by the Polish National Science Centre project 2014/15/B/ST6/05186 and partially as a part of the investment in the CLARIN-PL research infrastructure funded by the Polish Ministry of Science and Higher Education.

References

Beata Beigman Klebanov, Chee Wee Leong, E Dario Gutierrez, Ekaterina Shutova, and Michael Flor. 2016. Semantic classifications for detection of verb metaphors. In *Proceedings of ACL*, pages 101–106. ACL.

Erik-Lân Do Dinh and Iryna Gurevych. 2016. Token-level metaphor detection using neural networks. In *Proceedings of the Fourth Workshop on Metaphor in NLP*, pages 28–33, San Diego, California. ACL.

Agnieszka Mykowiecka, Małgorzata Marciniak, and Aleksander Wawer. 2018. Literal, metphorical or both? detecting metaphoricity in isolated adjective-noun phrases. In *Proceedings of Workshop on Figurative Language Processing*. ACL.

Jeffrey Pennington, Richard Socher, and Christopher D. Manning. 2014. Glove: Global vectors for word representation. In *Empirical Methods in Natural Language Processing (EMNLP)*, pages 1532–1543.

Sunny Rai, Shampa Chakraverty, and Devendra K. Tayal. 2016. Supervised metaphor detection using conditional random fields. In *Proceedings of the Fourth Workshop on Metaphor in NLP*, pages 18–27, San Diego, California. ACL.

Gerard J. Steen, Aletta G. Dorst, J. Berenike Herrmann, Anna Kaal, Tina Krennmayr, and Trijntje Pasma. 2010. *A method for linguistic metaphor identification. From MIP to MIPVU*. Number 14 in Converging Evidence in Language and Communication Research. John Benjamins.

Philip J. Stone, Dexter C. Dunphy, Marshall S. Smith, and Daniel M. Ogilvie. 1966. *The General Inquirer: A Computer Approach to Content Analysis*. The MIT Press.

Kristina Toutanova, Dan Klein, Christopher D. Manning, and Yoram Singer. 2003. Feature-rich part-of-speech tagging with a cyclic dependency network. In *Proceedings of NAACL HLT*, NAACL '03, pages 173–180, Stroudsburg, PA, USA. ACL.

Yulia Tsvetkov, Leonid Boytsov, Anatole Gershman, Eric Nyberg, and Chris Dyer. 2014. Metaphor detection with cross-lingual model transfer. In *Proceedings of ACL (1)*, pages 248–258. ACL.

Aleksander Wawer and Agnieszka Mykowiecka. 2017. Detecting metaphorical phrases in the Polish language. In *Proceedings of the International Conference Recent Advances in Natural Language Processing, RANLP 2017*, pages 772–777, Varna, Bulgaria. INCOMA Ltd.

Michael Wilson and Informatics Division. 1997. Mrc psycholinguistic database: Machine usable dictionary, version 2.00. 20.

Multi-Module Recurrent Neural Networks with Transfer Learning.
A Submission for the Metaphor Detection Shared Task

Filip Skurniak
Samsung R&D Poland
pl. Europejski 1
00-844 Warszawa, Poland

Maria Janicka
Samsung R&D Poland
pl. Europejski 1
00-844 Warszawa, Poland

Aleksander Wawer
Samsung R&D Poland
pl. Europejski 1
00-844 Warszawa, Poland

`{f.skurniak,m.janicka,a.wawer}@samsung.com`

Abstract

This paper describes multiple solutions designed and tested for the problem of word-
level metaphor detection. The proposed systems are all based on variants of recurrent neural network architectures. Specifically, we explore multiple sources of information: pre-
trained word embeddings (Glove), a dictionary of language concreteness and a transfer learning scenario based on the states of
an encoder network from neural network machine translation system. One of the architectures is based on combining all three systems: (1) Neural CRF (Conditional Random
Fields), trained directly on the metaphor data
set; (2) Neural Machine Translation encoder of
a transfer learning scenario; (3) a neural network used to predict final labels, trained directly on the metaphor data set. Our results
vary between test sets: Neural CRF standalone
is the best one on submission data, while combined system scores the highest on a test subset
randomly selected from training data.

1 Introduction

1.1 Shared Task

This paper is focused on the problem of automated metaphoricity classification of verbs.
It describes a system aimed at the Shared
Task `https://competitions.codalab.`
`org/competitions/17805` on metaphoricity classification co-organized with the Workshop
on Figurative Language Processing.

The task is based on VUA Metaphor corpus
(Steen et al., 2010). The data set, as its authors claim, is the largest available corpus hand-
annotated for all metaphorical language use, regardless of lexical field or source domain. The
method of metaphor labeling is consistent with
systematic and explicit metaphor identification
protocol MIPVU. The corpus consists of altogether 117 texts covering four genres (academic,
conversation, fiction, news).

Our submissions and results are for the all POS
(part-of-speech) part of the task.

2 Existing Work

2.1 Predicting Metaphoricity

The VUA Metaphor Corpus has been previously
used to automatically predict the metaphoricity
of verbs. In the baseline paper (Klebanov et al.,
2016) authors explore multiple feature spaces,
based on VerbNet and WordNet databases, clustering distributional similarity data of verbs. Tested
classifiers included Logistic Regression, Random
Forest and Linear SVM. The best of reported F1
scores averaged over four document types in the
VUA corpus reach 0.60 for a feature space combined of lemma unigrams and WordNet data.

In another study (Rai et al., 2016) authors use a
Conditional Random Field algorithm and a feature
space of MRC and WordNetAffect dictionaries.

In Do Dinh and Gurevych (2016) a neural network based on word embeddings is used to detect
metaphorical words. The network is a multi-layer
one, but not sequential as in our approach.

In a similar manner, (Sun and Xie, 2017)
use four sequential recurrent neural networks (bi-
LSTM) to predict metaphors. The first three models use a sub-sequence as the input to BiLSTM
network, each with a special kind of sub-sequence
extracted from the input sentence. The last model
is an ensemble model which aggregates the outputs from the first three models.

2.2 Transfer Learning

The idea of transfer learning has not been
widely explored in the context of predicting the
metaphoricity, especially in the context of verbs.
We do not consider the method described in Bizzoni et al. (2017) to be fully transfer learning.

In our understanding, the term transfer learning
refers not only to finding representations of words

Proceedings of the Workshop on Figurative Language Processing, pages 128–132
New Orleans, Louisiana, June 6, 2018. ©2018 Association for Computational Linguistics

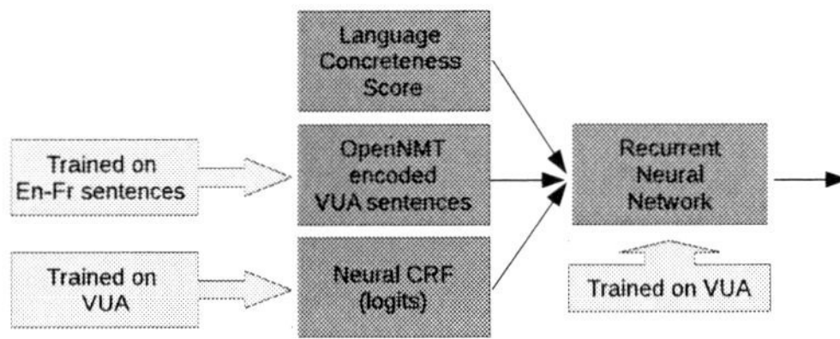

Figure 1: System design

in some vector space, but also to training full models that solve some non-trivial sequential problem, in order to apply them later to another one. Our approach is similar to Conneau et al. (2017) where authors investigate transfer learning to find universal sentence representation. The concept is to use datasets originally compiled for different applications, such as question answering, textual entailment or sentiment analysis, to finally apply them to some other task (in Conneau et al. (2017), to find sentence representation).

3 System Design

We test multiple systems and components on the task of word-level metaphor recognition. The architecture is based on multiple components that constitute input space for a recurrent neural network, which produces output labels. It combines the following elements: (1) Neural CRF (Conditional Random Fields), trained directly on the metaphor data set; (2) Neural Machine Translation encoder, used in the transfer learning scenario; (3) a neural network to predict final labels, trained on the metaphor data set. Figure 1 illustrates the system. Elements (1) – the neural CRF and (3) – the recurrent network can be used to predict the output labels and we test them both in subsequent sections.

3.1 Neural CRF

We used a sequence tagging model (Ma and Hovy, 2016) to generate scores (logits) for each tag. We used those logits for directly predicting the output labels as well as for input features into another recurrent network. The model is based on both word representation and contextual word representation. The former uses pre-trained word embeddings (GloVe (Pennington et al., 2014) trained on Wikipedia 2014 and Gigaword-5 corpus) as well as features on the character level extracted using bidirectional LSTM (Hochreiter and Schmidhuber, 1997). The latter is based on bidirectional

LSTM on the word level, which captures information about the context. In the decoding phase, the vector of scores corresponding to each tag is generated with a fully connected neural network. Finally, predictions are made with linear-chain CRF which, in contrast to a simple softmax function, make use of the neighboring tagging decisions.

We fed the presented model with training data from the VUAMC corpus. The model has been used in two settings: standalone, to directly predict the output labels, and in another mode, where we used the extracted logits (the output of a fully connected neural network on an encoded state of bidirectional LSTM on words level) as an input for another recurrent neural network, as illustrated in Figure 1.

3.2 Concreteness Score

We used the concreteness score from Brysbaert et al. (2014) database, which provides ratings for nearly 40,000 words. For each word, its mean concreteness rating, ranging from 1 to 5, was computed based on at least 25 observations. In the task instructions, concreteness was defined as a feature of words related to things and actions which can be experienced directly through senses. In addition, the task designers put stress on all 5 modalities, providing examples of concrete words connected with different senses.

In our data set we found concreteness scores for nearly 66% of words. For those that could not be found in Brysbaert et al. (2014) database we assumed a mid value of 2.5 as a neutral score. We later normalized these values.

MIPVU (Metaphor Identification Procedure VU University Amsterdam) (Steen et al., 2010) is based on investigating if there is a more basic, concrete, body-related, precise or historically older meaning of a given word compared to its contextual meaning. The concreteness score may indicate if the contextual meaning of a token is also its basic meaning.

3.3 OpenNMT encoded VUA Sentences

OpenNMT (Klein et al., 2017) `http://opennmt.net` is an initiative for neural machine translation and neural sequence modeling. It offers a set of tools dedicated for machine translation, which enable end-to-end translation process are offered.

In our solution the OpenNMT implementation is used in a transfer learning fashion: a model

	Measures			Features				
	P	R	F1	Conc.	Logits	Encoder states	GloVe 100	GloVe 300
bi-GRU 3 layers	0.57	0.67	0.62	x	x	x	x	
bi-GRU 3 layers	0.61	0.51	0.55	x	x	x		
bi-GRU 2 layers	0.61	0.63	0.62	x	x	x	x	
bi-GRU 2 layers	0.59	0.5	0.54		x	x	x	
bi-GRU 2 layers	0.66	0.52	0.58	x	x			
bi-GRU 2 layers	0.57	0.58	0.57				x	
neural CRF	0.58	0.57	0.57					x

Table 1: Best training phase scores (all POS).

trained for machine translation is used to generate a representation of an input sentence. Then, instead of translating the sentence into another output language, we use the intermediate representation for metaphor recognition.

Thus, the overall procedure was to (1) train the translation model; (2) translate Metaphor Shared Task sentences and capture the hidden states of a machine translation encoder for each sentence and (3) extract the hidden vector for every word.

1. Training translation model

   With the aim to maximize usability of the model and consequently, quality of the extracted encoder states, we decided not to use pre-trained models available in the web but rather to use an open source dataset of parallel sentences instead. The corpora are provided by Tiedemann (2012) and are commonly used in the machine translation tasks.

   The translating model is trained on one million English sentences with their French translations.

2. Translation and hidden states

   The translating model consists of a encoder-decoder approach. The model used in the solution is built with simple unidirectional LSTM. The hidden states of the LSTM were captured during the translation process. Typically, the outputs of the encoder play the role of an intermediate layer in the translation pro-

cess. The encoded states capture the meaning of a sentence.

3. Word vectors extraction

   Extracting word vectors is the last step of the process. Finally, each word is represented by a 500-dimensional vector.

3.4 Bidirectional GRU

To predict metaphors in a given text we used bidirectional Gated Recurrent Units (GRU). Previously described features - concreteness score, logits from neural CRF and OpenNMT hidden states - as well as pre-trained words embeddings (GloVe) served as an input to our neural network.

4 Results

All reported results were obtained for all part-of-speech data.

4.1 Training Phase

Initially, we evaluated different versions of our model on the provided training set - randomly shuffled and divided into three subsets (15% test / 15% - validation / 70% - training). The results on this test set (not the Shared Task official test set) are presented in Table 1.

We tested the models with a different number of layers and sets of features. Models with all features showed the best performance. Omitting any of them led to a considerable decrease in F1 score. We also tried class weighting which slightly increased the performance. Finally, we tested neural

	Measures			Features					
	P	R	F1	Conc.	Logits	Encoder states	GloVe 300	GloVe 100	class weighting
bi-GRU 3 layers	0.722	0.312	0.435	x	x	x			
bi-GRU 3 layers	0.705	0.343	0.461	x	x	x			x
bi-GRU 3 layers	0.675	0.371	0.479	x	x	x		x	x
bi-GRU 2 layers	0.655	0.237	0.348					x	
bi-GRU 2 layers	0.638	0.407	0.497	x	x	x		x	x
bi-GRU 2 layers	0.621	0.362	0.457					x	
neural CRF	0.547	0.575	0.561				x		

Table 2: Best submission scores (all POS).

CRF and bidirectional GRU with GloVe embeddings. Those more basic models served as a point of reference.

The best score was generated by a bidirectional GRU with all the features. A difference in layers number did not show any significant change in performance.

Batch sizes for all models were set to 64 or 128 during experiments. Models were trained using Adam optimizer and a binary cross-entropy loss function.

The network named 'bi-GRU 2 layers' in Table 1 contained two bi-directional LSTM layers. Dropouts were applied after each layer with rates in range from 0,5 to 0,6. Bi-directional layers were followed by two dense layers of size 500 with dropouts (rate 0,5) placed after each of them. The last layer of this network was a sigmoid one. All GRU layers had 'tanh' activation functions, dense layers 'relu' activation functions.

The network named 'bi-GRU 3 layers' in Table 1 contained three bi-directional LSTM layers followed by a sigmoid layer. Dropouts were applied after each bidirectional layer, with rates in range from 0,5 to 0,6 as before.

4.2 Submission Phase

Table 2 shows our submission scores obtained by the best performing models chosen in the previous step. We tested them on the all part-of-speech task.

Interestingly, scores from submission differ significantly from those observed in the training phase. Here, the Neural CRF model applied standalone came out as the best solution. Three layer bidirectional GRU generated a better F1 score than two layers model. However, both models gained much lower scores than noted in the training phase.

This discrepancy can be possibly explained by different character of our test set (random sub-part of the training data set), compared to the official test set in the shared task.

5 Conclusions

In this paper we have discussed solutions for metaphor detection built for Metaphor Detection Shared Task. We described different features and architecture combinations along with their scores, measured on a test set randomly sampled from training data and on official submission procedure.

Due to discrepancies between scores obtained in from the training set and scores obtained in submission, it is not easy to draw straightforward conclusions.

When tested on a subset of training data, our results indicate that all proposed features: those captured in OpenNMT encoder states, concreteness ratings and tag scores from neural CRF, all had an impact on the performance of our system, which resulted in a better F1 score than simple models using GloVe. These results seem to go along the lines of results reported in Do Dinh and Gurevych (2016).

Submission results, as measured on the official

test set of the Shared task, provide an entirely different picture. They also show the advantage of bidirectional GRU including all features over one trained on GloVe only. Yet, it is neural CRF standalone, which included only pre-trained embeddings, that outperformed other more complex models.

References

Yuri Bizzoni, Stergios Chatzikyriakidis, and Mehdi Ghanimifard. 2017. "deep" learning : Detecting metaphoricity in adjective-noun pairs. In *Proceedings of the Workshop on Stylistic Variation*, pages 43–52, Copenhagen, Denmark. Association for Computational Linguistics.

Marc Brysbaert, Amy Beth Warriner, and Victor Kuperman. 2014. Concreteness ratings for 40 thousand generally known english word lemmas. *Behavior Research Methods*, 46(3):904–911.

Alexis Conneau, Douwe Kiela, Holger Schwenk, Loïc Barrault, and Antoine Bordes. 2017. Supervised learning of universal sentence representations from natural language inference data. *CoRR*, abs/1705.02364.

Erik-Lân Do Dinh and Iryna Gurevych. 2016. Token-level metaphor detection using neural networks. In *Proceedings of the Fourth Workshop on Metaphor in NLP*, pages 28–33, San Diego, California. Association for Computational Linguistics.

Sepp Hochreiter and Jürgen Schmidhuber. 1997. Long short-term memory. *Neural Comput.*, 9(8):1735–1780.

Beata Beigman Klebanov, Chee Wee Leong, E. Dario Gutiérrez, Ekaterina Shutova, and Michael Flor. 2016. Semantic classifications for detection of verb metaphors. In *Proceedings of the 54th Annual Meeting of the Association for Computational Linguistics, ACL 2016, August 7-12, 2016, Berlin, Germany, Volume 2: Short Papers*.

Guillaume Klein, Yoon Kim, Yuntian Deng, Jean Senellart, and Alexander M. Rush. 2017. Opennmt: Open-source toolkit for neural machine translation. In *Proc. ACL*.

Xuezhe Ma and Eduard Hovy. 2016. End-to-end sequence labeling via bi-directional lstm-cnns-crf. In *Proceedings of the 54th Annual Meeting of the Association for Computational Linguistics (Volume 1: Long Papers)*, pages 1064–1074, Berlin, Germany. Association for Computational Linguistics.

Jeffrey Pennington, Richard Socher, and Christopher D Manning. 2014. Glove: Global vectors for word representation. In *EMNLP*, volume 14, pages 1532–1543.

Sunny Rai, Shampa Chakraverty, and Devendra K. Tayal. 2016. Supervised metaphor detection using conditional random fields. In *Proceedings of the Fourth Workshop on Metaphor in NLP*, pages 18–27, San Diego, California. Association for Computational Linguistics.

Gerard J. Steen, Aletta G. Dorst, J. Berenike Herrmann, Anna Kaal, Tina Krennmayr, and Trijntje Pasma. 2010. *A Method for Linguistic Metaphor Identification*. John Benjamins Publishing.

Shichao Sun and Zhipeng Xie. 2017. Bilstm-based models for metaphor detection. In *National CCF Conference on Natural Language Processing and Chinese Computing*, pages 431–442. Springer.

Jrg Tiedemann. 2012. Parallel data, tools and interfaces in opus. In *Proceedings of the Eight International Conference on Language Resources and Evaluation (LREC'12)*, Istanbul, Turkey. European Language Resources Association (ELRA).

Using Language Learner Data for Metaphor Detection

Egon W. Stemle
Eurac Research
Bolzano-Bozen, Italy
`egon.stemle@eurac.edu`

Alexander Onysko
Alpen-Adria-Universität
Klagenfurt a.W., Austria
`alexander.onysko@aau.at`

Abstract

This article describes the system that participated in the shared task (ST) on metaphor detection (Leong et al., 2018) on the Vrije University Amsterdam Metaphor Corpus (VUA). The ST was part of the workshop on processing figurative language at the 16th annual conference of the *North American Chapter of the Association for Computational Linguistics* (NAACL2018).

The system combines a small assertion of trending techniques, which implement matured methods from NLP and ML; in particular, the system uses word embeddings from standard corpora and from corpora representing different proficiency levels of language learners in a LSTM BiRNN architecture.

The system is available under the APLv2 open-source license.

1 Introduction

Ever since conceptual metaphor theory was laid out in Lakoff and Johnson (1980), the most vexing question has remained a methodological one: how can conceptual metaphors be reliably identified in language use? Although manual identification was put on a stronger methodological footing with the Metaphor Identification Procedure (MIP) ("Pragglejaz Group", 2007) and its elaboration into MIPVU (Steen et al., 2010), fuzzy areas remain due to the fact that conceptual metaphors can vary between primary metaphors and complex metaphors (cf. Grady, 1997). Furthermore, highly conventionalized metaphorical expressions might not be processed in the same way as novel metaphors. The core process of manual metaphor identification is not completely unproblematic either since it can be difficult to establish whether the meaning of a lexical unit in its context deviates from its basic meaning or not. In the face of

that slippery terrain, automatic metaphor identification emerges as an extremely challenging task. An increasing volume of research since the start of annual workshops at NAACL in 2013 has shown first promising results using different methods of automated metaphor identification (see for example Shutova et al. (2015) and Klebanov et al. (2016) for previous events). The current shared task of metaphor identification provided a further opportunity to put the computational spotting of metaphors to the test.

Our bid for this task combines (cf. Section 2) `fastText` word embeddings (WEs) with a single-layer long short-term memory bidirectional recurrent neural network (BiRNN) architecture. The input, sequences of WE representations of words, is fed into the BiRNN which predicts metaphorical usage for each word.

The WEs were trained (cf. Section 4.2) on different large corpora (BNC, Wikipedia, enTen-Ten13, ukWaC) and on the Vienna-Oxford International Corpus of English (VOICE) as well as on the TOEFL11 Corpus of Non-Native English. The latter corpus was used, among others, in the First Native Language Identification Shared Task (Tetreault et al., 2013) held at the *8th Workshop on Innovative Use of NLP for Building Educational Applications* as part of NAACL-HLT 2013.

We were led by the idea (cf. Section 2.3) that metaphorical language use changes while gaining proficiency in a language, and so we hoped to be able to utilise the information contained in corpora of different proficiency levels.

The paper is organised as follows: We present our system design with related work in Section 2, the implementation in Section 3, and the experimental setup with an evaluation in Section 4. Section 5 concludes with an outlook on possible next steps.

133

Proceedings of the Workshop on Figurative Language Processing, pages 133–138
New Orleans, Louisiana, June 6, 2018. ©2018 Association for Computational Linguistics

2   Design

Generally, our design builds upon the foundation laid out by Collobert et al. (2011) for a neural network (NN) architecture and learning algorithm that can be applied to various natural language processing tasks. The most related task specific design is given in Do Dinh and Gurevych (2016) who used a NN in combination with WEs to detect metaphors. In contrast to our study, they used a dense multi-layer NN while we adapted the design of Stemle (2016a,b), who combined WEs with a recurrent NN (RNN) to predict part-of-speech (PoS) tags of computer-mediated communication (CMC) and Web corpora for German and Italian. RNNs are usually considered to be more suitable for labelling sequential data such as text.

2.1   Word Embeddings

Recently, state-of-the-art results on various linguistic tasks were accomplished by architectures using neural-network based WEs. Baroni et al. (2014) conducted a set of experiments comparing the popular word2vec (Mikolov et al., 2013a,b) implementation for creating WEs with other well-known distributional methods across various (semantic) tasks. These results suggest that the WEs substantially outperform the other architectures on semantic similarity and analogy detection tasks. Subsequently, Levy et al. (2015) conducted a comprehensive set of experiments that suggest that much of the improved results are due to the system design and parameter optimizations, rather than the selected method. They conclude that "there does not seem to be a consistent significant advantage to one approach over the other".

WEs provide high-quality low dimensional vector representations of words from large corpora of unlabelled data. The representations, typically computed using NNs, encode many linguistic regularities and patterns (Mikolov et al., 2013b).

2.2   Bidirectional Recurrent Neural Network

NNs consist of a large number of simple, highly interconnected processing nodes in an architecture loosely inspired by the structure of the cerebral cortex of the brain (O'Reilly and Munakata, 2000). The nodes receive weighted inputs through their connections on one side and *fire* according to their individual thresholds of their shared activation function. A firing node passes on an activation to all connected nodes on the other side. During learning the input is propagated through the network and the actual output is compared to the desired output. Then, the weights of the connections (and the thresholds) are adjusted step-wise so as to more closely resemble a configuration that would produce the desired output. After all training data have been presented, the process typically starts over, and the learned output values will usually be closer to the desired values.

Recurrent NNs (RNNs), introduced by Elman (1990), are NNs where the connections between the elements are directed cycles, i.e. the networks have loops, and this enables the NN to model sequential dependencies of the input. However, regular RNNs have fundamental difficulties learning long-term dependencies, and special kinds of RNNs need to be used (Hochreiter, 1991); a very popular one is the so called long short-term memory (LSTM) network proposed by Hochreiter and Schmidhuber (1997).

Bidirectional RNNs (BiRNN), introduced by Schuster and Paliwal (1997), extend unidirectional RNNs by introducing a layer, where the directed cycles enable the input to flow in opposite sequential order. While processing text, this means that for any given word the network not only considers the text leading up to the word but also the text thereafter.

Overall, we benefit from available labelled data with this design but also from large amounts of available unlabelled data.

2.3   Language Learner Data

Our experimental design also utilizes data from language learner corpora. This is based on the intuition that metaphor use might vary depending on learner proficiency. Beigman Klebanov and Flor (2013) indeed found a correlation between higher proficiency ratings of learner texts and a higher density of metaphors in these texts. Their study is also one of the few in the field of automated metaphor detection that are concerned with learner language. Their aim, however, is quite different to the current study as they try to establish annotations for metaphoric language use that can help to train an automated classifier of metaphors in test-taker essays. The current study, by contrast, utilizes learner corpus data to build WEs among other corpora representing written standard language. Learner language could be a particularly helpful source of information for automated metaphor detection via WEs as learner language provides different usage patterns compared to WEs derived from standard language corpora.

3   Implementation

We maintain the implementation in a source code repository[1]. Our system uses sequences of word features as input to a BiRNN with a LSTM architecture.

3.1   Word Embeddings

We use gensim[2], a Python tool for unsupervised semantic modelling from plain text, to load pre-computed WE models and to compute embedding-vector representations of words. Words missing in a WE model, i.e. out-of-vocabulary words (OOV), are first estimated by looking at a fixed context of their non-OOV words. If this fails, OOVs are mapped to their individual, randomly generated, vector representations.

3.2   Neural Network

Our implementation uses Keras (Chollet, 2015), a high-level NNs' library written in Python, on top of TensorFlow (Abadi et al., 2016), an open source software library for numerical computation.

The number of input layers corresponds to the number of employed feature sets. For multiple feature sets, e.g. multiple WE models or additional PoS tags, sequences are concatenated on the word level such that the number of features for an individual word grows.

Input sequences have a pre-defined length and represent original textual sentence segments. In case a sentence is longer than the sequence length, the input is split into multiple segments. And if a segment is shorter than the sequence length, the remaining slots are padded, i.e. they are filled with identical dummy information.

Each input layer feeds into a masking layer such that the padded values from the input sequence will be skipped in all downstream layers.[3] The masked input is fed into a bidirectional LSTM layer that, in turn, projects to a fully connected output layer that is activated by a softmax function.

The output is a single sequence of matching length with labels indicating whether the corresponding word is used metaphorically or not.

During training, we use dropout for the linear transformation of the recurrent state, i.e. the network drops a fraction of recurrent connections, which helps prevent overfitting (Srivastava et al., 2014); and we use a weighted categorical cross-entropy loss function to counteract the fact that far fewer words in our sequences are labelled as metaphorical than non-metaphorical, which usually hampers classification performance (cf. Kotsiantis et al., 2006).

4   Experiments and Results

Participants of the ST could either participate in the metaphor prediction tracks for verbs only, all content part-of-speech only, or both. For a given text in VUA, and for each sentence, the task was to predict metaphoricity for each verb or content word respectively, and submit the result to CodaLab[4] for evaluation. Results were calculated as the harmonic average of the precision and recall (F1-score) of the metaphoricity label. We participated with our system in both tasks.

The remainder of this section introduces the official data set, our WE models and describes our fixed hyper-parameters. The results of different combinations of WE models are shown in Table 1. Also note that *all results* in this paper refer only to the all content part-of-speech task.

4.1   Shared Task Data

The VUA, the corpus that was used in the shared task, originates from the British National Corpus (BNC). Altogether, it is comprised of 117 texts covering four genres (academic, conversation, fiction, news). For the ST, VUA was pre-divided by the organisers into a training and a test set. The training set was labelled and could be used to train classifiers, while the participants were supposed to label the test set and submit it. The distribution of metaphorical vs. non-metaphorical labels was imbalanced with a ratio of roughly 1:6 (11044 : 61567).

4.2   Word Embedding Models

We use pre-built WE models of the following corpora: *BNC* and *enTenTen13* web cor-

---

[1] https://github.com/bot-zen/
[2] https://radimrehurek.com/gensim/
[3] This is considered good practice and speeds up processing with long sequences and many padded values – with our rather short sequences it did not help much.

[4] http://codalab.org

	Tokens (Mio)	min Cnt	dim	T11 (low)	T11 (med)	T11 (high)	T11 (l+m+h)	VOICE	BNC	enTenTen13	ukWaC	ukWaC T11-size	Wikipedia17	F1-score on Test Set	10-fold CV Accuracy on Training Set μ	σ
T11 (low)	0.3	1	50	X										0.207	0.917	0.016
T11 (med)	1.8	1	50		X									0.526	0.924	0.011
T11 (high)	1.4	1	50			X								0.514	0.930	0.007
T11 (l+m+h)	3.5	1	50				X							0.541	0.928	0.008
VOICE	1	1	50					X						0.495	0.923	0.010
BNC	100	5	100						X					0.597	0.942	0.005
enTenTen13	19,000	5	100							X				0.594	0.947	0.004
ukWaC	2100	5	100								X			**0.598**	0.945	0.004
ukWaC T11-size	3.5	1	50									X		0.564	0.933	0.009
Wikipedia17	ca 2300	5	300										X	0.586	**0.947**	0.003
	7			X	X	X						X		0.576	0.941	0.003
	7						X					X		0.567	0.936	0.008
	103.5			X	X	X			X					0.596	0.944	0.008
	103.5						X		X					**0.613**	0.945	0.005
	103.5								X			X		0.597	0.948	0.003
	104.5			X	X	X		X	X					0.601	0.950	0.004
	107						X		X			X		0.586	0.951	0.002
	108						X	X	X			X		0.550	0.948	0.003
	19,004.5			X	X	X		X		X				0.603	0.947	0.006
	21,400								X	X			X	0.605	0.951	0.003
	21,401							X	X	X			X	0.594	**0.953**	0.003
	21,404.5			X	X	X		X	X	X			X	0.597	0.952	0.003

Table 1: Overview of the word embedding models we used, and evaluation results for individual models and some combinations on the metaphor prediction track for *all content part-of-speech*.
Number of tokens in the original corpus, parameters `minCount` and `dim` for `fastText` during training of the models. Our calculated F1 scores on the official labelled test set (they should coincide with the organisers' results). The mean accuracy as well as the standard deviation in the accuracy for 10-fold cross validation runs on the training set.

pus (Jakubíček et al., 2013) from SketchEngine[5], as well as *Wikipedia17*[6] from `fastText` (Bojanowski et al., 2016).

We trained WE models using `fastText`'s SkipGram model with the default parameters[7] except for the two parameters `-minCount` (the minimal number of word occurrences) and `-dim` (size of word vectors). The two parameters were altered to take the smaller sizes of our corpora into

[5] `https://embeddings.sketchengine.co.uk/static/index.html`
[6] `https://fasttext.cc/docs/en/pretrained-vectors.html`
[7] `https://github.com/facebookresearch/fastText/archive/v0.1.0.zip`

account. See Table 1 for details.

Three individual models were trained for the different proficiency levels low, medium and high of the training subset of the *TOEFL11* (Blanchard et al., 2013); another model was trained for the full training set comprising all three proficiency levels. One model was trained for the *VOICE* (Seidlhofer et al., 2013), a corpus of English as it is spoken by a non-native speaking majority of users in different contexts.

Two models were trained for ukWaC (Baroni et al., 2009), a corpus constructed from the Web using medium-frequency words from the BNC as seeds. The first model for the full corpus and the second model for a random sample of documents approximating the token count of the full TOEFL11 training set.

4.3 Hyper-Parameter Tuning

Hyper-parameter tuning is important for good performance. The parameters of our system were optimised via an ad-hoc grid search in 3-fold cross validation (CV) runs.

Parameters were: NN optimizer (*rmsprop*, adadelta, adam), recurrent dropout rate for the LSTM layer (0.1, *0.25*, 0.5), dropout for the input layer (*0*, 0.1, 0.2), sequence length (5, 10, *15*, 50), learning epochs (3, 5, *20*, 32) and batch size (16, *32*, 64), and the network architecture, e.g. introducing a second LSTM abstraction layer or using a Gated Recurrent (GRU) layer instead of the LSTM layer. Furthermore, we trained WE models with different values for the `dim` (25, *50*, 100, 150, 200, 250) and `minCount` (*1*, 2, 5, 10) parameters.

The weight for the categorical cross-entropy loss function is calculated as the logarithm of the ratio of number of words vs. metaphorical labels. The context for estimating OOV words was set to 10.

Once set, we used the same configuration for all experiments.

5 Conclusion & Outlook

The combination of WEs with a BiRNN is capable of recognizing metaphorical usage of words better than many other already tested approaches. More importantly, our design does not rely on WordNet or VerbNet information, and does not need concreteness or abstractness information like many successful architectures from previous annual workshops at NAACL. Besides VUA, our system only needs running text.

The best result on the test set was achieved with a combination of TOEFL11 learner data and data from the BNC. So far, the results are encouraging—but also mixed—regarding our initial idea that metaphorical language use at different proficiency levels could be utilised to recognizing metaphorical usage of words. To this end, we are looking forward to output from the *European Network for Combining Language Learning with Crowdsourcing Techniques*[8], where poten-

tially more and more fine-grained language learner data will be collected and made available.

Acknowledgements

The computational results presented have been achieved in part using the Vienna Scientific Cluster (VSC).

References

Martin Abadi, Paul Barham, Jianmin Chen, Zhifeng Chen, Andy Davis, Jeffrey Dean, Matthieu Devin, Sanjay Ghemawat, Geoffrey Irving, Michael Isard, Manjunath Kudlur, Josh Levenberg, Rajat Monga, Sherry Moore, Derek G Murray, Benoit Steiner, Paul Tucker, Vijay Vasudevan, Pete Warden, Martin Wicke, Yuan Yu, and Xiaoqiang Zheng. 2016. TensorFlow: A System for Large-Scale Machine Learning. In *12th USENIX Symposium on Operating Systems Design and Implementation (OSDI 16)*, pages 265–283, Savannah, GA. USENIX Association.

Marco Baroni, Silvia Bernardini, Adriano Ferraresi, and Eros Zanchetta. 2009. The WaCky wide web: a collection of very large linguistically processed web-crawled corpora. *Language Resources and Evaluation*, 43(3):209–226.

Marco Baroni, Georgiana Dinu, and German Kruszewski. 2014. Don't count, predict! A systematic comparison of context-counting vs. context-predicting semantic vectors. In *Proceedings of the 52nd Annual Meeting of the Association for Computational Linguistics (Volume 1: Long Papers)*, pages 238–247. Association for Computational Linguistics. http://www.aclweb.org/anthology/P14-1023.

Beata Beigman Klebanov and Michael Flor. 2013. Argumentation-Relevant Metaphors in Test-Taker Essays. In *Proceedings of the First Workshop on Metaphor in NLP*, pages 11–20. Association for Computational Linguistics.

Daniel Blanchard, Joel Tetreault, Derrick Higgins, Aoife Cahill, and Martin Chodorow. 2013. Toefl11: A corpus of non-native english. *ETS Research Report Series*, 2013(2):i–15.

Piotr Bojanowski, Edouard Grave, Armand Joulin, and Tomas Mikolov. 2016. Enriching word vectors with subword information. *CoRR*, abs/1607.04606.

François Chollet. 2015. Keras: Deep Learning library for Theano and TensorFlow. https://github.com/fchollet/keras.

Ronan Collobert, Jason Weston, Léon Bottou, Michael Karlen, Koray Kavukcuoglu, and Pavel Kuksa. 2011. Natural Language Processing (almost) from Scratch. *Journal of Machine Learning Research*, 12:2493–2537. https://arxiv.org/abs/1103.0398.

---

[8]http://www.cost.eu/COST_Actions/ca/CA16105

Erik-Lân Do Dinh and Iryna Gurevych. 2016. Token-Level Metaphor Detection using Neural Networks. In *Proceedings of the Fourth Workshop on Metaphor in NLP*, pages 28–33, San Diego, California. Association for Computational Linguistics.

Jeffrey L. Elman. 1990. Finding structure in time. *Cognitive Science*, 14(2):179–211.

Joseph Grady. 1997. *Foundations of Meaning: Primary Metaphors and Primary Scenes*. Ph.D. thesis, University of California, Berkeley.

Sepp Hochreiter. 1991. *Untersuchungen zu dynamischen neuronalen Netzen*. diploma thesis, TU München.

Sepp Hochreiter and Jürgen Schmidhuber. 1997. Long short-term memory. *Neural Computation*, 9(8):1735–1780. http://dx.doi.org/10.1162/neco.1997.9.8.1735.

Miloš Jakubíček, Adam Kilgarriff, Vojtěch Kovář, Pavel Rychlỳ, and Vít Suchomel. 2013. The TenTen corpus family. In *7th International Corpus Linguistics Conference (CL 2013)*, pages 125–127, Lancaster. http://ucrel.lancs.ac.uk/cl2013/.

Beata Beigman Klebanov, Ekaterina Shutova, and Patricia Lichtenstein. 2016. Proceedings of the Fourth Workshop on Metaphor in NLP. In *Proceedings of the Fourth Workshop on Metaphor in NLP*. Association for Computational Linguistics.

Sotiris Kotsiantis, Dimitris Kanellopoulos, and Panayiotis Pintelas. 2006. Handling imbalanced datasets: A review. *GESTS International Transactions on Computer Science and Engineering*, 30.

George Lakoff and Mark Johnson. 1980. *Metaphors we Live by*. University of Chicago Press.

Chee Wee Leong, Beata Beigman Klebanov, and Ekaterina Shutova. 2018. A report on the 2018 VUA metaphor detection shared task. In *Proceedings of the Workshop on Figurative Language Processing*, New Orleans, LA.

Omer Levy, Yoav Goldberg, and Ido Dagan. 2015. Improving distributional similarity with lessons learned from word embeddings. *Transactions of the Association for Computational Linguistics*, 3:211–225. https://tacl2013.cs.columbia.edu/ojs/index.php/tacl/article/view/570.

Tomas Mikolov, Kai Chen, Greg Corrado, and Jeffrey Dean. 2013a. Efficient Estimation of Word Representations in Vector Space. *CoRR*, abs/1301.3781. http://arxiv.org/abs/1301.3781.

Tomas Mikolov, Ilya Sutskever, Kai Chen, Greg Corrado, and Jeffrey Dean. 2013b. Distributed Representations of Words and Phrases and their Compositionality. *CoRR*, abs/1310.4546. http://arxiv.org/abs/1310.4546.

Randall C. O'Reilly and Yuko Munakata. 2000. *Computational Explorations in Cognitive Neuroscience Understanding the Mind by Simulating the Brain*. MIT Press. http://books.google.com/books?id=BLf34BFTaIUC{&}pgis=1.

"Pragglejaz Group". 2007. MIP: A Method for Identifying Metaphorically Used Words in Discourse. *Metaphor and Symbol*, 22(1):1–39.

M. Schuster and K.K. Paliwal. 1997. Bidirectional recurrent neural networks. *IEEE Transactions on Signal Processing*, 45(11):2673–2681.

Barbara Seidlhofer, Angelika Breiteneder, Theresa Klimpfinger, Stefan Majewski, Ruth Osimk-Teasdale, Marie-Luise Pitzl, and Michael Radeka. 2013. The Vienna-Oxford International Corpus of English (VOICE).

Ekaterina Shutova, Beata Beigman Klebanov, and Patricia Lichtenstein. 2015. Proceedings of the Third Workshop on Metaphor in NLP. In *Proceedings of the Third Workshop on Metaphor in NLP*. Association for Computational Linguistics.

Nitish Srivastava, Geoffrey E. Hinton, Alex Krizhevsky, Ilya Sutskever, and Ruslan Salakhutdinov. 2014. Dropout : A Simple Way to Prevent Neural Networks from Overfitting. *Journal of Machine Learning Research (JMLR)*, 15:1929–1958.

Gerard J. Steen, Aletta G. Dorst, J. Berenike Herrmann, Anna A. Kaal, Tina Krennmayr, and Trijntje Pasma. 2010. A Method for Linguistic Metaphor Identification: From MIP to MIPVU. 00:238.

Egon W. Stemle. 2016a. bot.zen @ EmpiriST 2015 - A minimally-deep learning PoS-tagger (trained for German CMC and Web data). In *Proceedings of the 10th Web as Corpus Workshop (WAC-X) and the EmpiriST Shared Task*, pages 115–119. Association for Computational Linguistics.

Egon W. Stemle. 2016b. bot.zen @ EVALITA 2016 - A minimally-deep learning PoS-tagger (trained for Italian Tweets). In *Proceedings of Third Italian Conference on Computational Linguistics (CLiC-it 2016) & Fifth Evaluation Campaign of Natural Language Processing and Speech Tools for Italian. Final Workshop (EVALITA 2016)*, Napoli, Italy.

Joel Tetreault, Daniel Blanchard, and Aoife Cahill. 2013. A report on the first native language identification shared task. In *Proceedings of the Eighth Workshop on Building Educational Applications Using NLP*, Atlanta, GA, USA. Association for Computational Linguistics.

Author Index